# THE
# TREASURE
# HUNTER

# THE TREASURE

*Other Books by Robin Moore*

PITCHMAN
THE DEVIL TO PAY (with Jack Youngblood)
THE GREEN BERETS
THE COUNTRY TEAM
FIEDLER
THE FRENCH CONNECTION
COURT MARTIAL (with Henry Rothblatt)
UNTIL PROVEN GUILTY (with Henry Lowenberg)
THE KHAKI MAFIA (with June Collins)
THE HAPPY HOOKER (with Xaviera Hollander
                              and Yvonne Dunleavy)
THE FIFTH ESTATE

# HUNTER by Robin Moore
## and
## Howard Jennings

PRENTICE-HALL, INC.    *Englewood Cliffs, New Jersey*

*The Treasure Hunter* by Robin Moore and Howard Jennings
Copyright © 1974 by Robin Moore and Howard Jennings
Copyright under International and Pan American
Copyright Conventions
Printed in the United States of America
Prentice-Hall International, Inc., London
Prentice-Hall of Australia, Pty. Ltd., North Sydney
Prentice-Hall of Canada, Ltd., Toronto
Prentice-Hall of India Private Ltd., New Delhi
Prentice-Hall of Japan, Inc., Tokyo

10  9  8  7  6  5  4  3  2  1

Library of Congress Cataloging in Publication Data
Moore, Robert Lowell.
The treasure hunter.
1. Treasure-trove.   2. Jennings, Howard.
3. Moore, Robert Lowell.   I. Jennings, Howard,
joint author.   II. Title.
G530.M74        918'.04'0922   [B]        74-576
ISBN 0-13-930529-7

Designed by Linda Huber

*For our daughters, Lynn and Margo*

We both express appreciation to our mutual
friend of many years, Al Dempsey. Al was
the firm Miami base to which we turned for
help, and his help was of inestimable value in
the preparation of this manuscript.

# HOW IT ALL BEGAN

Howard Jennings is my friend. I prize him both for what he is and for what he represents.

It is not hard to find the obvious reasons for liking Howard. He is charming, easy-going, intelligent, and humorous. I admire his suavity and his devastating way with women. Even more, I admire his toughness, his integrity, and his courage. He is a good man to drink with and a very good man to have on hand in an emergency.

But above all, I like and envy Howard for doing so many things that I wish I could have done myself. We all have our private dreams of freedom and adventure, dreams that ignore or, rather, deny the realities that hedge in our lives—the next mortgage payment, the next promotion, or, in my case, the next book. In a very real sense, Howard has lived my dreams for me—occasionally letting me take part in his adventures, just to prove, as it were, that those dreams weren't pure fantasy. For this, I owe him not only my affection but my gratitude.

I first met Howard Jennings in Jamaica, where we had both fled from the confines of the business world. It was in 1960, before the tourist boom, and I had left my public relations job with Sheraton Hotels to settle there, near Port Antonio, and to devote all of my time to writing. Howard had left an oil company job in Tulsa the year before, and when we met he was involved in organizing the Jamaica Air Service, the first commercial airline to run scheduled flights internally within Jamaica. We shared many interests, from airplanes to women, and we spent many a memorable evening together over the next few years.

As you will see in the chapters that follow, I was involved in Howard's first foray into treasure hunting, and in a few others that followed. Our first "expedition" was a boozy adventure that was close to slapstick comedy, but for Howard it was the small beginning of a new life that would ultimately take him into places few civilized men had seen. Over the next thirteen years we met often, and finally, in London, in January, 1973, I learned that he was interested in writing his memoirs.

As a writer, I found his story irresistible. Since I had known Howard from the beginning of his life as a treasure hunter, we agreed to share the telling of the story, with me writing of those adventures in which I shared and Howard taking over to recount the exploits in which I had no part. For the sake both of old friends and old enemies we have had to change a good many names, and in order to accommodate our scheme of alternating narration, we have taken some small liberties with chronology. But that apart, the incidents we recount are absolutely true. I've edited Howard's portions somewhat, since no writer can ever leave things alone, but, for the most part, Howard's voice is that of the real Howard Jennings, and Robin's voice is that of a writer who simply could not stay outside a story that had at times personally, and always in his imagination, involved him deeply.

I think you'll agree that Howard Jennings is a very special kind of man who has packed more into his life than most of us ever dream of. This is his story. I am pleased and proud to have been a part of it.

Robin Moore
Westport, Connecticut, 1974

# CONTENTS

# 1 THE MORANT KEYS FIASCO

The bar overlooking the main runways of Palisados Airport outside Kingston, Jamaica, was once a classic among international watering holes. Sitting there, waiting for a current companion to depart or the next to arrive, one could look out to the west and see the maritime bustle of Kingston Harbor. Eastward, grey-white clouds of dust rose from the huge cement plant, which was pouring out the basic ingredient for Jamaica's building boom. Still further east, a plush, radiant explosion of flora covers the Blue Mountains, which climb to seven thousand feet and produce some of the most exotic-tasting coffee beans in the Western hemisphere. Beyond the mountains, on the northeast tip of the island, lies Port Antonio, where I was living at that time.

After one had exhausted the scenery, there was always the lively diversion of people watching. Actress Patrice Wymore, better known in Jamaica as Pat Flynn, Errol's widow, was a frequent visitor to Jamaica in those days. And one might pass the time, during the waits for the inevitably delayed flights, chatting with other regulars such as Noel Coward, Ralph Bunche, Bill Paley, Ian Fleming, Ginger Rogers, or a former Vice President named Richard Nixon and his chum William Rodgers. After several years in New York television and several more running the public relations operation for Sheraton Hotels, I had developed at least a casual acquaintance with most of these people.

On this particular occasion, Howard Jennings and I had driven into Kingston together. He was shipping a girl out and I was receiving one in, and neither of us was in the mood for table hopping. Even as we waved goodbye to the plane taking his girl home, he began to bemoan the prospect of spending Christmas week alone.

1

I laughed. Howard seldom went more than three or four days without female companionship, and it was hard to imagine him alone during Christmas week, one of the most active social times of the year in Jamaica.

I had met Howard in Jamaica a short time back, and we had been friends since, two bachelors who shared a common interest in good food, good wine, and not-too-good women, all of which Jamaica provided in profusion. Howard had all the charm necessary to support his constant quest for females. He was a tall, handsome, rangy man who seemed to epitomize the popular image of a Texan, though his speech, his sophisticated knowledge of the world, and his fastidious dress had little of his East Texas background left in them. His effect on women was—and still is—nothing short of devastating. I got to know him well over the years, and I found him a fascinating, often perplexing man, part tough adventurer and part elegant *bon vivant*. He seemed to have left his Texas boyhood far behind him, yet the marks were there, beneath the polished urbanity. He was a loner, a man with a need to move on, to see what the next ocean or jungle had to show him. He was—although neither of us knew it that day in Kingston—the stuff of which treasure hunters are made.

Howard was born in Tulsa, Oklahoma, on February 27, 1925, though his boyish looks still belie that date. He came of people who had participated in the Oklahoma Land Rush of 1889, and who had lived their first year in a sod hut on the prairie. His father, Kelse E. Jennings, represented that second generation of southwestern frontiersmen in whom the thirst for land had given way to the thirst for oil. Kelse was a wildcatter, and when an oil boom fulminated in the Texas Panhandle in 1927, he hurriedly moved his wife, Dorothy, and two-year-old Howard to Amarillo, Texas. Then, following the great East Texas discoveries of oil, the family, now enlarged to include two more children, Dorothy Jeanne and James Robert, settled in Texarkana in 1933.

Texarkana is a twin city smack on the Texas-Arkansas line, with two separate and independent city governments and with

2

a long-standing friendly rivalry across the state boundary. Howard grew up and attended school in Texarkana, on the Texas side, and although he was interested in high-school sports —he played basketball—hunting and fishing were his real loves. In those days, there was still plenty of open land around Texarkana, and he and his friends seized every opportunity to go off on camping trips.

Like many young boys in the Southwest, Howard grew up on a diet of adventure yarns: stories of gunfighters, of Indian wars, of fabulous lost gold mines, and of hidden treasure hoards dating back to the time of Cortez and Coronado. He read of the great privateers and pirates who followed the Spanish conquest, and names such as Hawkins and Drake, Morgan and Kidd, the cruel L'Ollonais and the maniacal Blackbeard, ran through his imagination. Among them, one name stood out, with reason: Captain Henry Jennings, an early privateer who operated in the Bahamas and who founded the pirate stronghold of New Providence, on the present site of Nassau. Family legend had it that Captain Jennings was an ancestor, and even though there was no real proof of this, Howard read of the captain's exploits with a sense of immediacy that other stories did not bring.

Captain Jennings got his start by raiding the salvage operations then in progress in the Florida Keys. These operations were an attempt to recover the vast treasures lost with the Spanish Plate Fleet in the previous year, 1714. (Oddly, a present-day treasure hunter named Kip Wagner has continued the salvage operations that Captain Jennings so profitably interrupted two and a half centuries ago, and Wagner has recovered a fortune in Spanish treasure from that same wrecked fleet of galleons.) The captain went on to assemble a sizable fleet of buccaneers, and they preyed quite successfully on the rich merchant vessels that sailed the Spanish Main from Veracruz and Portobelo up through the hazardous waters of the Caribbean. Henry Jennings accepted a royal pardon after a few adventurous and profitable years at sea, and retired to a respectable life in Bermuda to produce a family whose descendants might well have included a gangling kid who roamed the

3

hills of East Texas. The stories of old Captain Jennings, and of the Spanish treasure galleons he looted, were never far from Howard's mind, and he was to think of the captain often in later years, as he sought some of the very same treasures that had enticed the pirate more than two centuries before.

When World War II came, Howard, who had always been fascinated by flying, joined the U.S. Army Air Corps. Thanks to an accelerated training program that commenced at about the time of his enlistment, he received his commission while he was still eighteen. Thus, when he was assigned to operations, he became the youngest aircraft commander in the Eighth Air Force. Howard piloted a big four-engine Liberator bomber in the 329th Squadron of the 93rd Bomb Group. Between the Flying Fortress and the Liberator pilots there was—and still exists—a violent division of opinion about the relative merits of the two planes. Howard defends the Liberator vehemently, and to this day, any criticism of the Liberator will bring an angry edge to his normally well-controlled voice.

On February 6, 1945, while on his twenty-fifth mission over Europe, Howard's plane was hit by flak from a small four-gun battery near Alkmar, Holland. Howard began to feel his aileron control going, and as the Liberator slid out of formation, Howard jettisoned his bombs. The last bomb had hardly cleared the racks when the plane was hit again, this time directly in the bomb bay. One waist gunner was immediately killed, and the second died a few seconds later in the fire that swept through the fuselage. Howard and the remainder of the crew bailed out. Ten seconds later, the Liberator blew up.

Howard admits that he had become a bit casual with his flight equipment, as many combat pilots did. This time he had failed to harness his parachute properly, and he had several horrible minutes to regret it as, at 17,000 feet, he hung from one shoulder, twirling about wildly in the air, his body at about 45° to the vertical. He landed, with a dislocated shoulder, and was eventually taken prisoner. He was held as a P.O.W. until April 29, 1945, when he was finally liberated by Patton's Third

4

Army at Moseburg, near Munich. In a few more days the war in Europe was over.

Howard talked very little of the years following the war, but during the many days we spent together I pieced together a picture. After he returned from Europe, he took advantage of the G.I. Bill to enroll at the University of Oklahoma, majoring in geology. When his girl friend announced that she was pregnant, he dropped out of school and married her. By the time they discovered she wasn't really pregnant, Howard had accepted his obligation to support a wife. Instead of returning to the university, he got a job as a "roughneck" in the oil fields.

His recollections of the months on the drilling rigs are vivid, and he educated me on the specific duties of the roughneck, one of three men who handle the huge wrenches that tighten and loosen the pipes during drilling operations. It is hard manual labor, and it is extraordinarily well-paid as unskilled jobs go. Howard and his new bride were living rather well. Then one day he severely injured his hand while working one of the wrenches, and his well-paid days as a roughneck abruptly ceased. This financial blow was evidently enough to undo what remained of his disintegrating marriage, and the couple agreed to divorce.

Alone again and unable to work in the oil fields, Howard wandered from job to job, as many of us have done. He once passed a harrowing stint as a crop duster flying ancient BT-13's. When we swapped stories about our experiences in flying rattletrap planes, these wretchedly maintained, obsolete aircraft were Howard's most horrible memories. After cracking up twice, he left that job behind and drifted back to Tulsa.

It was there that he got lucky. He landed a good job as a scout for Amerada Petroleum, and a short while later fell in love and married a second time. He was at last prepared to settle down, but two weeks after the wedding he was recalled to active Air Force duty in the Korean War. The dislocation was not as great as it might have been: He was assigned to Kelly Field in Texas, flying big four-engine C-47's for the Military Air Transport

Service. However, the job entailed long absences while he flew men and supplies across the Pacific, and possibly this was a contributing factor in the erosion of his second marriage.

Howard left the Air Force in 1952, returned to Amerada, and found himself assigned to the staff of the company's Land Department. This job took him on many long exploration expeditions into Utah, Wyoming, and other parts of the Northwest, and helped to revive both his boyhood interest in lost treasures and his enthusiasm for living in the wilderness. He roamed through sparsely settled areas of the Northwest, occasionally making side trips into old ghost towns or prospectors' settlements and poking around with an army surplus mine detector. On one of these jaunts up in South Pass, Wyoming, he ran the detector around the hearth of a burned out log cabin and got a strong signal. Grabbing a spade from his jeep, he began to dig, and in minutes he had collected quite a pile: 15 twenty-dollar gold pieces, 153 silver dollars, and a well-preserved .41 caliber Remington Derringer.

In time, Howard rose to become head of the Land Department's Canadian operation, and soon learned he was to be offered an important corporate staff job back in Amerada's Tulsa headquarters. He also learned that his second wife was suing for divorce. At thirty-five, he faced a professional future of security, advancement, and solid success in a major corporation. He also faced the end of his second marriage, and a number of disturbing questions about the kind of life he wanted to live. There was something gnawing at Howard Jennings' guts, something that would not be confined to the meetings and board rooms of the business world. And so one day he walked out of his office, assigned his income and most of his savings to his wife, and cancelled his subscription to the *Wall Street Journal*. As he left his job and his home behind him, he also put the conventional life behind him forever. Though he could not have known it fully then, his break with routine was the beginning of a rebellion that was to carry him from the comfortable center of middle-class society to the dangerous outer edges of civilization.

But that was still in the future. From Tulsa he drifted to Jamaica, where we met and shared some good times, including many trips to this airport to receive or deliver female visitors. Now, as we waited to receive my incoming girl, Howard began to suffer from his own post-partum depression.

"Dammit, Robin, *think* of someone," he demanded as the New York flight's arrival was announced.

"Mmmmm," I mumbled over the rim of my glass. It was rather flattering to have this make-out artist turning to me for ideas, but I was distracted by the anticipation of Barbie, my French-born, New York girl friend who, along with her other memorable talents, was also a great typist. I was finishing one of my novels, and I needed all of her skills.

"Mmmm, hell!" Howard crabbed. "This is serious."

Back in 1960, Customs and Immigration in Jamaica were fast and easy; Barbie was in my arms within ten minutes of her plane's landing, and within ten more we were piled into my Morris station wagon and heading for Port Antonio.

There are two ways to go to Port Antonio from Kingston. The coast road is pretty, but it takes about half an hour longer than the route through the mountains, and I was in a hurry. Howard chatted with Barbie as I wheeled the car along the winding road, screeching the tires on the curves and hoping not to smash into one of the huge trucks that frequently break down and park on the narrow highway.

We had crossed the mountains and were wheeling down a fairly straight piece of road along a magnificent stretch of coastline when I nearly sideswiped a small car parked on the side pointing in the same direction in which we were headed.

"Damn fool!" I yelled.

At that same instant, Howard screamed, "Stop the car!"

I hit the brakes and the car slid to a halt. Before the dust had settled, Howard was out the door and jogging back toward the stalled car.

I craned around, really expecting some horrible accident scene, but all I could see was a tall, slim, auburn-haired girl wearing a thin yellow dress. I looked at Barbie and Barbie

7

looked at me and we both began to laugh. I put the car into reverse.

The girl was standing beside Howard, who had raised the hood of her car and was peering into the engine. I stepped out of the Morris and walked over to them.

Howard said, "Robin, I'd like you to meet Linda."

Just like that; as if he had known her for years, as if she had come to spend her Christmas holiday with him.

I leaned over to see what Howard was looking at.

"Looks pretty bad to me," Howard said.

I am no mechanical genius, but even I could see that the lead into the distributor was hanging loose, and even I knew it simply needed to be slipped back into place and the girl's rental car would be running again.

"Well, Linda," Howard said, "it looks like you'll have to come in our car. We can send a garage truck out to fix this."

I looked at him in disbelief. Then, before I could bring an end to this farce, the girl cooed, "Well, if that's what you think, Howard."

Linda Bradford turned out to be the daughter of a missionary couple who lived in West Africa. She was in Jamaica for a three-week vacation, and had been driving toward Port Antonio for a visit to our picturesque harbor town when her car broke down. Within an hour of our return, Howard had cancelled her hotel reservations, sent the car back to the rental agency, and moved her into a spare bedroom in his house. As we all learned about Howard, when he puts his mind to something, it gets done.

The Blue Lagoon is one of the most breathtakingly beautiful spots in the world. In a bowl-shaped lagoon, with a channel to the sea, surrounded by dark green foliage and glowing yellow beaches, shimmers some of the bluest, clearest water on this earth. I had purchased the property two years previously and built a lovely gathering spot, which I named the Teahouse of the Blue Lagoon. During the day, tourists would stop by for a dip in the crystal water and a few drinks, and at night, I would frequently have dinner parties for my friends. Two nights before Christmas Eve I had a party, and naturally, Howard showed up with Linda.

The Teahouse was constructed as a large, thatch-covered, open-sided dining/drinking area. At one end was a shed that housed a small kitchen and large bar. The air was soft and the glow of candles flickering in the night complimented the women. In addition to my Barbie and Howard's Linda, there were Peggy Oxenbury, with her husband, Lieutenant Colonel Tony Oxenbury, a retired British Army officer; Penny and Allen Langley from Miami; Iris and Scotty MacRowland, and finally, pretty Wren Warren and her husband, Des, my boat captain.

Tony Oxenbury had made quite a bit of money early in his life in London and then had retired to Jamaica to use his money to make more through land speculation. Tony was a strong, vibrant person who lived life to the fullest and relished the company of others.

Allen Langley was director of the Lloyd Merlin Art Gallery in Miami. He was more of an archaeologist than an authority on art, but careers in archaeology are limited. Through his connections with the University of Miami, which has developed extensive collections of pre-Columbian art, he maintained contact with both fields.

Scotty MacRowland was a gambler whose profitable construction business supported his less profitable hours at the card table. Both Howard and I found his addiction to poker entertaining and rewarding.

Des Warren was a rare Jamaican who could fix an engine, navigate a boat, and distinguish between my possessions and his own. His real name was not Des, but he so reminded me of Phil Wylie's *Des and Crunch* series in the old *Saturday Evening Post* that I had to call him by that name.

After a few drinks, I found Barbie emphatically explaining to Allen Langley the duties of a gallery director, and it occurred to me that we all had had too much to drink. It also struck me

9

that Howard had been trying for an hour to turn the discussion into an area which was of concern to him. When Howard is concentrating or frustrated he begins stalking. Other people have described it as "pacing the floor" or "hovering like a helicopter" or "fidgeting back and forth," but to me it was stalking, and he was doing it that night.

Finally, during a momentary lull, he pounced.

"Penny, does Allen ever buy any Caribbean gold for the gallery?" he asked.

Penny Langley was no woman to stay on the fringes of her husband's life; she was nearly as qualified as he was in the field of museum purchases and exhibitions.

"Allen has found that the gallery just can't get too involved in Gulfstream treasure finds," she said. "The costs involved are really beyond our grants. We mainly work toward the pre-Columbian artifacts out of the Yucatán or other digs in Central America."

Allen joined us. "Actually, Howard, gold for the sake of gold is really out of the question for art galleries," he said. "Most of the Spanish gold out on the wrecks was melted down from Indian artifacts and minted in Lima. The wrecks off Florida and in the Bahamas have little interest for us; doubloons are for the treasure hunters, not for the academicians."

I finished my martini and smiled at Howard. "Morant Keys?" I asked him.

He nodded. "Exactly."

I turned to my guests and said, "Howard and I have a theory. Let's see what you think."

For the past several weeks, over drinks on quiet evenings, Howard and I had evolved a theory that the Morant Keys, about forty miles off the Jamaican coast, were an ideal spot to find buried treasure. A pirate ship that had been plundering up in the Bahamas—or off the Florida Coast, or north of Havana Harbor—would pass closely by the Keys after coming through the Windward Passage between Cuba and Santo Domingo.

"Our idea is that the traffic in and out of Port Royal was heavy enough so that we can assume that some of the pirates

10

would rather have trusted their treasure to a hiding place on the Morant Keys than to take it into the den of thieves working with Henry Morgan in Port Royal."

Howard then went on to describe the physical location and topography of the tiny islands. The archaeologist nodded but seemed bored.

Finally I asked him, "What do you think, Allen? Any possibility?"

He smiled and took a sip from his glass. "Sure," he said. "There are millions of dollars of gold coins, bullion, and treasure in the Caribbean. Maybe hundreds of millions. But it's only money. There's little of value to the archaeologist."

As we pondered that, Tony Oxenbury surprised us all by saying, "Well, I don't care. I'd love to go."

"Why?" Allen asked. "You'll go out, work your backsides off, and come back discouraged. Dozens of trained archaeologists go out to find legitimate antiquities and come home empty-handed."

I could tell that Howard wasn't convinced. In the weeks since he and I had first begun talking about the possibility of treasure on the Keys, he had finished up the land development scheme he had been working on for the past few years. He had risked money, worked long hours, and fought local labor inefficiencies. The rugged land he had bought was cleared, he had built a road up the side of a hill that had been inhospitable to mountain goats, and most surprising of all, he had sold off all of the building sites to reasonably wealthy Americans for vacation homes. Now Howard was anxious to get on with a new project. The idea of hunting the treasure of the Morant Keys had excited him beyond anything I could remember during all the time I had known him.

The idea had found fertile ground in my mind, too. I imagine every man at some time in his life has daydreamed about the possibility of finding treasure, and I am no exception. But when someone plants the seed of an honest-to-God treasure possibility, then the mind really begins to churn. At odd times, mostly when I was supposed to be grinding out words on my typewriter, I would find my imagination wandering ahead to that moment when I would break open a crusty chest and slip my hand in among shining gold doubloons. It takes me a couple of years, maybe longer, to finish a novel, and for that effort I could receive quite a few thousand dollars. But just imagine, in one treasure chest I could dip my hands into hundreds of thousands, maybe millions of dollars in gold and silver and . . . Well, that's the way the mind works.

Howard was hacking away at Allen's theory. "First off, Allen, there is nothing illegitimate about finding treasure. Quite a few reasonably honorable men have become involved up to their necks in searching for missing treasures. Besides, not all of the gold and silver artifacts were melted down into bars or even minted. The Spanish did send quite a few artifacts back along the Spanish Main intact for their own museums."

"Ah, the Spanish Main," said Allen. "What a romantic ring. Think of all those Spanish ships, traveling the same routes from the Caribbean mainland back to the national treasuries of Spain, bulging with treasures from plundered lands. Wonderful! Trouble is, the Morant Keys don't fall onto the routes. Sure, there is some logic to your idea about gold being left by pirates. But you have to remember that the possibility is very small."

"Why?" Howard asked.

"Well, for one thing, the major pirate period was only from the mid-sixteen hundreds until the early seventeen hundreds. That's a relatively brief span. For another, there was the problem of secrecy. An average pirate ship carried a crew of fifteen to twenty-five men who were all deeply involved in a nefarious business. Just imagine trying to keep a group of socially maladjusted thieves banded together. Once a man left the group, loyalties would switch and secret locations would be compromised. Don't get me wrong; we are talking about millions of dollars in raw gold and silver, but we are also talking about a very low possibility of any substantial treasure being left alone for years and years. Many of those pirate crew members were in their teens; they would have had quite a few productive years to go back and dig it up."

12

Allen surveyed his quiet, somewhat sullen audience, and then continued, "Stevenson wrote a highly imaginative work called *Treasure Island,* and history was kind enough to him to provide wide distribution of his works. And to leave us all with visions of evil pirate captains killing all crew members who knew where the booty was hidden. In reality, such incidents would be extremely improbable. Truth is, Stevenson and his publishers are probably the only men in subsequent history who have really profited from the Brotherhood of the Coast."

"I assume you're suggesting there is little treasure in the world?" Howard asked.

"Essentially, yes."

"Sir, I think you're full of shit," Howard said quietly.

I was really shocked. Not at the language, but at the fact that Howard Jennings, whose strict East Texas Protestant upbringing prohibited vulgarity in mixed company, had said it. In retrospect, I have a feeling that that moment may have marked a turning point in Howard's life, and what seemed like a crude social lapse was really the defense of a dream.

Tony Oxenbury broke the uncomfortable silence.

"Well," he said in his best Sandhurst manner, "I think it would be jolly-good fun to have a crack at the Morant treasure."

Howard said, "I'd by-God drink to that, Tony . . . If I had a drink."

Relieved that the nasty moment had passed, I shouted, "Creole! Dammit, Creole! Where's the wine?"

When the wine had been poured, Howard raised his glass and toasted the treasure venture.

Allen Langley drank and smiled in good humor, but he added, "And here's to another group of poor souls bitten by the treasure bug."


The next five days were involved with hectic preparation, conducted in deadly earnest and bordering at times on pure farce. Howard's prime concern was metal detection equipment. He had his old World War II mine detector, a clumsy-looking device and very heavy, but surprisingly accurate during our experiments out in Howard's back garden. We had buried and "found" a dime at six inches depth, a screwdriver at eighteen inches, and a frying pan at three feet. We did not realize till later that a freshly dug hole gives a pretty good reading all by itself. We were jubilant.

Not to be outdone by Howard, I jumped on a plane to Miami in search of equipment for our trip. Asking around, I found out that a chap in West Palm Beach was making a new detector, so I whipped up there and paid $285 for the machine and a cram course on its operation. Then I chartered a flight to rush me and the detector back to Port Antonio. After all, what were a few hundred bucks in relation to the millions in gold we intended to find?

Tony and Peggy Oxenbury had been assigned the task of laying on our provisions for the one-week expedition. Tony had been a World War II tank commander, and we figured if he could help move an army across France, he could surely plan food for six treasure hunters and five workers. Our logic failed to account for Peggy Oxenbury, who was used to hostessing social parties in London's chic Belgravia area and who managed to spend $980 on such necessities as smoked oysters, fresh artichokes, and canned *paté tendre*. Luckily, Tony also bought some steaks, hamburger meat, and cans of baked beans.

We aroused a certain amount of curiosity at the local general store when we purchased shovels, picks, rope, buckets, lanterns, and several dozen other oddments to the tune of another $462. A gross inventory of other purchases—bush jackets, pith helmets, jungle boots, and safari stools—came to over $1,000. I splurged $11 on a diving mask, fins, and a Hawaiian sling spear gun, probably the only sensible purchases made by the whole wacky group.

At last we were ready. We would rendezvous at 6 A.M. at the Blue Lagoon.


We had cleared the Blue Lagoon by 6:30 in the morning, and we were out of the Port Antonio Harbor area within an hour. It was 7:45 when we passed Longitude 76°30′ West, the position I had fixed on my radio direction finder. I took up a new heading of one-seven-eight degrees, bearing due south toward the Morant Keys.

My boat, *Intermezzo*, was a 38-foot Evans Sport Fisherman. Besides Barbie and myself, I had brought Creole along to cook and three Jamaican laborers to do the heavy digging—and to help carry the treasure. A quarter of a mile astern was the 56-foot *Belaire*, a luxurious, brand-new Chris Craft Constitution that Howard and Tony had borrowed from friends in Port Antonio. It was piloted by Des Warren, who knew Jamaican waters as well as anyone we could have hired, and it carried, in air-conditioned splendor, Howard and Linda, Tony and Peggy, several cases of booze, a freezer full of steaks, and cupboards crammed with assorted goodies to ease the rigors of the treasure hunt. We did not intend to suffer unduly while finding our fortune.

As I was at the wheel of *Intermezzo*, Barbie was reading aloud to me from *The Lore of the Wreckers*, an academic book I had picked up to learn a bit more about the history of treasure in the Caribbean; below deck, Creole was cooking up bacon and eggs for our first breakfast at sea. Things just seemed to be going right. I did not know that back on *Belaire* my boat captain, Des, was transporting a load of trouble. Howard and Tony were both well on their way to an early morning drunk; with each succeeding bloody mary, the emotional fuse grew shorter and shorter. Five hours later, when we dropped anchor in the shelter of the Morant Keys, tempers were nearing explosion.

As we eased up to our anchorage near the largest of the three tiny islands, Tony broke out Howard's mine detector and began waving it toward the main island, shouting, "Now you bloody gold! Where the bloody hell are you?"

As I throttled back on *Intermezzo*'s engines, I heard Howard shouting at Tony, "Put that by-God machine away! You'll ruin the batteries."

Tony yelled, "Bugger off, Jennings!" And at that moment,

15

the two boats gently bumped together, Tony lurched off balance, and the detector slipped out of his hand and splashed into the water.

I threw my boat into reverse and eased quickly away from *Belaire*. Howard lunged for the side of the boat, colliding with Tony and sending him crashing to the deck. Without breaking stride, Howard dove right over the side of *Belaire,* and from the speed with which he moved I suspect he caught the detector before it even touched bottom. Des wisely cut his engines and allowed *Belaire* to drift. Grabbing a line in one hand and a long boat hook in the other, he waited. After what seemed like minutes, we could see Howard struggling upward with his detector, and at last his head broke the surface of the crystal-clear water.

As Des reached toward him with the boat hook, Howard snapped, "Not me, dammit. Pull in this damn detector."

We spent the next hour mooring the boats, drying out Howard, and trying to get his detector to work. We succeeded in the first two, but the detector was lost to us for the rest of the trip.

Our first lunch consisted of vichyssoise, asparagus mayonnaise, salmon poached in oyster juice, and strawberry parfait with coffee. We then took a nap while our workers transported our equipment ashore. This was the way to treasure hunt.

We awoke at about four in the afternoon and assembled for cocktails aboard *Belaire*. With drinks in hand and the British Admiralty Chart Number XIX spread out on the table in *Belaire*'s main salon, we reviewed our plan of attack.

The Morant Keys consist of two larger islands and one smaller one. Looking at them on a map, they vaguely resemble the front anatomy of a woman wearing a bra, the small island being her belly button. We had anchored by the largest island, the one farthest east, about one mile from the western island. "Belly Button," as we began to call the little island, was the southernmost of the three, about a half a mile from our anchorage. The larger island we were going to search first had a small fishing camp or village on the western shore which was deserted during

16

the holiday season. (The only real research we had done on the Keys was to determine that the fishermen all went home to Jamaica from before Christmas until after New Year's.) There were no docks, since the Jamaican fishermen pulled their craft right up onto the beach at high tide, and the eight or ten huts proved to be dark, smelly, and dirty.

All the Keys were on the sea route into or out of Port Royal, Jamaica, but our assumption was that Morgan or other pirates stopping off to bank treasure rather than take it into what was then the "wickedest city in the world" would stand off at anchor, put over a longboat, and head for the nearest point of land. There was just such a point, the eastern tip of the largest of the three Keys.

By then it was too late to begin our hunt, so we decided to have an early dinner and begin fresh in the morning. We polished off another Lucullan feast, had brandy under the stars, and turned in.

The sun rose at six-thirty. Howard, Tony, and I were fed coffee and toast by Peggy—Barbie and Linda had slept in. Howard was working on his detector, trying feverishly to get some spark of electronic life back into the thing. All he could raise was a feeble tweeting sound. The illness seemed terminal, and we decided to use my new detector instead. Tony was quiet, still embarrassed about his foolish prank.

The three of us had gone ashore by seven o'clock, leaving Peggy to play mother hen to the younger girls. The three laborers and Des were waiting for us on shore. They had slept right on the ground, wrapped in thin blankets, and were finished with breakfast by the time we arrived. We struck out directly for the eastern point, the Jamaicans hacking a path through the brush.

Upon reaching the eastern point of the island at seven-thirty, we had my detector assembled and "tuned" in a few minutes. The type of metal detector we were using was essentially a transmitter and a receiver. A signal is sent from the transmitter down into the ground, where it "bends" back up to the receiver. By placing a metal object on the ground and holding

17

the detector a couple of feet above it, you can adjust a knob and instruct the machine how to react when the signal is interrupted by metal. Once the machine is delicately tuned, it should detect metallic substances below the surface. When the signal encounters metal, a needle jumps and there is a loud *wheeee-owwuulll* in the headset.

Howard took the first turn, sweeping the machine back and forth across the test area. There were no trees, but some scrub brush grew as high as two or three feet, and Howard had to negotiate a pattern around the bushes, moving in close to the root base, probing into the ground.

The area we had chosen to search was about 250 yards from the shoreline, and Howard was working an area about one hundred feet by one hundred feet, moving toward the sea. For a short while, Tony and I followed closely behind him, waiting anxiously for some indication of a signal. As we nearly collided, Howard stopped, and with a tinge of impatience in his voice said, "Look, why don't you go sit down? I'll call you if I hear something."

It was then that I experienced my first flash of treasure-hunting anxiety: "He has found something and doesn't want us to know," a nasty voice whispered inside my head. That's one of the greatest hazards of treasure hunting: suspicion. The feeling passes quickly as sanity prevails, but that first pang of doubt is a horrible sensation.

Just before nine o'clock, Howard shouted, "Hey!"

We required about ten seconds to run to where he stood, tense, slowly moving the detector back and forth over a small area covered with tufts of grass.

"By God!" he said softly, and he whipped off the headset and urged the detector at me. "Give a listen."

I slipped the headset over my ears, took the handle, leveled the detector, and swung forward slowly. Suddenly, the high pitch of the warning indicator howled in my ears.

I continued to move forward. In about two feet, the signal stopped abruptly. I backed up a foot and turned 90°. I moved forward and lost the signal again, this time only five or six inches from my starting point. I closed my eyes and eased backward, gently coaxing the machine to give us a profile of the strong signal area. About eighteen inches back, the signal stopped again. Swinging the front probe of the detector in a slow arc, a picture began forming in my mind. Down there, below my feet, something was raising hell with the detector; the measurements were roughly two by three feet. A perfect size for a treasure chest!

I pulled the headset off and stood there grinning.

Howard took the detector and said, "You mark it, okay?"

I grabbed a stick and dropped to one knee. Howard moved the detector and said: "Mark." I scratched a small reference point in the soft soil. "Mark," he said and I moved my stick again. In a couple of minutes we had outlined the rectangular shape, and the three of us stood staring at the suggestive figure we had marked in the dirt.

Tony called to Des and the work crew, and they came running. I've been involved in a lot of exciting things in my life—the last-minute hustle before a bombing mission, the frantic activity at the opening of a new Sheraton Hotel, the experience of the best man and ushers trying to get a groom ready for the ceremony—but nothing could compare with the total chaos of seven men pouncing on that little patch of earth on one of the Morant Keys. It was a battle of asses and elbows, until Howard said, "Now, let's take it easy." In a minute, he had the rest of us out of the way and had assigned one of the Jamaicans to take the first turn starting the hole.

I was staring intently at the shovel tearing into the ground, but when I glanced up at Howard I saw that he wasn't watching; he was looking out at the sea. Later I came to know that stance and the look in his eyes. It was as if Howard were already searching for tomorrow. He was sure there was going to be a bonanza in that hole, and now his mind was racing ahead to new adventures, to new hoards of gold hidden in God-knew-what remote corners of the world.

The hole was nearly two feet deep, and the digger was sweat-covered from head to foot. Des ordered another man to take

19

his place, but before the new digger could begin Howard said, "Let's check it."

I really didn't see any point, but I picked up the detector and turned it on. To my surprise, the signal seemed weaker, but it covered a slightly larger area.

It was strange, but no cause for concern. The signal was still there, still strong. I climbed out of the hole and told the digger to expand the area.

Two diggers later, the hole was about four feet square and over four feet deep. Water began showing up in the dirt.

Howard ordered the digger out of the hole and jumped in with the detector; the signal had faded still further, but it was still there, still indicating metal presence. Digging continued for another half-hour, until the hole was over five feet deep and the leather-tough bare feet of the digger were hidden in three or four inches of water.

Howard jumped into the hole again.

The signal was gone!

Without a word, he climbed out and went to one of the supply sacks we had brought from the boat. He took his time replacing all of the batteries, even though the indicator showed that the batteries were strong. He closed the case, came back to the hole, and checked it again. No signal.

Looking up at me, he said, "I want a drink."

We headed back to the boat.

Drinks helped a little bit, but they did not give us any answers. We had done everything right; what had gone wrong? In desperation, I reached for the marine radio-telephone.

"What the hell are you going to do?" Howard asked.

"I'm going to call Palm Beach and find out what kind of Mickey Mouse machine I bought from that sonovabitch."

"And as soon as you do, everyone in Jamaica is going to know," he said. "The radio-telephone is the most public communication possible. We'll have the police on us, we'll have other treasure hunters here, we'll have a dozen sightseers hanging around by tomorrow."

"I'll use a code. The guy will know what I'm talking about, but no one else will."

Howard gave up trying to stop me; he wanted to know just as much as I did.

The call was placed through the Kingston Marine Operator; in five minutes, I was talking to the man in Palm Beach who had sold me my detector.

I managed to get across the idea that people might be listening. I told him that the "radio" I had bought worked fine for a while, that it came in good and strong. But when we came closer to the station, the signal faded.

He said, "You're calling from a boat?"

I said, "Right."

He said, "And you're trying to use the 'radio' near salt water?"

"Yes."

The bastard began to chuckle. "Mr. Moore, I'm sorry. If you had only told me, I might have saved you a great deal of trouble. I hope I can make myself clear to you, but you must realize that salt is a mineral, a stable compound of sodium and chloride. It gives off one hell of a 'radio' reaction under the right circumstances."

I found I didn't want to talk to him any longer. I thanked him and signed off.

All of the group on the boat had heard. It was a depressing lesson for us, but I think it was especially important to Howard. He would never treat treasure hunting lightly again.

We didn't search any more that day, but, after a good night's sleep, we started working other areas of the island. The pattern repeated itself: great booming signals followed by hours of digging, followed by a nasty puddle of salt water. Surprisingly, we all cut back on our drinking. We worked another four days and left a lot of the island looking like a pockmarked battlefield.

That night, Tony and Peggy Oxenbury announced that they were leaving in the morning. Howard and I decided to stay, so the next day we transferred the supplies from *Belaire* to *Intermezzo* and the Oxenburys headed back with Des and two of the diggers.

That day, while Linda slept late, Howard took the detector

and worked a different part of the island. I took Creole and Barbie with me in the dory and we rowed to the island opposite the one we had been working. It was desolate, but strangely refreshing.

As we walked the beach, Creole suddenly stopped dead in his tracks and fell to his knees, clawing at the sand. I thought he had gone bonkers. In a minute or two, he had dug a hole about ten inches deep and two feet wide, and there in the hole was a squirming mass of newly-hatched baby turtles, only a day or two from digging their way to the surface and heading out to sea. Creole had brought along a sack, and we lugged one hundred wriggling baby turtles back to the boat. We put them into the live-well in *Intermezzo,* to form the foundation for a revitalized turtle population in the Port Antonio area. (Of course, I caught hell from the conservation people in the Jamaican Government, even though I hadn't known it was illegal to disturb nests. Anyway, I still feel the turtles found better homes in and around the Blue Lagoon.)

The next day, without much discussion, we loaded everything on board *Intermezzo* and headed for home.

I've thought about the Morant Keys down through the years, and I'm still convinced there is gold there. Now that the engineers have designed detectors impervious to salt water signals, it might be a good idea to go back and work the island. But I'm not sure I have the heart to try. Perhaps Howard will do it some day, for old times' sake.

In a sense, our expedition to the Morant Keys was nothing much better than an expensive piece of nonsense. But I remember it with affection—I will never forget the incomparable thrill of hearing that electronic howl when our metal detector sent out its first false message of treasure.

As for Howard, the experience must have had implications much deeper than either of us could have guessed at the time. It was, as I have said, perhaps a turning point. In my mind's eye, I can see him still, looking back at that pockmarked little island and saying, "It's there. By God, it's there. . . ."

# 2 THE EMERALDS OF CHIQUINQUIRA

⚎

KINGSTONJAM VIA CABLE & WIRELESS
FROM BOGOTÁ THRU PANAMAPANA
84914  LT     orm/wrk/     CAW  906PM

ROBIN MOORE
BLUE LAGOON
JAMAICA WEST INDIES

ARRIVING JAMAICA TOMORROW STOP MIGHT
NEED SOME HELP STOP WILL SEE YOU AT
TEAHOUSE PPMM
REGARDS JENNINGS

That was the cable I had sent to Robin; he had it right there on the bar in front of him when Linda and I arrived back at the Blue Lagoon, where the Colombian emerald hunt had begun. Robin had been in on it from the start, and he would be the first to hear the wild details.

Ten days after the Morant Keys fiasco, Linda and I had dropped into Robin's Teahouse of the Blue Lagoon. It was much too early for gin or whisky, so we were looking for a cold beer. At that time in Jamaica—at least around Port Antonio—the only place you could find a cold beer served in a frosty glass mug was at Errol Flynn's Jamaica Reef Hotel or at Robin's Blue Lagoon. Robin was there, pounding at his typewriter, but he quickly pushed it aside and set up beers.

We had been chatting and joking for thirty or forty minutes when a car pulled up to the Blue Lagoon. It was Abe Levy, a mutual friend who ran a string of fine jewelry shops on the island.

"You boys ready for another adventure?" Abe asked innocently.

Just about everyone on the island knew about our Morant

23

s disaster, all because of Robin and those damn turtles. I
l warned him to leave the turtles there, or at least to keep
mouth shut, but Robin is a storyteller. He'd bragged about
nem, and the authorities had jumped on him with both feet.

"No," I told Abe. "And we don't need any turtles, either."

"Hmm. Then I guess you're not ready for another purchase?"

"As a matter of fact, I might be," I answered.

I had given quite a bit of business to Abe, buying gifts for
young ladies who spent their vacations with me at my home.
Linda had no idea that she was in for an expensive present,
but she'd have to know soon. All good things must end sometime.

Abe smiled and reached into the inside pocket of his jacket.
He pulled out a thin chamois bag and spilled a half dozen brilliant emeralds onto the bar. "Look at these," he said. We were
looking. Linda's eyes sparkled as she examined the stones, and
I began giving some serious thought to having one of them set
for her.

"How much?" I asked.

"Emeralds can run up to five thousand a carat," he said. He
saw me wince and quickly added, "I could cut up one of
these, say about two carats, for twenty-five hundred . . ." My
eyes told him that he was still way out of the ball park, and
he finished the sentence, ". . . but a lovely pair of earrings
could go as low as eight hundred."

I shook my head, but my curiosity was aroused. "Where'd
you get these stones?" I asked.

"They're Colombian," he said, and he then unfolded a fascinating story of the emerald trade.

He told us about the mines in the Cordillera Oriental Mountains, north of Bogotá, where more than ninety percent of the
world's quality emeralds are found. Abe's stones came from
the Muzo Mines near the city of Chiquinquira, about a hundred miles north of Bogotá. There are about ten thousand
people in Chiquinquira and three thousand in Muzo, and
most of the people in those towns virtually worship emeralds
because the industry supplies so many jobs.

24

"Worship?" Linda asked.

Abe smiled. "Actually, emeralds have a history of worship." He explained that the stones have, at one time or another, been credited with preventing epilepsy, curing dysentery, assisting in childbirth, preserving chastity, and driving away evil spirits. The ancient people of Manta were said to have worshipped an ostrich-egg-size emerald as the "Mother of Emeralds." Abe added that though most emeralds are relatively small, a Leningrad museum has a stone weighing six pounds.

I asked, "Were those stones of yours smuggled?"

Abe nodded. "The route is involved and treacherous, though. It begins in the mines themselves."

He explained that the mines are government-controlled and that security is tough. Occasionally, the peasant miners can hide a stone or two on their persons, but they must be very careful; the armed guards will shoot a worker on the spot for possession of a stolen stone.

Once smuggled out of the mines, the illegal stones are then taken to nefarious dealers in the small towns, where the first value is placed on them—usually about one-twentieth of the wholesale value of the stone. From that point on, the price begins to jump in algebraic progression as the stones pass from hand to hand.

The small-town buyers have regular markets in Bogotá, but transporting the stones to this city is no small trick. The roads and train routes are peppered with checkpoints, each one manned by ill-trained, well-armed, hot-headed Army troops. Other routes to Bogotá are well-populated with *banditos* who relish capturing, killing, and stealing from smugglers.

Once the stones are in the capital, the danger diminishes considerably. Tourists pass through outgoing Colombian customs inspections with only cursory checks. A hundred thousand dollars' worth of emeralds could be smuggled out in ladies' underclothing in a suitcase; Latin civil servants are timid about despoiling *gringo* ladies' undergarments. These particular stones of Abe's had been flown to a distribution point in Panama, then had been carried by a banana boat deckhand to

25

Port Antonio, where Abe had bought them for $4,000. He expected to double that figure in the retail market.

"Is there a solid market?" I asked Abe.

"Is a pig's ass pork?"

Robin was quick to latch on to my thinking. We were both disappointed and slightly embarrassed by our failure at Morant Keys, and here was a chance to recoup.

Robin said, "What Howard is asking, Abe, is would you buy some emeralds if we got them here for you?"

Abe waved his hand and finished off his beer. "Robin, I'll guarantee you a solid profit on every good stone you can bring to me," he said.

That word "good" caught my attention. "How could we be sure that we were bringing you good stones?" I asked. "We'd need an expert along for advice."

Abe shook his head. "Howard, I can make you an expert buyer in just a few hours in my shop in Kingston. If you get serious, give me a call."

As you might guess, we got serious.

As soon as Abe left, Robin and I began bouncing ideas around. Our first scheme was an involved plan to sail *Intermezzo* down through the Caribbean to the port of Barranquilla on the north coast of Colombia. It sounded great at first, but we had to discard the plan. The trip would probably have eaten up all our profits in gasoline for the boat. A Sports Fisherman is great for a day's outing after blue marlin, but it is no practical way to travel a thousand miles round trip on a smuggling project. Anyway, Linda didn't really like boats, it would take a long time, and Robin's publishers were pressing him for delivery of his new novel. In addition, I was still busy with the formation of Jamaica Air Service.

The second plan involved Robin's plane, a twin-engine Piper *Apache* that he used for charter purposes. It was a beautiful plane for that sort of an operation. We would only be gone for three or four days, and Linda loved flying in private planes.

So it was settled. We'd fly to Bogotá, buy some emeralds, make our fortune, and salvage our pride. We were all quite excited about the prospects.

That is, we were excited until the next day, when Robin's agent flew into Jamaica and delivered an ultimatum: Robin had to finish his book forthwith. Robin argued, but the agent was adamant.

So Robin had to stay behind in Port Antonio. But he nevertheless remained a partner in the operation. Robin and I each put in $8,000, giving me $16,000 with which to make purchases. Considering that we were going to eliminate the smugglers, the transporters, and the in-between brokers, I guessed that we could double or maybe triple our investment. As Robin went back to writing his book, I packed up Linda and headed for Abe Levy's jewelry shop in Kingston.

We checked into the Myrtle Bank Hotel and phoned Abe. In fifteen minutes we were sitting in his cluttered office.

When you spend your time as a treasure hunter, as I have over the past years, you get to see places and things that most people never dream exist. But even for me, the back room of a major jewelry dealer is still startling. There are dozens of solid gold settings lying about, collecting dust; there are diamonds and rubies scattered in the most curious places, folded in Kleenex tissue, or just sitting innocently in an unused ash tray.

But there is also organization in the jeweler's business. Abe pulled out a red-velvet-lined tray holding two dozen emeralds in various stages of processing. He dumped half a dozen innocuous-looking stones into a Kleenex.

"Here's what they can look like coming out of the mine."

I looked at the green stone, which had been cupped by nature in a nondescript setting of yellow material called matrix. Abe handed me a jeweler's loupe—one of those funny little magnifying glasses that you place to your eye—and I peered down into the cold beauty of the stone. Lines ran through it like the canals on Mars, and shades of green glowed and changed as the gem was turned under the light. There was *life* in this stone. Then and there I fell in love with the subtle, shifting beauty of emeralds.

Abe broke the spell. "Don't imagine that it's easy to be a gem expert, Howard. Even men who have been in the business for years must often rely on educated guesswork. Still, I'd say you can guess as good as anyone. I've seen you play poker."

"Guesswork?"

"Just that," Abe replied. He explained that one tap of a jeweler's hammer could shatter a poor emerald into a thousand worthless pieces of chromium-impregnated beryl. It all depended on how you read those stress lines. "But it is not as much of a gamble as you might think. First off, the quality factor out of the Muzo Mines is extremely high. If you are sure they are from those mines, the odds are they are good."

"Guesswork." "Gamble." I did not like to think in those terms. I was getting ready to play around with $16,000, not a few bucks on a poker table.

I spent hours with Abe Levy that day, peering through the loupe while he explained the finer points of emeralds. At last, with my head spinning with terms—"refraction index," "cleavage," "specific gravity," and a dozen others—I pulled the loupe from my eye and shook my head. "There's just too much to know, Abe," I said. "I'll end up with worthless stones for sure."

Abe reached down into a drawer and pulled out a small pouch. Taking a piece of chamois, he shook out ten or twelve stones. Then, from the tray sitting in front of me, he mixed in the uncut gems we had been examining. He spread the chamois on the tabletop and said, "Now, pick out an emerald, and I'll cut it. The ones from the sack are worthless."

I knew that Abe could sell an uncut but badly flawed emerald for $1,000 or $1,500. But not if the stone was shattered.

I spent ten minutes looking at each stone. Finally, full of apprehension, I selected one and handed it to him. He placed the loupe in his eye, delicately seated the rough gem on the tiny anvil before him, and studied it carefully, hammer and chisel poised.

Then the hammer came down with a sharp smack, and there on the table were three lovely emeralds and dozens of tiny chips. The stone I had selected had been a good one. My confidence soared, and my mind raced ahead to the adventure in Colombia.

Our Avianca DC6B landed at Bogotá's El Dorado Airport just before eleven the next morning. Linda and I checked into the Tequendama Hotel and we quickly discovered why some rooms are provided with oxygen tanks: Making love above eight thousand feet is literally a breathtaking affair.

A light lunch of native fruits and a bottle of the local white wine eased us into a relaxed mood. I called down to the front desk and ordered another bottle of wine with an oxygen bottle chaser; after both bottles had been properly employed, we joined the rest of Bogotá in that extremely civilized custom, the afternoon siesta.

We awoke at about seven o'clock, dressed in the one fairly formal outfit we had each brought, and headed downstairs. Back in those days, when U.S. oil men still ran the petroleum industry there, the Tequendama Country Club was the place to meet. I had a standing invitation at the club due to my previous connections with Amerada Petroleum, and I thought I'd show Linda how the *gringos* live in foreign lands.

"*Buenas noches, señor,*" the taxi driver greeted us as we left the hotel.

In Latin America you can pretty well plan on becoming the temporary employer of an English-speaking taxi driver, usually the one who picks you up at the airport on arrival. Ours was named José.

"*Buenas noches,* José," I said. "We want to go to the . . ."

". . . Country Club?" he finished, already anticipating where two fancily dressed Americans would want to go. We laughed and got in.

29

The Tequendama Country Club turned out to be an oasis of U.S. chrome and Formica, filled with talk of cars, kids, television, and politics—all American. Bored with drilling equipment and the Baltimore Colts, we left after two drinks.

As we headed back into the city, José cautiously asked, "Are you here on business?"

Just for fun, I said, "I'm here to buy emeralds . . ."

He laughed, but I guessed that he knew I wasn't kidding. He slipped into silence.

I asked him to take us to a nice local restaurant, and he did. The lights were bright, the table cloths were clean, and the food was good. When we came out of the restaurant, José was standing by his taxi with a "friend."

He said, "Señor, I'd like you to meet Palacio."

I imagine everyone has his own impression of what a Latin American crook must look like. All of them fit Palacio. He was not the kind of a character you would want to do business with on a dark street, especially when you are carrying $16,000 in cash.

"Do you deal in emeralds?" I asked Palacio.

"Does he deal in emeralds?" José replied. "Señor, this is Colombia; *naturally* he deals in emeralds."

"Do you have any to sell?" I asked Palacio.

José said, "Does he have any to sell? But of course he does, señor."

I looked sternly at José and said, "Let him do his own answering."

José looked hurt. Then in an injured tone he said, "Palacio does not want to talk to you."

Of course. That's why he was there. Patiently, I asked, "Why?"

"Señor," José replied, "Palacio thinks you are the police."

At that point I assumed I was dealing with an amateur; surely any pro would know most of the police. I pulled a tight rein on my temper and said, *"He* came to *me,* José. Tell him I am only a typical tourist who wants to buy some typical em-

30

eralds at typically low prices. Now, dammit, José, let's do business or take us back to the hotel."

Palacio came to life. "How many do you want?" he asked. That was better.

Palacio slipped his hand into his pocket and pulled out a leather pouch. Loosening the drawstring, he poured a half-dozen cut stones into the dirty palm of his hand. In the darkness, they could have been cut beer bottle glass. I suggested we go to the hotel where I could examine the quality. Palacio balked.

"Sorry, señor," he said. "That I cannot do. The police, you know."

"No, I do not know, señor. To begin with, those stones are cut. I want uncut stones. Second, there are not enough. I want more, many more. Third . . ."

Palacio raised his hand. "*Si, señor*. I will meet you in your hotel room. The number please?"

"I'll meet you in the lobby," I replied. I was not anxious to have this bandit arrive during an oxygen-inhalation session with Linda.

"*Si, señor*," Palacio said, "I will meet you there in one hour."

We never saw Palacio again, but sometime around midnight the phone rang. A man identified himself as Rojas and said that he was Palacio's boss. He veiled his comments just enough to confuse a hotel telephone operator who might be eavesdropping, but I recognized the voice of a man ready to talk business. We arranged to meet for an eight o'clock breakfast.

The next morning I slipped quietly out of bed, allowing Linda to sleep. I showered, dressed, and was in the hotel dining room in time to have a cup of coffee before Rojas joined me. We ordered eggs and made small talk. Then, as we finished, I said, "Do you have any stones with you?"

Rojas was a pudgy, round-faced man with olive skin. His face elongated in shock and his color went pink. He whispered: "Here?"

I smiled. "I'd like to see them in my room." He untensed,

31

and we headed toward the elevator. I noticed two men sitting in the lobby, trying to hide their faces and gun bulges behind the morning newspapers. Rojas noticed my reaction and said, "Do not worry, señor. They are my men."

I worried. Those young punk hoods were armed.

I decided to let them know they hadn't cornered the gun market. Opening my jacket, I reached for the handkerchief in my hip pocket, accidentally exposing the .38 Smith and Wesson I was wearing in a shoulder holster.

In the corridor, Rojas said, "Señor, you are not supposed to carry a gun in Colombia."

I said, "I am also not supposed to get myself killed in Colombia."

Linda was asleep and uncovered when we entered the room. She gasped and clutched the sheet, but the brief glimpse had not been lost on Rojas.

I tossed Linda's peignoir to her and seated Rojas at a small table by the window, where he had an unobstructed view of Linda as she struggled into the flimsy clothing.

"Now, let us talk," I said.

Rojas fumbled two large leather envelopes out of his pocket and displayed three dozen various-sized stones on the desk top. I held the jeweler's loupe below my eye and began concentrating on the stones. Rojas concentrated on Linda.

At that time in my life, I don't think I could have been considered a lapidary, but one tends to learn quickly when there is $16,000 at stake. I immediately excluded all but seven of the gems Rojas offered me—the others had obvious flaws. Although I knew that emeralds are frequently cut *en cabochon,* with a rounded head to cover flaws, the stones I was looking for were destined for rings or pins cut in the classic "octagonal step cut." A skillful buyer might have found salvageable value in the stones I rejected, but I was working on only sure things.

The seven remaining emeralds looked good to me. Their shape and color were excellent and the refraction index seemed high, although I would have needed a spectograph to check the color dispersion. The cleavage seemed to promise flat surfaces when they were split. Assuming the stones were from the Muzo Mines, I did not have to worry about their hardness.

I had devised a simple method to help me evaluate the important specific gravity of the stones. I carefully measured water into a chemist's beaker, then dropped the stones in. They displaced ten millimeters of water, which I calculated to be just over one third of an ounce avoirdupois. I then removed the stones and placed them on an inexpensive postage beam scale. The stones weighed barely over one ounce. Figuring the water reference as one, I then determined that these stones had a specific gravity of 2.9, a number indicating good quality in emeralds. Once satisfied that I was probably examining seven good stones, I looked at Rojas, who was staring at Linda.

"Señor Rojas, I want two things from you," I said.

"*Sí,* Señor Jennings." He returned to mundane things reluctantly.

"Rojas," I said in my best businesslike tone of voice, "first, I want you to supply me with the names of two or three emerald brokers in Chiquinquira; second, I want you to pick out five hundred dollars' worth of emeralds from these seven I have set aside."

I am quite sure he had little interest in letting me know how to deal directly with the illegal brokers in Chiquinquira; but, for the moment, he was completely shocked at my purchase offer.

"Señor Jennings," he whined. "It is illegal to even possess emeralds without authorization in Colombia. If I sell stones to you for a mere five hundred dollars, I would not have enough money left to pay off the police, and if you were to expose me, I would be ruined financially trying to pay for a lawyer. No, señor, a sale is out of the question at that price."

We negotiated.

Unless you have ever done business with Latins, you cannot appreciate what "negotiation" really means. It involves pleading, begging, threatening, and crying, all punctuated with melodramatic gestures of the hands and eyes. Finally Linda, who understood that a distraction was needed, appeared in the room and began pouring drinks.

After many drinks and an hour of rather confused haggling, Rojas agreed to select four stones at a total price of $1,500. He seemed reluctant to leave.

"Why do you wish to go to Chiquinquira?" he asked.

I smiled and said, "Because I am greedy, just like you."

There was another session of extravagant discussion, with Rojas torn between glimpses of Linda and his desire to get my $1,500 in hand.

I was reaching the end of my patience. I said, "Come on, dammit, Rojas, give a name."

"I can get in much trouble for this, Señor Jennings," he moaned.

I waited. Finally he said, "The man you want to meet . . ." He paused, looked around the room, leaned closer to me and whispered, ". . . his name is Don Oswaldo Lopez."

I paid him his $1,500, let him take one more hungry look at Linda, and then ushered him out of the room.

An hour later, we had checked out of the hotel and were headed toward the train station in Bogotá.

The train itself was primitive, filled with pigs, chickens, naked children, and a generally nauseating odor. The hundred and five miles to Chinquinquira were made just bearable by the liberal application of one of the bottles of gin we had brought along as part of our survival kit.

"There seem to be lots of soldiers out there," Linda remarked after half an hour.

There were. She had spotted the first of three military checkpoints between Bogotá and Chiquinquira. The trains did not stop on the outward trip, but they would stop at all three on the way back.

"Are we coming back by train?" she asked.

"I don't know yet."

The soldiers were standard issue for a Latin American army: dirty, unshaven, undisciplined, with rumpled, ill-assorted uniforms. Their armament consisted of equally ill-assorted pistols and a few vintage rifles. Nothing was standard and most of it could be called junk. But it was lethal junk.


The only thing missing from Chiquinquira was John Wayne.

It was a town out of the old American Wild West, complete with horses and burros tied up to hitching rails around the windblown, unpaved main square. Soldiers were everywhere. The population was technicolored—white men, brown men, black men, Indians, mulattos—but the one thing they all had in common was that they openly carried guns. With mine tucked under my armpit, I began to feel positively prudish.

"You think this is such a good idea, Howard?" Linda asked faintly.

"No, it isn't a particularly good idea," I replied. "You want to go back?"

"No."

"Neither do I."

I studied the saloon doors across the packed dirt street. They swung open and shut as drunk civilians and drunk soldiers staggered in and out, every one of them packing enough armament to exterminate a small village single-handedly. We did not visit the bars.

Castro's message had reached these parts, we noticed. *"Castro sí, Yanqui no,"* was daubed on a few outhouses with all the admirable brevity of the sloganeer. Castro was still something of a revolutionary hero in those days, and the Colombians had just had another revolution of the classic sort. The pundits calculated the next one wasn't due for six months at least.

There were only two taxis in town—both Chevrolets, both ancient. I chose the one that looked least likely to self-destruct. With a bit of luck, it might even survive a trip back to Bogotá, in the event we found reason not to catch the train. In fact, the taxi worked better than it looked. The driver, something of a relic himself, took pride in the interior of his twenty-year-old tragedy in tin.

35

"Take us to the best hotel in town," I commanded.

"Of course, señor."

The owner of this establishment was either a romantic or an optimist. He called it the Hotel Paris. In the years since, I have seen many a bedbug academy in South America, but few as disastrous as this one.

"Oh, my God," Linda gasped as we were shown our room.

"Yeah," I said. "Me too. Never mind. With any luck, we'll be out of here tomorrow."

"What are those things on the floor?"

I recognized the rat droppings. "Just dirt," I said nonchalantly.

She pointed across the room. "Are those things cockroaches?"

"I'll fix them."

"Where's the wash basin?"

"There isn't one. No running water."

"What about the toilet?"

"Under the bed."

"Howard, we can't sleep here." Linda was near tears.

"Just wait a while. I'll go get some sheets and a few other things."

I came back with curtain material and a can of insect killer, which I purchased in a shop on the square. The whole can *might* discourage the hotel's native wildlife from attack for one night—the curtain material we could sleep in.

When we had made the room barely habitable, Linda said, "Howard, I was thinking."

"What?"

"If this is the best hotel in town, what's the jail like?"

"Don't think."


I had no problem finding my contact. There was a store facing the dirt square with a sign that said, DON OSWALDO LOPEZ, HARDWARE AND GENERAL SUPPLIES. Mentally I added to the sign: "Stolen Emeralds to the Trade, Casual Murders Undertaken. Reasonable Rates?"

In Latin America, the term *don* indicates a man of some stature in the community, so Don Oswaldo had to be the rather distinguished-looking, white-haired old gentleman parked on a high stool near the rear of the store.

"Don Oswaldo?"

"*Sí.*"

"*Habla inglés?*"

"*No.*"

He called out, and his young, very pretty, black-haired granddaughter appeared to act as interpreter. Her fine features and intelligence made her a rare creature in this town, and her grandfather was obviously very fond of her.

Boldly, I said I was there to buy uncut emeralds. A flurry of Spanish ensued.

"Don Oswaldo says you are to come back tonight. He will show you what you have come to see," the girl announced.

"Fine. Will you come to the hotel to meet us?"

"My grandfather says that is not necessary."

"Tell him I said it *is* necessary."

After another discussion: "My grandfather says he can meet you only here."

I did not want to walk into a trap. We had almost $15,000 on us, motive enough for a dozen murders. But I did want to make the emerald buy. If Don Oswaldo was as fond of his granddaughter as he seemed to be, I reasoned, he was unlikely to risk involving her in a gunfight in his store. I would have to do it his way or go home empty-handed.

That evening, the rendezvous occurred as planned. Don Oswaldo held court in the living quarters behind the store, flanked by two young half-breed thugs, both equipped with low-slung Colt .45's. The smaller the gunman, the larger the gun.

One of them spoke broken English, but I ignored him. I had no desire to lose the presence of the girl. It did not improve the punk's temper, but the girl remained as our interpreter.

Glasses of rum and water were handed out, and we got down to business. The old man pulled out a suede bag and upended it on the table. Even in the dim light of the room, the dark green sparkle of several hundred small emeralds made Linda gasp. I thought they were pretty too, but I wanted big ones.

"Tell your grandfather I want larger stones."

The girl translated and the old man nodded. He spoke a few words of Spanish. The ill-tempered gunslinger disappeared. We heard him going down steps into a cellar, then moving around below us. Their own private emerald mine, no doubt. He soon returned with another suede bag and handed it to Don Oswaldo.

This time it was exactly what we wanted—huge, uncut stones of fine brilliant quality. I took my time and examined them, and even Don Oswaldo seemed impressed with my home-grown techniques and procedure. Each stone could be cut up into several gems good enough to keep Liz Taylor happy for a week. I chose what I considered to be the eight best.

Then the fun started. The rest of the night was taken up with negotiating a price. Sometime around dawn I made a final take-it-or-leave-it offer of $12,500. Complaining, they took it.

That left only the minor problems of how to affect the exchange without being shot, and how to get out of the country without being arrested.

I turned to the granddaughter, who was bleary-eyed from lack of sleep. "Tell Don Oswaldo we must take the noon train to Bogotá, but we are having our driver take us to Lake Fuquene, because we hear it is beautiful."

"Yes, it is very beautiful," she said.

It was also, I had taken pains to discover, on the road to Bogotá.

"Ask him where he would like to make the exchange."

After yet another conference she turned to me. "There is a village near the lake called Susa. He says he will be there at nine o'clock this morning."

"Good. He is to have no one with him but his driver. And he must bring you as well. Agreed?"

The two-man goon squad seemed definitely unhappy about this.

38

"He says he agrees."

"Good. See you later. Good night." Linda and I wearily stood up.

We strolled back to the hotel, where the insects were putting up a gallant fight against the chemical warfare—and they seemed to be winning. But we were not to have the experience of hand-to-hand combat with Chiquinquira cockroaches after all.

It was now six in the morning. Linda and I sat on the bed as I took stock of the situation. Don Oswaldo and his cowboys now knew that I carried at least $12,500 on my person. They also knew that I was now aware of the identity of at least one middleman, Rojas, between emerald smugglers and the Bogotá marketplace. Wouldn't it make great sense for Don Oswaldo to ambush the American somewhere out of town, destroy this menace to his security, and at the same time relieve the dead American of his considerable bankroll? The answer came to me instantly. It would indeed make great sense.

I stood up abruptly and pulled Linda to her feet. "Let's go," I said. "I'll carry our bags."

"Where? Why?" she asked groggily.

"We're going to find our intrepid cab driver before Don Oswaldo gets to him, and then we're going to see the countryside by early morning light."

Leaving the hotel, we walked along the dirt street to the open garage where we had hired the ancient car and driver. The window of the old Chevrolet was open, and I reached inside and tooted the horn. The sounds of grumbling in Spanish came from the shack behind the garage.

"Hey, wake up, señor," I called out as a head appeared in the window. "Time to be on the road." I fanned a sheaf of dollar bills for emphasis.

"Sí. Momento," he called back as I threw our bags into the back of the taxi.

Our driver reported to the car ten minutes later, dressed in his threadbare dark chauffeur's uniform, which appeared to give him a feeling of stature in the village.

I pulled out a map of the area and pointed to Lake Fuquene. In my limited Spanish, I made him realize that my lady and I had heard much about this beautiful lake, and that we wanted to visit it and still get back to Chiquinquira in time to take the noon train back to Bogotá. I wanted to be very sure he understood that we must be back to catch that train out of here.

Our driver nodded. There was plenty of time to see the lake and still get back by noon, he said. Then he opened the back door of the cab for us and we stepped in.

Linda snuggled up against me in the back seat of the car. "Nap time, Howard," she sighed, closing her eyes.

"Not now, darling. Sorry." I leaned forward and made the driver understand that we wanted to go first to the local *cantina*.

"I'd rather sleep than eat," Linda protested.

"We're going to be all *turista*, darling. We'll have ourselves a nice, leisurely breakfast, just as casual as can be, right where everybody in town can see us."

A breakfast of doubtful origin was put in front of us, and somehow we were able to wash most of it down with black coffee.

As I had expected, our taxi driver entered into conversation with a passing friend. I picked up enough of it to gather that Linda and I were the subjects of this discussion. Where was the *gringo* going? Out to the lake. When is the *gringo* coming back? Eleven, in time for the train.

When he climbed back into the cab, I peered over our driver's shoulder and noticed that the gas gauge showed the tank to be half full. Not enough to make it to Bogotá, but hopefully enough to get us to the first gas station on the way.

As we approached the shores of the beautiful Lake Fuquene, I handed our driver the first of several surprises in store for him this day. We would forget the lake, I explained, and drive on to the quaint little town of Susa, which we had always wanted to see. The driver grumbled a bit, but kept on going past the lake.

Susa is composed of three dusty, rutted streets, two of them

40

running parallel to the main road, the third perpendicular to the other two. We parked the car on the perpendicular road so that it was hidden from what passed along the main drag. We were, as I had planned, an hour early. From now on I would watch every person and vehicle that entered the town from the direction of Chiquinquira.

There was a *cantina* with a window fronting onto the main road, and for the second time that morning we risked dysentery with a couple of cups of coffee. There was hardly any traffic on the road. Halfway through the second cup of coffee, a battered old pick-up truck rattled into town from the direction of Chiquinquira and came to a halt in a swirl of dust.

Two men got out, both carrying rifles, and went into a house across the road from us. I recognized both of them: One was the English-speaking cowboy of the night before, the other was the gentleman who had been so interested in our itinerary over the breakfast table.

"What are we going to do, Howard?"

"Well, we could bolt for Bogotá now, but why waste all the effort we've gone to? Best thing to do is let them keep thinking we're going back for that train and wait till the old man shows up. Maybe we can twist his arm a little."

"You really think so?"

"It's the best plan I can come up with. If we can get those two out of town and make our deal with Don Oswaldo, they're still going to have the ambush set up in the wrong direction."

Don Oswaldo turned up just after nine. I took my .38 out of its holster, stuck it in my belt, and then walked across to his jeep—which was parked in front of the house that the two gunmen had entered.

The girl was in the car with her grandfather.

"Tell your grandfather he has five minutes to get those two *caballeros* out of that house or the deal is off."

"My grandfather is very sorry. He does not understand you."

"Tell your grandfather that if he does not immediately understand me I am going to the soldiers." The old *don* understood.

Without a word, he climbed out of the jeep and walked into

41

the house. The two gunmen came out, equally silent, piled into their old pick-up truck, and headed off in the direction of Chiquinquira. I assumed that they would drive only a few hundred yards in that direction.

"Now, Don Oswaldo," I said, "are you still interested in selling your emeralds?"

"Why not?"

We made our deal on the side street while sitting in the back of the taxi. I put the gun in my lap and handed the old thief $12,500 in $100 bills. The girl gave me the emeralds. I studied them to be sure they were the same emeralds I had picked the night before while the old man counted out the money, bill by bill, three times. There was probably a $10,000 profit for him, but I have never seen anyone look so unhappy at making $10,000.

"Okay," I said, all bright and cheerful. "I hate to rush you, it's just that we had hoped to see your beautiful Lake Fuquene before we catch the train."

Don Oswaldo had not said a word all morning, but he looked suspiciously happier as he strode off to his car.

We watched as Don Oswaldo's jeep headed back toward Chiquinquira, disappearing in a cloud of dust. Our driver turned to us and asked when we wanted to return to catch our train. I noticed that his eyes were fixed on the revolver, now lying on the seat beside me. Reaching into my wallet, I removed a $100 bill, which I slowly pushed in his direction.

His eyes swiveled from the gun to the bill and back to me. I gave him a friendly smile and said one word: "Bogotá." I pointed down the main street in the opposite direction from Chiquinquira. His eyes went back to the gun and then he gave me a weak smile as he took the $100.

"Si," he said. "Bogotá."

The taxi coughed itself to life and started out of town. As we gained the road and started on our trip back to Bogotá, I looked behind us frequently, but the billowing dust made it impossible to see whether or not we were being followed.

The first checkpoint would be ten miles south of Susa. At the speed we were going, I figured we had twenty-five minutes to hide our emeralds securely. I had been giving this matter some thought.

"Let me have your camera," I said to Linda. She handed me her old-fashioned Kodak. Taking out the film, I opened the bellows and pulled out most of the works. Then I filled the inside with the emeralds—there was just enough room. I snapped the back into place again. "Happy photographing."

We reached the checkpoint, a ramshackle building propped up by half a dozen decrepit Colombian soldiers.

Linda was wearing the shortest skirt in her wardrobe, and on descending from the taxi, she stretched first one long leg and then the other out the door. Finally, she stood beside the car, a bright smile on her pretty face.

El Presidente himself could hardly have hoped for as smart a reception as Linda found. Shirttails were tucked in, hands run through hair, brown-stained moustaches wiped with backs of greasy hands. Two of the soldiers got busy with a half-hearted search of the car while keeping their eyes on Linda, who was doing an absurd amount of hip-swivelling as she strolled about the car.

Then came Linda's *coupe de maître*. Through miming, she indicated she wanted to take a picture of all the handsome soldiers lined up against the building. They were delighted! With great smiles exposing their broken teeth, they arranged themselves in front of their guardhouse and looked straight at the camera lens. The camera did not even go click at the appropriate moment. But it didn't matter. She could have been looking through a toilet roll and they wouldn't have noticed the difference.

The soldiers took the barrier up for us and waved us through with many shouts of affection and esteem. For the first time in several hours, we felt we could relax.

"How did I do?" Linda asked

"You were great. You should be in the movies."

"You know, that's funny. I wasn't scared back in that village, even of those two guys with rifles. And that's why. It was too much like a bit out of a movie script."

The road was hot and dusty and winding, and we were both

43

close to exhaustion. We dropped off to sleep, Linda's head on my shoulder, my head resting atop hers.

I woke up an hour later with a vague feeling of unease. The cause of the worry was our driver—he was just ambling along. Why? Could it be that he saw a way to make more than just $100 out of the deal? A little insurance seemed in order. Clearing my throat, I stuck the gun in the back of his neck.

I didn't want to upset him too much, so there was another $200 in my left hand.

"Bogotá," I said. "Presto! Pronto!" I waved the gun. "Move over. I'm driving." When the car came to a stop, I climbed over the back of the seat and settled behind the wheel.

"What's this?" Linda murmured, waking up.

"What's left in the booze cupboard?" I asked from the driver's seat as we began rolling again.

"This is a hell of a time for a drink," she answered. "Let's see. We've got one bottle of vodka. That's all."

"Good," I said. "Give it to our friend here."

The old man stopped grumbling and attacked the bottle with some enthusiasm. The stuff he was used to was the local variety of white lightning rum, which is better measured in octane than proof. Vodka must have seemed as smooth as water.

"When is the next checkpoint?" I asked.

"Twenty minutes," he answered.

He was out for the count by the time we arrived. Half the bottle had disappeared in fifteen minutes!

The soldiers at the checkpoint were positively outraged. Poor *turistas,* their driver gets so drunk they have to drive the taxi themselves!

The officer in charge jerked the door open and out fell our taxi driver in a snoring heap, vodka bottle and all.

"This is a disgrace to our country," cried the officer, thumping his boot into the poor bastard's ribs for emphasis. "This one we will lock up for a long time."

"Hey, that's not necessary," I said. "Anyway, I can't just take his taxi. How will he get it back?"

"Don't worry. You tell the police in Bogotá. We'll tell him. You have had a most unfortunate experience. I hope it has not spoiled your stay in Colombia."

"Certainly not, Officer." I watched two soldiers drag our driver into the station house. "Thank you for your trouble."

"My pleasure, señor. *Adiós.*"

When the checkpoint was obscured in the dust storm that followed the taxi, Linda showed her nervousness. "We'd better get out of this country before they check out our poor driver's story," she said.

I drove along unconcernedly now. "I wouldn't worry about it. Who's going to back him up? Don Oswaldo? What do you think would happen to him if he was found either with emeralds or $12,500 worth of American currency?"

We found a rundown service station where an old, weathered, half-Indian attendant hand-pumped the tank full of gas, and then I drove the remaining distance to Bogotá at a fast clip. We made it, right back to the Tequendama Hotel. I pulled the taxi into a parking lot and joined Linda in the lobby. It was late afternoon and the next plane out of Bogotá for Jamaica would not leave until the following morning.

In our room, we took a long bath together. Later, we ordered dinner from room service, but barely managed to stay awake until the drinks and food arrived. Without finishing the whole meal, we both fell into bed, too exhausted to need oxygen.

We both had terrifying images of what a Colombian jail would look like if we were caught trying to smuggle the stones out of the country. The next morning, after checking in at the airline and being passed on into the custom's departure lounge, Linda repeated her act, snapping photographs of the officious-looking inspectors and swinging her hips. Despite our nervousness, we were greeted with nothing more than big grins.

By mid-afternoon we were in Kingston, and after the two-hour drive to Port Antonio, we were standing in the Teahouse of the Blue Lagoon.

Robin was annoyed by the blank expressions on our faces.

45

Linda playfully asked, "Robin, can I take your picture?"

"Screw your pictures; did you get the emeralds?"

Linda and I burst out laughing. She popped open the back of the camera and $12,500 worth of smuggled emeralds spilled out onto the bar.

"Damn!" Robin exclaimed. "You did it!"

We put in a telephone call to Abe Levy and invited him over to Port Antonio for dinner and an emerald shopping spree.

Robin, happy that the trip had been a success and also because he had just finished his novel that same afternoon, laid on a real feast.

Abe arrived shortly after seven, but we insisted on waiting until after dessert before showing him the stones. I was savoring the satisfaction of my first successful fortune-hunting venture.

With coffee and Tia Maria liqueur in front of us, the servants were dismissed and I unveiled our spoils.

Abe took out his jeweler's loupe. We sipped our Tia Marias as Abe examined the stones, and the first flurries of apprehension began to gnaw their way into my brain. Why in hell was he taking so long? Then, just when I was about to express my irritation, Abe lifted his head away from the stones.

"These gems are beautiful." There was genuine awe in his tone.

An audible sigh of relief came from both Robin and me.

Abe began making notations.

"I'll take two of the smaller stones for a thousand each," Abe said. I had included Rojas' stones in with the larger ones from Don Oswaldo.

I asked, "Twelve hundred?" and he said, "Okay."

Then, fondling the larger stones, he told me, "I'll take two of the eight. I'll give you five thousand each."

Robin and Linda gasped in excitement; we had not told Abe what we had paid for the gems. I said, "Six for each." Abe replied, "Fifty-five hundred," and I agreed. We had nearly covered our investment and expenses, and we still had a fistful of emeralds to sell.

46

Abe went on apologetically, "I'd like to take them all, Howard, but I can't right now. There is a buyer coming down next week, though, and I'll get you together with him."

Before Abe left, I slipped him the other two smaller emeralds and told him to make them into a pair of earrings for Linda. She would have an appropriate memento of her trip to Colombia and her stay with me.

The following week we all drove over to Kingston and met the New York buyer in Abe's office. In less than fifteen minutes, Robin and I had accepted $45,000 for the remaining uncut stones, and we left the office with the check in hand.

That afternoon, I put Linda on a plane back to her home in New Orleans and Robin on one to New York, where he was going into the jungle of the publishing world.

As I drove back to Port Antonio, visions of treasures and precious stones danced in my mind. I knew I was through as a land developer. Adventure, gold, and jewels were what I wanted, at least for a while. I had no idea, then, where that vision was to take me in the decade to follow.

# 3 PIRATE GOLD OF ROATÁN ISLAND

Dear Robin,

We're having some people in for lunch Easter Monday and we'd love you to join us. We can handle two or three of your friends with no problem. We hope to see you about one—come casual.

All the best,
Bruce

The note had been slipped under my door while I was away. It was Easter Monday morning and I had just arrived back from New York, wound up and ready to let go. A friendly luncheon at Bruce Kellock's would just do the trick. Two of the friends I could take would be Howard and whatever little lovely he had bunking in with him over the holiday weekend. The third would be Noel, a wispy little Paramount starlet who had come from New York with me to help me unwind.

My call to Howard was answered by a sultry British accent.

"My dear," I began, "is Howard there? I'm Robin Moore."

"I'm *not* your dear and he *is* here."

I thought the girl seemed touchy. As it turned out, I had interrupted one of Howard's "elevenses." The poor girl. She was a nurse on vacation, I learned.

Howard's voice came on the line. "Hey, Robin. When'd you get back?"

"Just arrived," I said. "I just had a note from Bruce Kellock. He's giving a luncheon today. You want to go?"

"Hell, yes," Howard said, "I've wanted to meet the Kellocks."

"Fine," I said. "Bring a girl and we'll meet you at his house in an hour. Okay?"

49

We all arrived there just before one-thirty. After my apologies for being late and introductions all around, we settled down to some catch-up drinking. There were four other couples there, the Oxenburys, a doctor and his wife, and some others whom I can't remember. What I do remember about the beginning of that luncheon was everyone's fascination with Bruce Kellock's son and his incredible collection of Erector Set toys. Bruce's son had a real talent for making all kinds of weird devices. While the women chatted, the men gravitated magnetically to the elaborate display. Bruce was really proud of the young man's ingenuity.

In a short time, the conversation swung around to the gadgetry of metal detectors, and our all-male group moved out onto the patio area.

"You two must have had quite an experience with your detectors," Bruce said.

After Morant Keys, I had worked very hard to push metal detectors and all that goes with them far out of mind, but Howard jumped into the subject with gusto.

"I just bought a new one in Miami," he said, "It works great. I've been exploring the St. Thomas area and I'm convinced that Morgan buried treasure on his land there."

Howard went on, explaining that after Morgan gave up piracy and become Lieutenant Governor of Jamaica, he was deeded thousands of acres in St. Thomas. "There just has to be treasure buried there."

Howard was beginning to sound like a man obsessed.

"I've come up with an idea about . . ." Howard went on and on. I drifted away to make sure that Tony Oxenbury wasn't getting too close to my starlet. After protecting my property and knocking back a quick drink with her, I drifted once again to the patio. Bruce Kellock was talking.

". . . and it seems that Morgan went to the Bay Islands off Honduras after the sack of Panama in 1671. At least, that's the story."

Howard was obviously excited.

"Robin," he said, "Bruce just told us about a huge treasure

find discovered in 1935. They found it by using a boat's compass as a detector."

I knew something about both airplane and boat compasses. While they can deviate slightly if a piece of metal is placed near the magnet, it would take one hell of a mass of metal to make a compass react if the metal was buried a couple of feet below the surface.

I must have looked skeptical.

Bruce smiled. "I forgot to mention that the treasure was in gold, silver, and emeralds, and was stored in three good-sized metal chests. Quite a mass concentrated in one spot. I think it would cause a compass deviation."

"I suppose so," I said. "It would also cause quite a stir when that much gold was introduced into the market, but it's a hell of a story."

Howard asked, "Bruce, what was the girl's name again?"

"Sammy Mitchell-Hedges."

Apparently Frederick Mitchell-Hedges had been a British archaeologist who had headed an expedition to explore the Mayan civilization of Honduras in Central America. Curious about island-living segments of the culture, Mitchell-Hedges went to the island of Roatán in the Honduran Bay Islands. He took along his stepdaughter, Sammy, and a man who is only identified as "Doctor Ball."

The three-person expedition, aided by several local native workers, began concentrating on an area which was named Port Royal. It had been given that name by the pirates, who had formerly operated out of the infamous City of Sin, Port Royal, Jamaica. The exploration began turning up quite a bit of pirate residue: cannon balls, musket parts, shoe buckles, and the like.

As either a diversion or a serious quest, Doctor Ball removed the compass of their ship, *Amigo,* and began crawling about on his hands and knees, using the magnetic flux principle to detect metal. He found the normal amount of junk, until one day a startling thing happened.

While working one of the larger sand islands out in Port

51

Royal Harbor, he saw the needle react with comparative violence. He discussed the find with Mitchell-Hedges and they dug. One foot down they unearthed a large iron chest. After breaking the rusted hasps, they pried the lid off and were confronted by a fantastic inventory of gold artifacts and jewels. All thoughts of archeology dissolved; the scientific exploration turned into a treasure hunt. Two more chests were discovered, and the trio then plotted their next moves. They reburied the chests and began to search for other signals. However, some of the natives had become aware of the find. Natives in the islands tend to talk, and these talked to the police at the main barracks twenty miles at the other end of the island.

Mitchell-Hedges was, I understand, a charming man, and he had made friends with many of the local civic leaders. One of them tipped him off that the police were planning to make an inspection of the digging area the next day.

Mitchell-Hedges and Dr. Ball decided not to wait around. In an exhausting all-night operation, they dug up two of the chests, and just as dawn broke, they hoisted *Amigo*'s sails and made for British Honduras, 150 miles to the northwest.

Near the port of Belize, *Amigo* anchored off a small cay. Mitchell-Hedges took the ship's skiff into the port, and returned some hours later with a load of timber. Feverishly, they built new crates, transferred their trove, and threw the empty metal chests overboard. They then booked space on a steamer to New York with the treasure innocently tucked into their cabins, labeled "Mayan Artifacts." In New York, Mitchell-Hedges presented part of his collection for auction, realizing, in the end, $600,000 from the sale.

Mitchell-Hedges' life-style changed considerably when he returned to England. He bought a country castle and devoted the remainder of his life to collecting antique silver and hobnobbing with celebrities. Reportedly, General Eisenhower was a guest at his home during World War II.

Do stories like that make other men seek fortunes buried in the ground? You bet they do. Certainly Mitchell-Hedges' story propelled Howard and me into another adventure. But it didn't start right away.

It was over a year later. My little starlet had left me to marry a Broadway producer, and Howard's English nurse was flitting around maternity wards, diapering new little Englishmen. By that time, Howard had liquidated all of his holdings in Jamaica and had gone to England to spend his money more quickly. My book had been a modest success, and I was in London to negotiate rights with a British publisher. Howard was letting me use his flat while he traveled on the Continent.

I had two days to kill because British lawyers need that long to review a three-page contract. What does a footloose writer do with two days to kill in London? He goes to famous restaurants for bad food, makes passes at marginally attractive "birds," watches the changing of the guard at Buckingham Palace, is disappointed by Big Ben—and browses around the British Museum.

Browsing around the British Museum could take years, and I had only a couple of hours. But just as I was approaching the end of my self-imposed time limit, I noticed an incredibly beautiful display case, over-filled with Mayan artifacts—several of them that lovely, warm color of gold. The plaque discreetly attached to the case identified the finder of these priceless objects as Frederick Mitchell-Hedges. Wham!

There was the old urge back again, the treasure lust surging through my veins. I could picture the old man and his stepdaughter as they opened those chests and held those massive gold objects in their hands.

I've researched a good many books in my day, so the first thing I wanted to know was precisely where the treasure was found. I had a vague idea for a novel on the subject of the Mitchell-Hedges find, and I had to know more about the Bay Islands.

The British Museum has everything. Within fifteen minutes, a friendly, grey-haired maps custodian was leading me up to the map room. Politely pointing to a wide, floor-to-ceiling filing cabinet, he told me that five of the flat drawers had to do with the western Caribbean—I was welcome to study them at my leisure. Then he left me alone.

It was three hours later when the old man came back. The

museum was closing, he said, but I could come back in the morning. I had found five great old maps, such as the 1791 one by Lieutenant Jeremy Thorndyke, surveyor in the service of the Royal Navy. I checked the aging, yellowed diary card and discovered that the last time anyone had looked at Lieutenant Thorndyke's map was in September, 1843. The topographer had worked in a large scale. One inch on the map represented five hundred feet in the area around Port Royal Harbor—right where Mitchell-Hedges had made his find. There were three village sites indicated, with detailed locations of dozens of houses and buildings. It was as if I were a spaceman looking down on a community that had existed a couple of hundred years ago. I was now, more than ever, determined to search out any available information.

The next morning found me back at the museum as it opened. With the aid of the curator of the maps section, I discovered two more fine old prints. One showed the entire island of Roatán, the other was an engineering survey and building detail of old Fort Key, (or George Island, as some of the maps called it) which sits in Port Royal Harbor. I arranged to have high-quality photographic reproductions made of the maps and prints, then went back to the Mayan section. I found little information there on Frederick Mitchell-Hedges.

By the time two more days had passed, I had picked up duplicate maps, but I had also become re-enmeshed in tedious negotiations with my London publisher. My involvement with the Roatán treasure had diminished.

It was Saturday morning. I was sitting there in the breakfast nook of Howard's apartment, glancing back and forth between my brandy-laced coffee and the sculptured beauty of Lady Margaret Stokes-Manning. I had met her at a cocktail party the night before, and she had unexpectedly consented to spend the night with me. She was sitting there clothed only in one of Howard's pajama tops. Because I was in the presence of the aristocracy, I wore the bottoms.

We weren't saying much—there wasn't much to say. The night had been exciting and satisfying, the morning was bright and cheerful, and we would soon part. On Friday word had come from my agent in New York that I was finally cleared to begin preparations for my work on *The Green Berets.* That struggle had begun in Jamaica, when I had met Vice President Lyndon Johnson during the Jamaican Independence celebrations and the coincidental opening of the Sheraton-Kingston Hotel. The Vice President, or one of his staff members, had been kind enough to read my book, *The Devil to Pay,* and the Vice President had encouraged me to pursue my goal to write a book on Vietnam. He had set me off through the bureacratic labyrinth which must be navigated to obtain governmental permission for such a project. Now, finally, approval had come through for me to attend the U.S. Army Airborne School at Fort Benning, Georgia—a prerequisite for going on to the Special Warfare School training center for the Green Berets.

I was to leave this beautiful woman behind and report to Fort Benning, to spend several months training to be shot at by a bunch of murderous Viet Cong guerrillas. Lady Margaret leaned across to pour herself another cup of coffee. As she did, the loose-fitting pajama top separated slightly, and I began to calculate how much longer I had before I had to leave for my Pan Am flight to New York.

A grating *buzzzzzz* startled us, and suddenly we were not alone. Howard had come home from the Continent.

Lady Margaret allowed about four and a half seconds for an embarrassed "Charmed to meet you" to Howard, then flitted into the bedroom to dress. Howard gave me an evil grin and poured himself a cup of coffee.

He said, "She's very nice."

I said, "I'm going back to the States today."

"Damn, Robin," Howard said, "stay here. We can have a few days of fun."

I filled him in on my Green Berets project and he understood. He nodded his head toward the closed door of the bedroom and asked, "You wouldn't mind if I . . .?"

I laughed and said, "Anything the lady says is fine with me.

Where I'm going there's no room for women. And no treasure, either." Then, feeling proud of my research, I presented the map reproductions.

For the next hour Howard studied the maps, virtually ignoring the lady and me. I dressed, packed, and announced I was going to catch a cab for the airport. When Howard offered to drive me out to Heathrow, I knew he had something on his mind.

The three of us left his Marlborough Hill flat and went downstairs to his Jensen, $15,000-worth of the hottest car in England. He wasn't a car buff, but he did like to move around in style. He chatted amiably with Margaret during the drive, but did not mention the maps I had left him. He parked at a NO PARKING sign and we went into the check-in counter. The clerk informed me that we had nearly an hour to wait, so we headed up to the First-Class Clipper Lounge for free drinks. After a few more minutes of chatter, Margaret excused herself to powder her nose. As soon as she left the table, Howard lowered his voice and said, "Let's go after the missing chest."

" 'Missing chest?' What missing chest?" I asked.

Howard explained, and I was sorely tempted. But I had a plane to catch, so I left Howard there, with a beautiful lady and the other thing he lusted after—the scent of treasure.


Robin had no way of knowing that I had made contact with Sammy Mitchell-Hedges, the stepdaughter of the late archaeologist-treasure hunter who had discovered the trove on Roatán. There was also no way for him to know about the chest of gold which they had not been able to take with them. I had only found out about it myself, when I had visited Sammy Mitchell-Hedges in Reading.

A month before Robin and I had met in my flat, I had been to the races at Ascot with a young English girl who had invited me to join her family in their box. In the course of the conversation, I mentioned the name of Frederick Mitchell-Hedges. One of the guests knew his stepdaughter, Sammy, and suggested I call her. That evening my call produced an invitation to tea, and that tea led to an intriguing revelation.

Sammy's home in Reading was not the stately home that had been the center of Frederick Mitchell-Hedges' social whirl during the later years of his life. He had spent lavishly, and by the time of his death the fruits of his accidental find on the island of Roatán had shrunk considerably. Death duties had diminished them further. They say in England that a family fortune can be wiped out by three deaths within twenty years; actually, *one* death can chop away up to ninety-six percent of the property and capital. Sammy was living on the residue of a badly eroded estate.

She was, however, living graciously in a lovely home, one hour by train from London. We settled down in her parlor, and after she completed the wonderful ritual of "pouring," we began to talk.

She told me about the day they sailed *Amigo* out of Port Royal Harbor.

"It took us until nearly three in the morning to move the first chest onto *Amigo,*" she said. "You understand, Mr. Jennings, the chest was heavy and we had to dig it up, move it to the small boat, load it, row out to *Amigo,* then hoist it aboard. It was exhausting."

She said that they had had only a little less difficult time with the second chest. Then she went on to describe the hasty departure in the early dawn. Our talk went on for well over an hour. We warmed to one another and in that short period of time I felt we had established a friendly rapport. Finally, I asked, "Whatever happened to the third chest?"

She looked at me with those warm blue eyes as she sipped her tea. "Did I mention a third chest?"

I smiled. "No, Sammy, you didn't mention it. That's the trouble. What happened?"

My ploy paid off. We talked for another hour.

That morning, back in 1935, the sky had begun to lighten just as they hoisted the second chest aboard *Amigo.* Frederick Mitchell-Hedges was on the horns of a dilemma. Their expe-

57

rience with the first two chests indicated it would take about three more hours to load the third. He was fairly sure the authorities would arrive that morning, but he could not guess the exact time. They could be caught in illegal possession of treasure and have the whole trove confiscated. He considered staying and taking his chances, but in the end he decided to weigh anchor and sail out of Port Royal Harbor. It was probably the wisest decision he could have made, and one which was to have an effect on my own plans in the future, when I was faced with a similar decision.

I probed Sammy's memory and tried to piece together the fragments of all she could recall of the third chest. It was not as large as the others, but it did have the same varied assortment of cups, artifacts, coins, and bars. It was rusted iron and had been easily opened. As far as she knew, it was still there, right where she and her stepfather had left it buried nearly thirty years before. I reviewed every detail, hoping to jog her recollection, but we were hampered by lack of maps.

Roatán had slipped from her life. It had supplied a high standard of living, and she was not a greedy person. There had been times when she had thought of going back, but the real or imagined threat of arrest prevented her. After the auction in New York, the story had spread, and it surely must have come to the attention of the authorities in Honduras. Treasure-laden countries take a dim view of outsiders coming in and making off with their historical and archaeological wealth.

I thanked Sammy for her hospitality and information and went back to London, hoping to find some more data to support her story. I spent a day looking through old newspaper files and came up with a lot of recorded information on Mitchell-Hedges, but nothing about the missing chest. I cultivated a friendship with one of the custodians at the Royal Geographical Society and was able to find a few inadequate maps. My efforts with the Honduran Embassy in London were just as fruitless. Aside from a few navigation charts, all I discovered was that reports in the seventeenth century told of three forts, five hundred houses, and more than two thousand buccaneers operating out of Port Royal Harbor, and that the harbor was uninhabited at the present time.

Then came Robin's accidental find of the maps from the British Museum. I think I would have eventually gotten around to the museum, but Robin's natural feel for research surely saved me time. With these highly detailed maps in hand, I took another ride out to Reading to visit Sammy Mitchell-Hedges.

The meeting went well, but there seemed to be a tension that I had not felt with Sammy before—I just could not get her to open up. I had spread out the maps and about all I could get out of her was a noncommittal "Hmmmmmmm, isn't that interesting." She refused to speculate on where the chest might be, and even acted as though the chest did not exist.

Nearing exasperation, I asked what the hell was the matter.

Sammy became very serious, "Howard, I know you have been around a lot. I know you can handle yourself well. But I just don't want any part of getting you in trouble." Then, in a somewhat petulant tone she said, "If you want to rot in some filthy Honduran jail, be it on your own head."

I spent the next five minutes letting Sammy know that I appreciated her concern and that I would be careful. Finally, she sighed and said, "All right, Howard." Easing a delicate index finger down to one of the maps, she pointed to a small spit of land at the east end of Fort Key, at the edge of Port Royal Harbor. "It's there, Howard. Right there."

Staring down at the map, I felt the familiar exhilaration beginning to grow inside me. That's one thing you have to learn about treasure hunting. If you want to enjoy the life and keep from going loony, you have to find a way, at the very outset, to place limits on your sense of greed. I told Sammy that I hoped to arrange an expedition, and that she would certainly share in the proceeds if there were any.

She demurred, but seemed relieved. I doubt that she was much interested in the treasure, but, being a sensitive and in-

59

tuitive person, she was concerned about my attitude. From her point of view and from mine, I had my feelings adequately under control.

I occupied the remainder of the weekend with Robin's friend, Lady Margaret, and on Monday morning I whipped over to the British Museum.

Robin had only scratched the surface.

In three days, I had collected enough information to write a small textbook on the Bay Islands, especially the island of Roatán.


At that time putting together a treasure-hunting expedition was not too involved for me, though later in life I learned how to make things much more complicated. I began by buying $5,000 worth of travelers' checks, told my maid that I would be gone for a while, and bought an airline ticket to Miami.

I checked into Miami's jet-set hang-out, the Racquet Club, called a few old friends and looked up electronic supply houses in the Yellow Pages. I had dinner at Tony's Fish Market and over coffee began trying to figure out how to get some help on the trip. While I'm known as a loner, I did not think it would be advisable to go into the Honduran bush alone. After running down my mental list of possibles, I came full circle back to Robin.

First thing in the morning I put in a call to his family in Concord, just outside of Boston. Robin's mother told me that he was not yet in Vietnam, and that he was still training at Fort Bragg. She gave me a number at which to reach him. The number in Fort Bragg was in the administrative section of something called the Counterinsurgency and Special Warfare Staff Officer School. A gruff top sergeant told me that Mr. Moore was in class, that he'd be advised I had called, but that classes lasted until three in the afternoon. I left my number and went out to buy some equipment.

Miami, which sits right on an imaginary line between most

of Latin America and the east coast of the United States, is called "The Crossroads of the Americas." After World War II, the airline industry boomed in Miami. Eastern, National, and Pan Am developed major overhaul and maintenance facilities, and this attracted quite a few electronic technicians from the Army, some of whom set up private businesses dealing in specialized applications of electronics. I ended up at a hole-in-the-wall firm on Northwest North River Drive.

Ever since my oil exploration days, I had messed around with metal detectors. My favorite had been an army surplus mine detector, the one Tony Oxenbury had ruined fooling around out at Morant Keys. I had loved that old olive-drab detector, but it would have been ashamed to enter that shop in Miami. Despite the tattered outside appearance, the offering inside was incredible, including sonar devices, Loran navigation systems, and metal detectors. I purchased a Fischer M-Scope Explorer for deep penetration and a coil-type Detectron to spot small objects near the surface. I dropped the devices off in my room and headed for Sears, Roebuck, where I purchased boots, heavy-duty work clothes, work gloves, and insect repellent. I'd spent too much time in the bush to let nature make my expedition unbearable.

I was back at the Racquet Club by half past two and was well into lunch when Robin's call came in from Fort Bragg.

"Howard, old buddy," he said happily. "What are you doing in Miami?"

"I'm putting together a by-God expedition," I said.

"To where?"

"You know where. You found the maps."

There was a pause. Then he asked, "The Mitchell-Hedges thing?"

"Right."

I filled him in on what I had been able to establish, and I must admit I tried to infect him with my enthusiasm for the project.

Finally, I said, "Robin, why don't you come along?"

"Can't do it," he said. Maybe he could think of someone to accompany me, he added. I said goodbye with a tinge of annoyance in my voice. I hadn't called him for recommendations.

The next day was Friday and I devoted it to more shopping, finding a girl, and going to an afternoon movie. When the girl and I arrived at the Racquet Club for dinner, there was a message for me. Robin was arriving at ten that night. After dinner, the girl and I went to my room and found ways to pass the time until ten.

When Robin came to my room, he looked better than I had ever seen him. First Airborne and the Green Beret training had been demanding, but healthy. His skin was tanned, muscles hardened, and his carriage erect. He looked like a bloody soldier.

I introduced him to my girl, and the hungry look in his eyes evidently decided the girl that it was time to make her excuses. When she had gone, I brought up Roatán.

Robin had rejected the scheme out of hand because he was just about to graduate from the guerrilla warfare course and he needed to go to Washington for some research in the Pentagon. He had committed himself completely to the Vietnam project. He was on a weekend pass right now, he explained. "I have only thirty days before I report to Special Forces Headquarters in Saigon, Howard. I'd love to go with you but there just isn't time."

"You have thirty days," I said. "When do they start?"

Robin said, "Graduation is next Thursday. I have thirty days from then."

"That's easy," I said. "We'll just limit the Honduras trip to ten days. You spend ten days at the Pentagon, then ten days getting laid—add them up."

Robin considered. I had a feeling that I was winning, so I charged into the opening. "I promise you, Robin, just ten days, because I *know* where the damn treasure is."

I looked at his face for a reaction. In fifteen seconds, I knew I had won. As it turned out, our Roatán venture took a little more than ten days—as a matter of fact, Robin had only five days for the Pentagon and no days for the pleasures of the last blondes he would see until he returned from Vietnam. But if you ask him, I think he'll tell you it was worth it.

On Sunday Robin went back to Fort Bragg, and on Monday morning I caught the flight to Honduras. The plan was for Robin to join me on Roatán Island by Friday or Saturday.

If you were to travel to Roatán Island today, you would be able to select any one of three TAN jet flights from Miami and pick up a feeder line, Lansa, which operates two flights daily to Roatán. But when I made that first trip, I flew in a war surplus twin-engine C-46. There was only one other passenger on the flight and he deplaned at Belize, British Honduras. Two hours later, I climbed down into the sultry heat of a typical afternoon at the airport of San Pedro Sula, the main industrial area in the Republic of Honduras.

Tourism in Central America was on the rise in 1963, so customs and immigration clearance was fairly easy. The inspector began to study the bright red boxes which made up the housing and shipping cases for my detectors, but I explained that I was a surveyor on vacation and that I was probably going to try and find some gold mines. There were gold operations inland, so the inspector bought the story.

I located a small air charter service out at the airport and made arrangements to fly to Roatán. I have had to fly in some marginal aircraft in my career, but that well-used, twin-engine Cessna I chartered sent chills down my spine. While the sloppy ground crew was stuffing my luggage into the plane, the much-too-young pilot was vigorously pounding with a hammer on the left-engine propeller blade, apparently trying to correct a dent.

I walked over to where the intrepid Latin airman was pounding away and asked what he was doing. He replied, "Feexing dee prooop." I asked how it happened to be bent. He answered, "I keeled a sheep on my last landing."

With no real enthusiasm, I climbed into the cockpit next

to my alleged pilot. The plane vibrated alarmingly from the bent prop, but it cleared the runway. We bounced up into the sky over Honduras.

To distract myself from the irritating throb-throb of the out-of-balance prop, I peered down at the countryside. The patchwork farms and dirt roads seemed to be fighting a losing battle with the heavy green jungle foliage at the foot of the mountains: Honduras has a lot of water and a warm climate, so vegetation grows rapidly. I estimated about 20 minutes' flying time to the island, 45 miles to the northeast. After about 15 minutes, I used my limited Spanish to ask the pilot how we were doing. He told me we were in good shape and that the island was directly ahead of us.

What I saw directly ahead of us was one monster cumulus, and off in back of it I could see another towering cumulus rising high into the sky. We were flying right smack into a cold front. The low stratus just over the sea promised a bumpy and dangerous ride. I had had enough. I reached across the pilot and picked up his navigation chart. On the chart, I spotted the small coastal town of La Ceiba southeast of us, in a direction opposite to the cold front. I had read that it was the principal port used by the people on Roatán. Emphasizing my wishes with a very angry finger, I pointed to La Ceiba and called out over the engine noise, "Land there. Put her down. Now!"

My pilot shrugged his shoulders and banked the plane over to the right. We landed on a dirt strip littered with rocks and cow dung, and I still remember holding my breath until we rolled to a stop. Hell, I didn't even hold my breath when I was shot down by the Germans over Holland.

Night was falling when I arrived at the main dock in La Ceiba via a rattletrap car hired at the dirt strip. I found a weather-beaten boat with a young captain, Riley Gough, who agreed to carry me and my baggage to Coxen Hole, the largest town on Roatán.

Several good-size boats ply the waters between the Bay Islands and the mainland carrying smelly fish in from the islands, provisions out from the mainland, and people both ways. Diesel exhaust mixed with decayed fish made for a fragrant trip, and the ominous sky I had refused to fly into had created a very rough sea, but the old tug of a boat made it to Roatán around dawn. The first human I saw was a sloppy-looking soldier, and in my imagination I saw another dawn, twenty-eight years before, when Frederick Mitchell-Hedges had watched the eastern sky come aglow and decided to leave a fortune in pirate treasure buried in the sand less than twenty miles from where I was standing.

Roatán had been settled by early English adventurers and convicts, who had become boat builders and pirates. They smuggled and they hired themselves out to work on the sea. In the mid-1800's, England ceded the Bay Islands to Honduras for a railroad right-of-way between the Atlantic and Pacific. Then, because the United States built the Panama Canal, the whole project was aborted and the white settlers were abandoned to a Spanish government. But even to this day, the islanders identify with the English-speaking world, and they still call anyone from mainland Honduras "Spaniards." In return for their taxes, the people of the Bay Islands are graced with small, undisciplined detachments of mainland soldiers to keep the peace. And, since the islanders are very peaceful, the dirty, slovenly soldiers spend their time drinking and getting dirtier and more slovenly.

When I arrived on Roatán Island, not one road had yet been built. I found the local grocery store proprietor just opening up his shop and asked the best way to visit historical Port Royal Harbor. He advised me to go to Oakridge, the village closest to the harbor, and told me whose boat could be hired for the trip. Within an hour, I was sitting in another boat, getting drenched by spray as we bore due east into an easterly sea and wind. By noon time, I was standing on a small wooden dock in Oakridge.

The words "unspoiled" and "virgin" are inadequate to describe Roatán as I first saw it. The beaches were long and covered with white sand, palm trees swayed gently, houses stood on stilts over the water's edge. It has changed in the years since then—but that is another story.

With the help of friendly villagers, I made my way to the

home of Miss Merle Cooper—her first name rhymed with Pearlie. She ran a clean, attractive, and homey guest house, a small building about one hundred yards from her home. It had three tiny bedrooms and one spotless bath. Merle served meals in the dining room of her own home. A room, three meals a day, housekeeping, laundry, and the use of a refrigerator to keep beer cold cost $3 per day. I cleaned up and fell onto my bed. I woke at four in the afternoon and headed for a cold beer.

Most activity in Oakridge centered around a tiny all-purpose store operated by a lady named Nonnie McNab. She was the sole source of "store-bought" chickens, and the local people joked that she had spent so much time with her hens that she had grown to look like one. Nonnie was pushing seventy, and her "store" was something to behold. She carried an inventory that would put a big-town variety store to shame. I found Eveready flashlight batteries at half the Stateside cost. U.S. cigarettes cost $1.50 per carton. (The Bay Islanders are not really smugglers, but they live by a maxim: "Screw the government; take what you can and get it to the island.")

The "bush telegraph" is a phenomenon found on islands in the Caribbean. It operates much more efficiently than any telephone service or newspaper. A friend of mine, the former Minister of Health for Jamaica, used to say: "I can sleep with a woman in Montego Bay, and by the time I drive the 120 miles to Kingston, someone is waiting there to ask me how it was." It works with similar efficiency on Roatán. I was chatting with Nonnie and drinking my second beer when I realized that there were nearly a dozen local men hanging around the store, and outside there were a number of young females strolling back and forth, glancing in for a peek at the new visitor.

As soon as I saw the geographical and sociological setup of Oakridge, I determined in my own mind that sex was out of the question. The village consisted of about thirty homes tightly crammed around a T-shaped lagoon. The people were close to each other physically and in family ties. It would be disastrous for an outsider to disrupt the local mores and relationships. The decision was a difficult one to sustain. Most of the young

66

men of Roatán are forced to seek a living by signing on with fishing boats, and consequently they are away for long periods of time, leaving the boy/girl ratio out of proportion. But I was not anxious to cause a scandal over a teeny-bopper and decided that hard work would have to substitute. Besides, it would only be for a couple of weeks; I'd catch up when I was in a looser social structure.

As soon as I realized that the group around me was hoping to learn my reason for being in Oakridge, I asked Nonnie to set up a round of beers for all those present. Within a short period of time, I had convinced them that I was a businessman on vacation and that my hobby was the history of piracy. I told them I was planning to spend a couple of weeks just "looking around" and that a writer-friend of mine was to join me soon. In the rambling conversation I was told that there were old pirate town sites up around Port Royal Harbor. I was careful not to indicate that from hours of intense research I probably knew the Port Royal Harbor better than they did. Several beers later I had managed to confirm all my opinions of the place.

I mentioned that I would like to hire a boat, and everyone suggested I go see Jeff Tree. The suggestion gave me an excuse to cut off the drinking bout and make my way to Jeff Tree's house.

Jeff is a typical Bay Islander. He works hard, he's strong, and he likes to keep his mouth shut when mainland authorities are around. As it turned out, Jeff had a further incentive. He took me out to the water's edge of his property, and there in his backyard was the 65-foot hull of a boat he was building, a strong-looking vessel which seemed quite near completion. He had been working on it for three years, and he told me he figured it would take "another year or two" to complete. He had cut the timber in the forest, floated it to Oakridge, and cut the entire keel from one 80-foot log, using only an axe and adz. It was exciting to find workmanship like that still in the world.

Jeff was running short of cash for the completion of the boat, and so he was anxious to hire on as my boatman and guide. His rate with his dory was five dollars per day, and a day in Roatán went from six in the morning until five at night.

I slept well that night, and the next morning I was up at 5:30. Merle, bright and chipper, cooked me eggs and made me a lunch to take along. Merle's lunch consisted of fruit, a small cake, and her "mystery meat" sandwiches. I never had the guts to ask her what the "mystery meat" was, but when you've been out on the water or hiking over hills, you realize the truth in the adage that "hunger is the best sauce."

The first day, Jeff took me around the various coves into the small creeks near Oakridge. Port Royal Harbor lies three miles to the east. We did some sightseeing, fished for a couple of hours with hand lines, and then knocked off at about three in the afternoon.

The second day we went out on the sea in Jeff's 16-foot boat and surveyed the coastline. Off to the east, I could see where the shore dipped in, and I asked Jeff about it. He said it was Port Royal Harbor, and he suggested we visit it the next day. My anticipation heightened.

My first look at Port Royal was an exhilarating experience. It must have looked about the same then as it did when Captain Henry Morgan arrived there after sacking Panama in 1671. From my research, I had calculated that his share of the loot, after murdering or paying off his fellow buccaneers on the raid, was worth in the neighborhood of $50 million by today's standards. Much of the booty ended up in the coffers of King Charles II, but far more than the amount Mitchell-Hedges had recovered is still unaccounted for.

Port Royal is a big, deep harbor, over a half-mile wide and three miles long, with an average depth of six fathoms and sufficient anchorage to accommodate a fair-size navy. The entire harbor is protected by barrier reefs through which bores a single natural access chanel sixty yards wide and ten fathoms deep. The remains of fortifications were evident as we cruised the length of the harbor.

Port Royal occupied a strategic position along the Spanish Main at the end of the sixteenth century. The Spanish were operating highly productive gold mines in mainland Honduras at the time and were destined to become an integral part of the Viceroyalty of New Spain, a New World empire built on the plunder of gold and silver and responsible for casting into oblivion the Inca, Aztec, and Mayan cultures, which had populated the area for thousands of years prior to the arrival of 34-year-old Hernando Cortez. With 500 men, 16 horses, and a lust for land and wealth, he had conquered Montezuma, the Aztec god-man-emperor, and consequently subjugated eleven million Indians to Spanish rule. To the south, Francisco Pizarro, with 188 men and 26 horses, similarly conquered the mighty Inca Empire.

From Central America and the northern coast of South America, boatloads of plunder began sailing the Spanish Main, first to Havana, then up the Gulfstream and across to Spain. All of the initial routes passed by, or were accessible to, Port Royal Harbor in the Bay Islands. Natural animosity between Catholic Spain and Protestant England provided a fertile field for conflict, and when the Spaniards began transporting treasure, Englishmen fought to take it away from them.

It is easy, when dwelling on buried or sunken riches from the past, to become obsessed with *the* missing treasure. There are dozens of legendary missing treasures, such as the chain of solid gold so heavy that two hundred men were required to carry it. The Incas talked of such a chain, supposedly one hundred yards long and containing more than ten tons of gold, fashioned by the great Huayna Capac to honor the seventh birthday of his son and heir, Huascar. The chain was said to have surrounded the great square at Cuzco until it was removed and hidden from the advancing Pizarro. It has never been found. Then there is the seven-foot-tall "Golden Virgin" that was cast in solid gold by Spanish artisans and placed in a Catholic cathedral. But the last record of it shows only that it departed the Panama port city of Colon in the mid-eighteenth century. No authority or researcher can explain why it never appeared in Spain, but there is a departure manifest on record showing that it did leave on its mysterious journey. I had dreamed of this incredible treasure often. Maybe Robin and I would find it here

69

beneath the surface of a sandy island in Port Royal Harbor. It was possible. At times it even seemed probable. I urged my mind to wander back, to take on the logic of a pirate who lived two hundred years before, to think like a brigand of the seventeenth century. (That whole mental process is not as far-fetched as one might imagine. There is a strong traditional belief within our family that one of our forefathers was a famous English pirate, Captain Henry Jennings, who operated out of the Bahamas.)

The hills around the harbor rise up sharply from the water's edge, stretching up over 800 feet less than a quarter of a mile inland. The foliage is dense, but I could see places that would seem natural sites for a town. In addition to our quest for the missing chest of Mitchell-Hedges, I was determined to explore other areas around the harbor which would undoubtedly produce other buried troves.

One such likely spot was Fort Key, a lovely island forming the east side of the harbor entrance. A substantial fort had been built there in the seventeenth century and was later improved by Royal Navy engineers in 1742. They had named it Fort George. I had studied the construction plans at the Royal Historical Society in London. Obviously, time had taken its toll of old Fort George. While some of the thick stone walls remained, most of the structure had been destroyed.

I mentioned this to Jeff Tree, and he told me that an American had come to Port Royal Harbor in 1940, looking for buried treasure. The man had spent only one day inspecting the fort, then decided to use dynamite to uncover any buried treasure. While he was setting the first charge, it accidentally detonated, blowing off his right arm. Finis one not-too-bright treasure hunter. I was the first American to enter the harbor since, Jeff added. We lunched on the site of the old fort's powder house, and off in the distance I could see the tiny, sandy island which had been the depository for the Mitchell-Hedges chests.

I spent the next two days trekking up through the bush with Jeff, unsuccessfully searching for possible sites of a pirate town.

70

We were returning to Oakridge at about four o'clock when Robin arrived.

I had been working very hard to assume a low profile on Roatán and in Oakridge. Trying to find and smuggle out a treasure chest of considerable size and value presents a problem, and visibility does not help. I had sent Robin a cable advising him of the rigors we might encounter and warning him to be prepared for a rough trip. His solution was to stop in Miami, go to Chalk's Flying Service on the MacArthur Causeway, and charter a twin-engine Grumman to fly him down. As the plane buzzed the Oakridge lagoon, scattering natives and their boats in every possible direction, I had horrible visions of another fiasco like the Morant Keys venture. I went to Nonnie's for a beer—let Robin find me if he could.

When he finally walked into Nonnie's store and gave me that sheepish grin, my anger subsided. When he said, "Hey, Howard, old boy," I completely forgot about the landing and was simply happy to have him there to help.

I had not shown the maps to any of the people on the island, but the next day Robin and I decided that it was vital to our plans to take Jeff Tree into our confidence. We were out in the middle of the harbor, near two spits of rock which all our maps identified as "The Cow" and "The Calf." (If you look on old Caribbean maps you will generally find a "cow" and a "calf"; cartographers seemed inclined to give us the big-little combination of islets that nomenclature.) We had Jeff anchor his boat at a rock landing on the Cow, and I began to show him the maps.

Robin said to Jeff, "We need your help, but we also need your silence."

I told him that he would be paid by us on the same daily basis, but if we discovered anything he would get twenty percent of the booty; Robin and I would divide the rest. Jeff found this a very attractive proposition; a lump of hard cash would give him all the money he needed to complete construction on his boat. We explained that we were searching for

71

the missing pirate town, but we still had not let Jeff know about the Mitchell-Hedges chest.

Our first objective was to locate the pirate headquarters of Augusta. Our maps showed that the town contained dozens of buildings, so we reasoned it would be the most logical place to find booty deposited with Mother Nature for safekeeping.

The chart indicated that the village had been situated on the west bank of a good-size stream or brook. Unfortunately, there were about two dozen streams feeding down from the hills into the harbor, so we simply selected the largest stream and landed our boat. All about us was jungle.

I wasn't inexperienced in coping with wilderness. I had done a lot of hunting in East Texas as a boy, and later on hunting trips in the Rocky Mountains, but the bush around Port Royal Harbor was as tough as anything I'd ever seen.

If you have ever felt a little lazy and allowed your front lawn to go a couple of weeks without mowing, then you can appreciate what nature could do to a town where no living being has set foot for over two hundred years. The jungle had become an imposing adversary.

If you are going to survive in a jungle, your fundamental weapon should be a sharp machete. "The Knife," as it's called, has a wooden or plastic handle and a blade from 24 to 30 inches long, which widens from about an inch and a quarter at the handle to about three inches at the outer end. The best ones are made from old railroad tracks, and many swear that the metal used in them has been tempered to an unusual hardness by the years of pounding under train wheels. They are heavy enough to pick up the momentum of your arm and slice through a sapling as much as three inches in diameter. You pick up a rhythm when you are hacking a path—back and forth, from right side to left, somewhat in the manner of a symphony conductor urging the brass section into a rousing passage. The thick branches fall easily—it is the vines and thorn-laden twigs that seem to dodge and weave as you try to chop them out of the way, then lash back to scratch your arms and legs. You must always be careful not to cut yourself with the machete itself.

And you sweat: Moisture forms in beads on your forehead and gathers into salty, stinging rivulets that run into your eyes. Robin and I were in good physical condition, but we began to develop blisters and unfamiliar aches.

By midday we were still working our way up inclines or down slopes, and I called a rest. Jeff had lugged along our "mystery meat" sandwiches and a plastic jug filled with Kool-Aid. Robin and I were both sirloin and champagne men, but that lunch tasted just great.

"We don't seem to be making any headway, Howard," Robin said, munching a sandwich.

"The maps show houses, Robin. Somewhere in that tangle are the foundations of a good-size village."

Robin looked down at his hands. Years of pounding out novels on a typewriter does not really equip a man to go into a jungle. Even his recently completed Green Beret training had neglected a course in the use of a machete. We were just going to have to put up with some sore hands for a few days.

I told Jeff, "What we're looking for is some level ground. The pirates would not have tried to build on the sides of hills—they were used to the flat decks of ships."

Jeff looked down at the map again. "The only flat spot I know in this whole harbor is right there," he said, indicating a point of land named Fort Frederick, over a half mile from where we were standing. I knew that we could not expect to make our discovery right away, but I also knew we would need some kind of encouragement. I suggested we go over and take a look.

After cleaning up our lunch area, we went back to Jeff's boat and crossed to Fort Frederick. As we approached a small, lovely beach, Robin tapped me on the shoulder and pointed down into the water. What he had spotted was a perfectly straight line of rocks, about three feet below the surface and extending out more than sixty feet into the water. I told Jeff to swing around so that we could take another look. That formation had to have been man-made. We decided to beach the boat and investigate.

The area was delightful. The sand was pure white and there

were a couple of dozen coconut palm trees and a spring-fed brook running down from the hill just behind. Jeff had an old, dirty, diving face mask tucked up in the bow of his boat. I borrowed it, stripped, and went into the water.

Below the surface of the harbor it was silent and beautiful, but bursting with life and color. I enjoy diving for pleasure, but despite the fascination of the underwater world, I've never been interested in diving for treasure. I know people, such as Kip Wagner in Florida and Gus Thompson in the Florida Keys, who have uncovered whole ships laden with gold and silver beneath the sea, but their accomplishments involve dozens of divers and sophisticated techniques as well as elaborate equipment. I am not an organization man, even in treasure hunting.

I spent only ten minutes examining the sunken stones. They had probably been part of a wharf of considerable size, but water erosion and the tides had broken it down over the years. At least we had found some sign of former activity.

When I returned to the beach I found that Jeff had opened a few green coconuts with his machete. If you have never done this difficult trick, don't try it—you can lose a finger or two in the process of learning. The coconut water was cool and sweet tasting.

Jeff told us that people from Oakridge frequently came to this little strip of beach for an afternoon holiday, and that he remembered there were flat pieces of land up above.

As soon as I had pulled on my boots, slacks, and shirt, we headed up a narrow path which led away from the beach. In contrast to our labors of the morning, this was sheer pleasure. We were up at the first level surface in minutes.

"This," I said, "is what we're looking for. Let's clear it."

One hour and several blisters later we had chopped out the undergrowth. Once the place had been bushed it was obvious that a building had stood there. We could see the heavy stonework of a foundation. I sent Jeff back to the boat for the metal detectors and, optimistically, a couple of shovels.

We assembled the large detecting device first, and I gave Robin the honors. The electronic search took his mind off his aching hands. He picked up a signal in less than ten minutes. I'd like to report that we found gold or silver, but unfortunately it was only a small four-pounder cannonball. It was of no value, but it was a relic of the pirates' past, and it raised our spirits considerably.

(It should be mentioned here that I did come upon a great treasure right there at the site of Fort Frederick, but that bountiful reward did not come in the form of valuable trinkets which I could hold in my hand. And it did not come into my life until later.)

Working just the small area we had cleared, we spent the rest of the afternoon digging up brass buttons, old shoe buckles, and a wonderful old flatiron for pressing clothes. The finds were not of great historic or financial value, but we continued to be encouraged.

Before we left the site that day, I took an exploratory walk around. I discovered that the area was actually terraced, and I located at least fifteen flat spots where buildings could have stood. On the ride back to Oakridge that evening, I told Jeff that I wanted to hire some local labor to clear the area. He said I could get some blacks from the other side of the island to work for a couple of dollars a day and I asked him to arrange for five men to meet us at Fort Frederick the next morning. We agreed to keep all of the metal detection equipment hidden from the workers—Jeff would tell them that "those crazy Americans" wanted a camp site cleared.

The next morning ten strapping workers showed up at the site just before seven o'clock.

I did not want the problems of supervising ten men, so I decided to try a technique I had used during my land development project in Jamaica. I assigned each man an area to clear and told them to go to work. I then sent Jeff and Robin off to try to find the site of Augusta while I watched the bushing operation. As soon as I saw the first worker slack off in his effort, I ran at him like a wild man, flailing my arms and shouting curses. I yelled out that this was a work project and that he could get the hell off the property. The other workers gaped at me as I ordered the man away. I repeated the performance as soon as I saw another man goofing off. By ten o'clock in the morning I had pared the group down to five of the workingest bush cutters the island of Roatán had ever seen.

It took the five men only two days to clear out the entire Fort Frederick area. I gave them all a day off with half pay while Robin, Jeff, and I used our metal detectors.

We found neither treasure nor the site of the village of Augusta that day, or the next, or the day after. I was beginning to worry—Robin had only another few days to spare for the Roatán adventure. We had uncovered a small village site that we at first thought to be Augusta, but there were only six or eight house foundations, which made it much too small for the pirate headquarters.

While our bushing crew cleared the last site, we took to Jeff's boat for another survey from the harbor. We cruised back and forth for a couple of hours, and I began to feel that there were some discrepancies in the actual locations of the creeks and streams as shown on the maps. I knew that such fresh water sources could have changed course over two hundred years, but *one* of them should have been right. Not a single one was. I suddenly realized that surveying instruments were not in use in those days, and that measurements would have been slipshod. I looked at the compass rose on the map. I was sure that that would be accurate, taken from the ship's dependable compass. I had Jeff maneuver our boat into a position from where I could take a fix off of two positive landmarks: the point of Fort Key and the area which we had cleared at Fort Frederick.

I was right! All of the stream beds were between five and six degrees *off* the actual compass bearing on the map. I ordered Jeff to head for a clump of trees across the harbor.

As he jammed the bow of the boat into a heavy growth of mangrove trees, we saw the mouth of a substantial stream.

Jeff was amazed. "In all of my life," he said, "I never knew this stream was here."

We splashed into the shallow water, and I felt as if I should be wearing jackboots and dangling a cutlass from my waist. Maybe there really is some of old pirate Captain Jennings in me. I certainly had a strange sensation at that moment.

By that time our hands had become hardened and our skill with the machete proficient. It took us ten minutes to hack a path up to the first level spot. Though covered in heavy grass and small trees, the top of the bluff appeared to have been leveled by man. As I stood on the edge looking over the area, I realized I was standing on a mound, and there were other mounds on either side of me. *This* was the old fort which had defended the village of Augusta—the mounds were protective embankments for the cannon emplacements. Walking along the edge, Robin and I counted nineteen separate locations where cannon had guarded the village; this had obviously been a sizable settlement.

Jeff was astonished. He had never seen this place and had never heard of there being a fort at this location in the harbor.

I wasn't particularly interested in the fort except as a guide to the old town site. We walked through the thick grass to a slight rise behind the fort. Within the first twenty feet, my machete uncovered a cut-stone foundation of an old building.

We had finally found Augusta!

That afternoon we cleared out a swath ten yards wide and nearly two hundred yards long. Enthusiasm generates incredible energy.

With our clothing drenched in sweat, our faces and hands grimy, and our backs weary from the labor, we looked at the discovery.

"Howard," Robin said quietly, "do you realize that we may be the first men to stand here since the village was deserted two hundred years ago?"

"Yeah," I replied. "Now comes the tough part."

Robin asked, "What's that?"

"Digging it up."

I told Jeff to have our bushing crew come onto the site the next day and asked him to supervise the clearing. I had some business I wanted to attend to the next day.

Jeff agreed, and we returned to Oakridge for much needed sleep.

The next day I walked into the village of Oakridge to ask some questions. Within an hour, I was sitting on an isolated dock talking to a craggy character named Billy Greenwood. After the nominal civilities, I came to the point.

"I understand you own some land in Port Royal," I said.

"Yep, 'bout twelve acres on the point sticking out in the harbor and fifty more a little to the west."

"Is it yours, free and clear?" I asked.

"Yep," Billy said, "my daddy left it to me. My brother owns another hundred right next to it."

"You want to sell some?"

Billy grinned and wrinkled up his face. "Hell, that land ain't no good for nothin'. Tried raising goats, but they don't even like the grass there. Anyway, I won't sell the west piece."

I wondered why, since the fifty acres had no beach. But no matter, because the twelve acres had old Fort Frederick on it.

Then I made my first mistake in a long history of negotiating. "Would you take a thousand dollars for the twelve acres?" I asked. The shock, pleasure, and surprise in his face let me know that I had probably offered two or three times what he would have taken.

"Let's go look at the maps," Billy suggested.

We went to his house, a loose term for the windowless eight-by-ten-foot shack with a corrugated tin roof. No wonder the thousand dollars sounded attractive—at that time a thousand dollars could build a fine little house on Roatán.

The deed to the property was incredible—it was a stack of string-tied papers over an inch thick. The first document was the original Spanish land grant, a beautiful piece of written legal history dated 1649. I studied the property boundaries and found that Billy's land was L-shaped with the longest part of the L fronting south in the harbor, the shorter part facing east. Both legs of the L met at the point where we had discovered Fort Frederick. That afternoon, Billy and I went

78

down to the title registrar's office and filed a transfer of title with the local government supervisor. I pecked out a comprehensive bill of sale on Robin's typewriter, and I became a landowner in Port Royal Harbor. Later that day, I tried to locate the owners of the property on which the old buccaneer village of Augusta had stood, but I learned that the land was tied up in an estate with fourteen heirs. It could take years to clear that title, but I did obtain permission for us to explore on the property from one of the heirs after paying him $50 for the right.

That night Billy came by to have a beer with Robin and me at Merle's. As we sat on the porch watching the evening sky settle over the sea, I asked Billy why he had refused to sell me the fifty-acre tract of land.

He hushed his voice and said, "You ever study up on treasures?"

I thought Robin was going to choke on his drink.

"A little," I answered.

"Well," Billy went on, "I had a dream . . ."

The story he unfolded was hard to believe.

Just about any small, isolated community or society in the world will evolve superstitions and odd beliefs, and the people on Roatán had developed the custom of dreaming about buried treasure. About a year before, Billy had experienced a dream indicating that there was a vast treasure buried on the larger of his two pieces of property.

"Did you look for the treasure?" Robin asked.

"Sure," Billy said. "We're still looking."

That should have been enough for Robin, but he continued on the subject. "Did you find anything?"

"Not yet," Billy said without one tinge of disappointment or doubt.

He told us that he and his brother had been digging a secret hole, and that they were sure they would have success. Flushed with the $1,000 check he had in his pocket, he offered to take us to the hole the next day. I admit my curiosity was aroused,

79

but another day lost in our own search was going to make us one day closer to when Robin would have to leave. Finally we agreed to meet Billy at his hole for a short time before going on to work Augusta.

The next morning Jeff nosed his boat in to the shore on Billy's property. When Billy saw that Jeff was with us, he made it clear that Jeff was not invited to see the hole. Billy had a reputation for being equally nice and rude to everyone in Oakridge. Jeff, an extremely easy-going person, smiled, gave us a friendly wave, and indicated he'd be waiting when we came back.

Billy then took us along a narrow path nearly three hundred yards back from the beach. What we saw was mind-boggling.

Billy and his brother, guided only by a weird dream, had dug a hole into the base of a ledge. The opening, after a year of difficult rock removal and earth excavation, was twenty feet across. The hole was dug down into the reddish-brown hard soil to a depth of over forty feet. The labor and effort seemed beyond human capacity, but they had done it.

Robin and I decided we should run a quick check on the hole with one of the detectors. Robin went back to the boat and brought up the most powerful one. I assembled the detector and spent about ten minutes sweeping the sides and bottom of the excavation. I didn't have the heart to tell Billy that there was not one single damn murmur, although I had turned the sensitivity up so high that it would have picked up a flea's wristwatch.

"Billy," I said, "I don't know. I can't say if there is a treasure or if there isn't. All I know is, I'd stop digging if it was my hole."

Billy smiled. "Like you say, Howard, them machines can't really tell—not like a dream. But thanks for trying to help."

We nodded, and left him there. I wouldn't be surprised if he was still digging that hole today.

We had our own dreams, but they were the kind you have in the daytime and they seemed very real to us as we headed for the village site. My five-man crew of chopping beavers had cleared nearly two acres by the time we arrived and we set right to work with the detectors.

We divided up the areas for search, but I cautioned Robin, "There is going to be a lot of metal junk around those building foundations. Don't expect every signal to produce a pot of gold."

Robin replied impatiently, "Okay, okay, but let's get on with it and find some holes to dig."

Minutes later I received a strong signal beside the first site I was working. We attacked the spot and found only a large brass shoe buckle just a few inches below the surface.

On our first day of operation in Augusta, we produced nothing more valuable than that shoe buckle, but I was not discouraged. I felt sure that somewhere in those ruins some pirate had hidden his fortune, then gone to sea and been killed, taking the secret of his hiding place with him.

Two more days of intensive and tiring work proved fruitless. On the third day our patience was rewarded.

It was Sunday, and Jeff was not along with us. The strong Protestant ethic of eighteenth-century England prevailed on Roatán, and virtually everyone went to church on Sunday. Robin and I wanted to work. We were already two days past his ten-day deadline, and he was so anxious that by six-thirty on that Sunday morning we had beached Jeff's boat at Augusta, and by seven, we were in operation. Robin was facing a dilemma: He needed to pursue his research on *The Green Berets,* yet he wanted to stay and feed his treasure-hunting bug. He began operating the detector with a vengeance.

Shortly before eight, I was working the foundation of a house that looked a bit larger than the others. I moved into what would have been the back garden, and stood there, trying to think with the mind of a pirate who had possibly stood there over two hundred years ago. I walked out from what would have been the back door of the house, stopping at a point that seemed like a safe location for a depository.

Old Captain Jennings must have really been reaching out

81

from the past to guide me—after only two passes I picked up the strongest signal we had heard.

"Hey, Robin, come on over here." I tried to contain my reaction, but the excitement in my voice was undisguisable. Robin ran full tilt from where he was working fifty yards away, charging like a man in battle, the shovel his weapon.

"Take it easy," I cautioned. "I picked up a good signal, but don't get carried away." I handed the detector to him and he swept the area. The pattern came in large and strong once again. Without a word, we both manned the shovels. Robin hit it first. The blade of his tool struck against metal and he dropped face first into the hole. Brushing away the dirt, he exposed about three square inches of flat metal. Within seconds, we had dug out the area around the chest.

Back in those early days, when I was first getting the feel of this treasure-hunting business, I made many mistakes. In the years since, I've studied how digs are handled, how careful records are maintained, how dirt is delicately removed with soft brushes and small trowels. But we banged that old chest and pulled at it and finally pried it open with a crowbar. The chest was damaged beyond salvage. Looking back, I wish we had been more careful. The container was heavily encrusted with oxidized iron, and the clasps and hinges were welded together with rust, but I think I could have restored it. What a great memento it would have made. However, one blow at the hasp with a sledgehammer finished any hope for posterity.

With the lid removed we could see the gleam of gold among the blackened silver coins that half filled the box. It was an incredible moment for us. If the trip to Roatán netted nothing more than this box and its contents, it was fully justified, not only for its value, but for the exhilarating thrill of discovery.

On close inspection we could see that the gold was in the form of a necklace—but it was partly imbedded among the silver pieces of eight. The surface corrosion of the silver in the coins had fused them all together, so we decided to take the entire mass back to Oakridge.

We had an early lunch of local rum mixed with our Kool-

Aid and left Merle's mystery meat sandwiches to the ants. Buzzing from the high-octane rum, we packed our booty into a knapsack and, with some benevolent guidance from above, navigated Jeff's boat back to the lagoon in Oakridge. We headed right to the dock at Merle's. It wasn't necessary to send word to Jeff. When he saw us going right to the guest house, he knew instinctively that we had something.

As soon as we reached the porch, I found that Merle had a new guest.

There, rocking peacefully back and forth in the early afternoon sun, was a tall, willowy brunette. Robin and I froze in our tracks.

She looked at us and said, "Good afternoon."

She could have said, "Your arm just fell off," and I would have smiled. Those long legs stretched out in front of her were totally distracting.

Her name was Gail Morton, she said. Noting my quick look at her left hand, she added, "My husband's name is Beau Morton. We're from Atlanta." I've always had a weakness for that charming accent of the South. Although I wasn't too keen about having any strangers concerning themselves with my affairs at that moment, the meeting was fortunate. I was to meet the Mortons again in another context.

By the time we had introduced ourselves, Jeff had arrived at the front porch, and we made our excuses and headed into my bedroom. Robin struggled with the weight of the knapsack, placing it carefully on the floor.

"Sorry you weren't with us, Jeff," I said, "but we found something and twenty percent of it is yours, just as we agreed."

Then we opened the knapsack.

The Spaniards operated silver mines in Mexico and Peru, and even had a mint in Lima, where many of the pieces of eight were coined. They were of the purest silver, and when pure silver is exposed to air containing a nominal amount of sulfur, it turns black through oxidation. Our coins looked like lumps of coal.

I knew that an accidental exposure to nitric acid or chloride can cause drastic changes in the physical characteristics of pure silver. Nitrogen can be produced by the ammonia and chloride found in many commercial cleaning agents, so I was careful to guard against any innocent-looking household cleansers coming near our lump of black wealth. Patiently, we used a jar of the best silver polish, which we diluted down into a watery liquid. We lifted coins away with plastic-coated tweezers and probed with toothpicks and cotton balls. We devoted two hours to the process of lifting the gold necklace out intact. At last we finished and looked down at our mini-display of antiquity and wealth sitting there on my bed.

There was respect in Robin's tone. "Makes it all seem worthwhile, doesn't it, Howard?"

I nodded and looked at Jeff. Here before him was probably enough cash value to buy the engine for his boat. His expression was one of intense satisfaction. There was no sign of greed—only pleasure.

The necklace was a fairly heavy chain, finely made, apparently of European manufacture, and was so long that it must have been worn in a double strand. There were 142 blackened pieces of eight, their dates ranging from 1635 to 1687. All were in good condition and could be easily cleaned. At the bottom of the mass, there was a thin, well-worn gold ring.

"Wouldn't it be interesting to know the history of that jewelry?" Robin said.

"Possibly the pirate was a widower and these things were his wife's." Then I smiled at my own romanticism. "More likely they were part of the booty taken from a Spanish ship."

In any case, after being buried for over two hundred years, the booty was now ours. I mulled over the problem of safekeeping. There was no such thing as a safe-deposit box on Roatán, and I knew that the treasure would be confiscated by the government if word leaked out. I mentioned the security problem to Jeff and Robin. Jeff pointed his finger upward. At first, I was afraid he was suggesting that we trust in the Almighty to protect us, but when I looked at the ceiling I noticed a trap door about eighteen inches square. Jeff had worked as a carpenter for Merle when she built the guest house, and the access in the ceiling was for any repairs that might be needed in the roof timbers.

This innocent hole in the ceiling became our bank. I was coming to appreciate the problems faced by the old pirates. When you don't have a bank vault nearby to protect valuables, it becomes a great problem; the temptation is to dig a hole and bury them.

The luscious Gail Morton flitted through my dreams that night, and I was half hoping to see her before we left. But we parted early the next morning, and by the time we returned from Port Royal that afternoon the Mortons had gone.

That night Robin and I agreed we should terminate our expedition. Our work that day had been fruitless, and we decided to go after the Mitchell-Hedges chest the next morning. We repaired to Jeff's house and found him working alone on his boat.

I told him, "Jeff, it is about time you knew. Robin and I came here looking for something specific, something big. I can't promise anything, but you will be in for your share."

We arranged to meet early the next morning.

We were on our way at dawn, headed directly for the islet, or key, which Sammy Mitchell-Hedges had positively identified as the location of the chest. It was a tiny lump of sand named Careening Cay. "Careening" is an old maritime process of beaching a boat broadside to the shoreline at high tide, thus exposing the hull to make cleaning or repairing possible at low tide. Then, at high tide, the vessel is refloated. This island was a careenage and might have been used by a captain who hid his treasure while the hull of his vessel was upturned on the shore.

We had studiously avoided examining Careening Cay because we did not want to tip our hands. Though we never mentioned Mitchell-Hedges, we were sure there were folk tales and rumors about his visit and the treasure find. We did not want any suspicion raised about us.

As we neared the beach and took our first good look at the

island, Robin and I stared at each other in mutual disappointment. The highest point on the island was less than three feet above water level, and the entire island was covered with a dense growth of mangrove trees. The bitter memory of our Morant Keys venture flooded back into our minds at the same time. As far as I was concerned, we might as well not have beached the boat, but Robin encouraged me to make a try. The results were as I had anticipated—the salt concentration in the water gave us loud signals. Even the modern, expensive detectors we had were useless on Careening Cay. Today you can buy equipment which will work in the presence of salt water, but back then, Robin and I knew that old Mother Nature had beaten us again.

I remember looking at Robin, standing there with shovel in hand, and saying to him, "Do you realize that that chest is probably within one hundred feet of where we are standing, but we aren't going to be able to find it?"

Robin retained his sense of humor. "Do you feel like digging up an island?" he asked.

"Not today."

"Neither do I," he said. "Screw it."

From where we stood, we could see the Cow and the Calf, the tiny islands I had observed on my first trip to Port Royal with Jeff. Robin wanted to check them with the detectors. They were the private property of other people, and I felt they were too small to be a good place to hide treasure anyway, but we decided to give it a shot.

We headed west in the harbor and arrived at the islands just as a shower began sprinkling down on us. We used tarpaulins to cover the detectors, not worrying about getting wet ourselves, because, though tropical rain storms may be violent, you can be dried by the sun within minutes after the rain stops. Jeff edged the boat in close to the Calf. The surface was so rugged that soil had never accumulated in any quantity sufficient to allow for hiding buried treasure, and the rough rock sides sheered up ten to twelve feet. I could not imagine pirates trying to haul gold chests up by rope.

86

Hoping that the nearby Cow would not be so formidable, we headed across the short span of water between the two islands. One side of the Cow revealed a small landing place cut out of the rocks. From the water, we could not see the interior of the island, but there were trees and we could see the tops of heavy brush. There had to be soil on the Cow. As Jeff eased the boat in, we could see the work that had gone into the stone steps. Maybe there wouldn't be treasure there, but someone had gone to a lot of effort a couple of centuries ago to provide an access to the island.

Using the worn and weathered steps, we climbed up the eight feet to the top of the natural rock wall. The center of the island was small, no more than one hundred feet square, but it was a beautiful and totally secluded spot. No more than a few feet inland, Robin made another discovery. In the small area he had cleared with his machete, we could see the corner of a cut-stone foundation.

With the three of us chopping, it took less than an hour to clear away the vegetation. The site revealed a foundation roughly 20 by 35 feet—quite a sizable building. We spotted more steps cut into the stonework and climbed them. About 12 feet up there was another level place, which provided a lookout for the resident of the island—the whole harbor was in view.

Jeff went back to the boat and brought up one of the detectors. Robin used it for about twenty minutes and decided the place was barren of signals. Taking the instrument from him, I found some old hardware attached to charred wood; obviously there had been a fire at some time in the distant past.

Feeling his hunch had proved worthless, Robin climbed up the wall and sat there with Jeff, watching as I searched. Fifteen more minutes passed.

Finally Robin called down impatiently, "Howard, let's pack it in."

I agreed, and the two of them headed back to the boat. Still I searched for a couple of minutes more. I was just getting ready to turn off the detector when a strong signal blasted my ears. I checked. It was a good signal and the size was promising. I looked around for Robin and Jeff, but they had climbed down to the boat. Going over to the rock wall, I shouted, "Hey, bring that damn pick and shovel up here."

In a minute or two, they joined me.

As we dug down, the signal increased considerably. Something was below us!

By now the rain was falling harder, the natural walls cut off any air current, and the heat was stifling. We were all drenched with rain and sweat. The hole was turning into a mud pond, but we kept digging.

Robin struck a solid piece of rock with his pick. "Son of a bitch," he said with disgust. "There's nothing but rock."

"Let me in there with the detector." I told him. "I know damned well there's metal here."

Again the detector's needle quivered with a high reading and the headset produced a loud signal in my ears. The indication was that we were digging slightly off center. I knew Robin believed we should give up, but he went back in that hole and dug.

He expanded the opening and dropped down onto his knees, his hands groping along the flat surface of the rock.

"I've got it!" he shouted. "I've found a crack in the rock. It's as straight as an arrow. It has to be man-made."

Jeff crowded down into the hole and took the pick. He felt around, took the point of the pickaxe, and wedged it into a crevice. He pulled and tugged on the pick handle, and finally he pulled away a flat, hand-cut slab of rock about three or four inches thick. He climbed out to show it to me.

"There's wood there," Robin shouted. "Painted. It's honest-to-God wood, Howard."

I put down the detector and jumped into the hole. Scooping out the loose soil with our hands, we finally identified the shape of a box. It was about two feet square. With all four of our hands yanking and prying, the box finally came free. We lifted it out to ground level, and immediately all the previous disappointments of the day were forgotten. All we saw was that

88

lovely box sitting there. It had been waiting two hundred years for us to unearth it.

Robin worked on the locks and hasps for several minutes, but he was getting nowhere. Age seemed to seal the chest from us. He looked up at me with a question in his eyes. I answered, "Go ahead, bust the son of a bitch open."

Using the handle of a machete as a hammer, Robin splintered the top and the rotten wood fell apart.

We could hardly believe what we saw.

In the top was a pair of decaying boots—the tall kind that Errol Flynn used to wear in pirate movies. Robin lifted them out and handed them to Jeff. They cracked as he tried to unbend them. Then there was some kind of material. It was hard to tell at first just what the cloth was—it was black and wrinkled, and it dissolved in the rain. On closer examination we saw that it was a dress, and then we realized why it was black. It was silver brocade.

Next we found a decayed wooden box, which contained a badly corroded navigation quadrant. Beside the quadrant was a small leather pouch in surprisingly good condition. It was heavy —because it contained two handfuls of bright, glittering gold nuggets.

"Now, that's one hell of a lot more like it," Robin said. "I never saw anything as beautiful in my life."

We figured the gold nuggets were it, and we were happy. We didn't have a half a million in treasure as Mitchell-Hedges had brought out, but we had found something—that was important.

About to shove the box back into the hole and cover it up, Jeff started to push it. "Damn," he said. "This devil is heavy." It was then that I noticed something strange. The rain falling into the bottom of the chest was not soaking into the wood—but the wood was old and rotten, and it should be absorbing the water. I bent down to make a closer examination. Jeff turned away to pick up the detector to get it out of the rain and Robin was busy examining the gold nuggets. I looked at the black bottom of the box. Taking out my knife, I scratched the surface.

I then sat back and stared. "Hey, Robin," I said, "if I let you take all the nuggets, can I have the box?"

"Why?" he asked, bending down. "What the hell have you found?"

I had found that what we thought to be the bottom of the box was, in fact, two layers of neatly stacked silver ingots—sixteen of them—65 pounds of nearly pure silver.

We didn't waste any time filling in the hole. To hell with it. We had found a treasure, and before anyone could discover what we had found, we'd better be off the island. We lugged the gear and loot down to the boat. Jeff had an old burlap sack and we slipped the gold and silver bars into it. As we did I handed Jeff two of the bars and a large gold nugget. We were all coming away from the venture a hell of a lot better off.

When we arrived back at Merle's guest house, she was standing on the porch with a worried look on her face. As the rain pounded down on the tin roof, she said, "Howard, there were two soldiers and an officer here looking for you this morning."

I didn't ask why—I could guess. Someone had finally become suspicious or jealous and had tipped off the authorities.

"Did they go back to their headquarters?" I asked. If they had gone to the police barracks in Coxen's Hole, then we should have some headstart.

"No," she said, still unable to shake the worried look off her face. "They were going to go to Port Royal, but the rain came. They plan to see you up there tomorrow. They want to see what you and Robin are doing."

"Did they say anything?" Robin asked.

"No," Merle replied. "I told them you were probably going to build a home there. But I don't think they believed me. I'm worried, Howard."

"Now you stop fretting, Merle." I tried to soothe her. "Everything will be all right."

I had not planned any particular escape scheme, but I started to develop one quickly. It took about thirty seconds. I told Robin to pack up our things, but to leave the brass buckles and buttons and the other things that had value only

90

as souvenirs. We'd have to pack the gold and silver into our suitcases with the clothing. Next, I headed over to Jeff Tree's house.

He had just secured his boat and was getting ready to bathe. I laid it on the line and told him we had to get the hell out of there.

The crossing from Roatán to the mainland is about thirty miles across perpetually rough seas. Columbus sailed this part of the Caribbean on his fourth voyage of discovery, and he had such a wicked time with the water between Roatán and the mainland that, when he finally cleared the rough seas, he said, "Gracias a Dios"—"Thanks to God." The place is still there on the maps, Cape Gracias a Dios. I knew the water was too rough for Jeff's small boat, so I reached into my pocket and pulled out two $100 bills. "Can you hire a boat that will get us to the mainland?" I asked.

Within an hour, Jeff pulled up to the dock at Merle's guest house with a sport fishing boat. It was old, but it was seaworthy and it had two working engines. Jeff had also found Riley Gough slopping beer in Nonnie's. Riley was quite used to the crossing, so he was sailing as Jeff's first mate. We loaded our baggage, settled up with Merle, jumped into the boat, and headed into the heavy seas.

On the trip to La Ceiba, I showed the gold nuggets to Riley, and he told me there were stories of a river of gold located right here in Honduras. If I was ever interested, he told me, I should look him up and we'd look for it together. I filed the yarn in my mind, but on that night, the most important thing was to get the hell away from the federals.

The crossing was rough, but we made it. Riley and Jeff headed back to Roatán, and we headed for the airport. It was eight o'clock when we arrived, and the airport was closed. I left Robin with the luggage and found Bill Earle in a local *cantina*. Bill is from Florida, by way of the Korean War, and owned the small charter service in La Ceiba. I dredged up the old camaraderie of the Korean War and finally talked him into flying us to San Pedro Sula. A plane bound for Belize,

91

British Honduras, was leaving there at ten o'clock. We made it with ten minutes to spare.

Until skyjacking became popular, there was no baggage inspection on departing flights, so we boarded immediately. We flew to Belize, switched to a BWIA flight, stopped off in Grand Cayman, and were in Montego Bay at one o'clock in the morning.

The Red Stripe Beer people in Jamaica are nice enough to keep the bar open late at the Montego Bay Airport. Robin and I wrapped ourselves around two tall drinks and tried to relax.

"What next, Robin?" I asked with a grin.

"Your ass, Howard," Robin said, breaking out into a laugh.

I said, "Want to go back and try to find that river of gold that Riley mentioned?"

Robin looked over the rim of his glass. "I'm going to get on a plane and find a nice peaceful war," he said. "After Port Royal, anything they've got over there will be a breeze. You go find your treasures. I'm going to do something easy."

So, that's just what we did. Robin headed off for a couple of years of research on *The Green Berets,* and I went off in search of treasure.

Vietnam was *not* a breeze.

Neither was Peru.

# 4 THE CHIMU TREASURES OF PERU

🐦

SAIGON: VIA ITT 18-2-64 006714—aarrnn 801

TO: H. JENNINGS—RACQUET CLUB 79TH STREET
CAUSEWAY MIAMI FLORIDA

HAPPY BIRTHDAY STOP IF MIAMI PACE TOO
HECTIC OVERHOP SAIGON STOP VERY QUIET STOP
VIETCONG USING REAL BULLETS STOP REGARDS

ROBIN

A kaleidoscope of experiences flashed through my mind as I
read Robin's telegram in my room at the Racquet Club. I
looked down at the gun-metal blue of the .38 revolver on the
table beside my right hand. I wished it weren't necessary to have
a gun always at hand, but then I quickly realized I would
live in no other way.

My thoughts suddenly fled back eighteen years. I saw a
German soldier there in front of me, raising his gun as I shot
him.

Robin had left me in Montego Bay a month before and had
flown to Washington for a cram course on the political situation and objectives of U.S. involvement in Vietnam, prior to
joining his Green Beret friends in Saigon. (At that time, late
in 1963, they were still known as U.S. Army Special Forces.
Robin had not yet tagged them with their more famous nick-
name.) I stayed behind to find a buyer for our Roatán loot.

Because I was a neophyte in the business, I really didn't know
where to begin. Figuring the closest likely market would be
Miami, I stabled myself at the Racquet Club. I found the out-
let for my treasure quite accidentally. A long-time friend of

93

mine, who had formerly been a *Time* magazine correspondent in Jamaica, now lived in Miami. We met for drinks at the Boom-Boom Room of the Fountainbleau Hotel, and I told him about our gold artifacts. He said that one of the nearby universities had a small but impressive collection of Central American artifacts, and suggested that maybe the director, Allen Langley, could help. Suddenly, that name clicked. Allen Langley was the man who had tried to argue Robin and me out of our Morant Keys venture. I called him the next morning and drove out to the university campus for a meeting.

The Lloyd Merlin Art Gallery is an endowed institution which is a quiet leader in the study of several areas of Central American cultural heritage. Entering the gallery, I was overwhelmed with an impression of solemnity. The gallery reeked of propriety, of an academic atmosphere, of an altruistic approach to art. I remembered Allen's reaction to the expedition Robin and I planned to the Morant Keys, and how distressed he was that we were so mercenary about the treasure, so naturally I had reservations about even discussing our latest treasure find. Surely such an academic institution, run by such a dedicated individual, was not the place to sell smuggled booty.

In my later days as a treasure hunter, I learned that academics are as likely to be interested in gold as anyone else; you only have to find the rope ladder to the top of the ivory tower. At the sedate Metropolitan Museum of Art in New York, the trustees bought a Greek calyx krater, a rare vase, and the damn thing was verified by the Italian government as stolen property. Many museum directors will publicly denounce the plundering of archaeological sites in Greece, Turkey, or Latin America, but put a great piece of treasure in front of them and they will ask "How much?" without a question about the method of its acquisition. I know, I've done it.

That morning in Miami, I was still an innocent, so I put off going into Allen's office and strolled through the gallery.

I'm not much for idle sightseeing—I visit museums for specific purposes—but looking around the Merlin Gallery that day, I suddenly became aware of the vast marketplace that must exist in America. Here, in this little gallery on a quiet campus in Florida, was a collection worth a great deal of money.

If you ever have the chance to visit the Wellington Museum in London, you will find an art collection worth millions. You will also find out that the very proper and very staid English proudly identify the stolen pieces of priceless art with tiny black stars on the identification cards. Most galleries in the United States are more devious—they disclaim stolen treasure with esoteric phrases, such as "On loan from a private collection" or "Certification not verified at present," printed in very small type.

A metamorphosis was taking place in my mind. I walked to the director's office with bolstered confidence. All of those pieces just could not have been obtained from Simon-pure sources.

The secretary asked me to wait a moment. She went through a door and soon returned with Allen Langley. He was wearing a smock and his hands were covered with a fine white powder.

Breaking out in a grin, he said, "Oh, hi, Howard. I just wanted to check that you were the same Howard Jennings."

He motioned for me to follow him.

We went through his office and into a brightly lighted workroom. He closed the door and we were alone.

"Excuse the mess. I just received a shipment and I was anxious to look at it, but that can wait." I told him I was in no hurry, and he went back to his bench.

"I've got some trinkets I want to sell," I said.

He smiled. "I have some too." He picked up a flat, round object covered with the same white powder. He blew on it, and there in his hands was a beautiful, glistening gold pectoral breast plate, ornamental jewelry of some ancient culture.

"Damn!" I exclaimed.

He laughed and asked, "Want to buy it?"

I knew he was joking. I said, "I'm selling, not buying."

Allen studied the pectoral and said, "Two days ago this was sitting in a smelly warehouse in Lima, Peru. Two weeks ago it was sitting on the chest of a Chimu Indian who probably died a thousand years ago. Now it's here."

He showed me another object, a solid gold nose ornament, which would have been a heavy load even for my craggy beak. I couldn't conceal my admiration, but I was also interested in my own problem. He cleaned up and we went back to his office.

I told him about the Roatán adventure. He listened and finally asked to see the trove. Opening my attaché case, I pulled out samples of each item.

After only a couple of minutes of cursory examination, he said, "Very nice, but not of much interest to us."

I cleared up his misconception. "I had no intention of selling this stuff to you. I realize it isn't your stock in trade. Do you have any suggestions?"

He became a bit pompous. "Actually, Howard, some of this stuff does have some intrinsic value, even real cash value. But these are—how shall I put it?—only trinkets, and—for want of a better word—stolen."

I could feel the blood rising in my neck. This arrogant academician was calling me a thief when right in the next room sat "objects of art" which were sure as hell stolen. Digging out Peruvian tombs is illegal—even I knew that. But I held my temper.

"Is there anyone . . ." I groped.

Thinking for a moment, he said, "Possibly. Where are you staying?" I told him and left, feeling angry and depressed. I was contemplating melting the gold down and selling it to a jeweler.

By the time I returned to the Racquet Club, a message was waiting for me to call a Mr. John Wilson.

The telephone conversation was guarded, and John Wilson asked me to come to his office that evening. He gave me the address, near Miami International Airport.

At about seven o'clock that night I drove along a road in northwest Miami, and turned off onto the street he had mentioned. I slowed down and looked at the area. I could see a shop that repaired airplane radios, another for recapping tires, another specializing in trailer hitches—the area was a grubby hodgepodge of small, marginal businesses. Finally I spotted the right number. The sign on the door said: MARINE FOOD PRODUCTS COMPANY—IMPORTERS.

I parked the car and noticed a Cadillac El Dorado in front of the windowless door. Some light showed around the edge. I knocked. Judging from the anti-burglary devices attached to the entrance, this could have been the front door to Fort Knox. When the door finally opened, I stood facing John Wilson, a short, balding, and well-dressed man with a pleasant face. After initial introductions, he asked me into the outer office, which was as grubby as the street outside. A couple of old chairs bore piles of old newspapers; cheap imitation paneling covered the walls. Wilson led the way into the next office, which had two desks and several filing cabinets crammed into it; printed forms and correspondence were scattered on the desk tops and spilling onto the floor.

We went through another door, and I stopped in shock.

The room was about twelve feet wide and twenty feet long. The paneling on these walls was solid mahogany, the floors were richly carpeted, and the lighting was low key and excellently executed. I know it was excellently executed because each beautiful gold artifact on display in that room was highlighted perfectly to show the detail and craftsmanship of ancient Indian workers. The sight was dazzling. John Wilson's office was a showroom for selling stolen and smuggled Latin American Indian artifacts.

Robin had explained the intricacies of how Mafia organizations "launder" cash from drugs, gambling, and prostitution, deviously running it through a cover operation and then investing it in legitimate businesses. I have discovered that the world of art and archaeology can be just as nefarious in its clandestine "laundering" of stolen treasures. An international trade estimated at $10 million a year makes the illicit traffic a small but lucrative enterprise.

For example: A tomb robber in Italy will sell his finds to

97

his *mediatore* or broker, who in turn smuggles the artifacts to Switzerland or Luxembourg. Papers for the object are forged, and it is then channeled to reputable or quasi-reputable dealers in Holland or Sweden. A classy operation will then move it to the plush galleries in London and thence to the lucrative market in the States.

The story in Latin America is much the same: Governments have stringent regulations prohibiting pillage of graves and archaeological sites; but try to convince a back-country peon that he should not dig out some artifacts and sell them for the equivalent of a couple of months' hard labor in his infertile fields. Who can blame the peasant?

John Wilson was a middleman and a smuggler. The operation he ran in Miami obviously had substantial sources of gold artifacts. After a few minutes of cautious probing, he showed signs of trusting me. The feeling, however, was not mutual.

He told me that he used his "import" company to ship in fish meal. The 100-pound sacks were used to conceal gold objects looted from Peruvian burial mounds. I was mildly interested by the story, but I was more interested in finding out if he would buy our Roatán pieces.

During our twenty-minute conversation, I kept trying to channel the discussion toward my offering, but he showed little interest. He poured us a couple of good belts of Scotch and I tried again.

"Would you like to see what I have?" I asked.

He reacted with slightly less enthusiasm than if he had been asked to view his neighbor's home movies.

I have to admit that what Robin and I thought of as a great find seemed insignificant compared to the elaborate display at this treasure hunter's showcase. But our loot *had* to be worth *something*.

After I spread out the treasure on his desk, John made a quick evaluation, scribbled some figures on a piece of paper, and said, "Very nice."

Impatient, partly angry, and nearly discouraged, I asked, "Well, will you buy it or not?"

He said, "I'll broker it for you. I'd say twenty-two thousand for the pieces of jewelry and the gold nuggets. We'll weigh out the silver. I can place it with a professional firm here in Miami."

I had reservations about the silver—the ingots were old, clearly stamped with mint marks, and I felt that their value as antiquities would be greater than the raw value of melted-down silver.

"I'll sell everything but the ingots." Then, "What about your commission?"

"I'll do it as a favor," he said. I was instantly suspicious—I had known him for less than half an hour and he was offering favors.

"Thanks," I said. "Why?"

He ignored the question. "How did you find this junk?"

I've since learned that in the treasure trade the vernacular for ancillary by-products of an expedition is "junk," but I was proud of our find and I decided I didn't like John Wilson. Still, he was talking about $22,000. I gave him a five-minute discourse on how we found the treasure on Roatán.

Finally, Wilson stated his proposition: "How would you like to go after some heavy concentrations of gold?"

Until that time I had been working with friends, people whom I trusted, people who were not hungry or greedy. John Wilson looked and acted greedy. I stalled for time, lighting a cigarette and sipping from my drink. I was, in fact, really in the mood for more treasure hunting, and since Robin was off to his war, I would have to deal with strangers if I was to continue seeking gold. John Wilson did not seem likable, but he was obviously substantial—one does not get a room full of pre-Columbian gold artifacts to display without having some wherewithal. I made my decision.

"I'd be interested," I said.

Even though we were in the confines of his private office, Wilson lowered his voice.

"For the past ten years I have represented a substantial family in Peru. I have used my import company as a cover to bring in about $2 million worth of gold in that period. The amount each year has been diminishing because the Peruvian government has clamped down on digging into the burial mounds. It is illegal to dig now, even if the mounds are on your own property. The police have taken to using aircraft for aerial surveillance, and the old method, using hundreds of peasant workers to dig out a mound, has become too risky. My source is drying up." He rose to pour us another drink.

I shrugged. "How can I help if the situation is so bad?"

He turned to me. "You know how to use detectors," he said, pointing to my pieces of gold sitting on his desk.

I watched him as he returned to the desk. The whole thing didn't ring true. "Detectors are easy to buy. I bought mine right here in Miami."

He offered a thin smile and said, "I bought some, too. I shipped them down to the site in Peru, and after my considerable expense and trouble, the people there broke them before they uncovered the first piece of gold. The family I am dealing with owns a huge piece of land, but they are really primitives as far as modern machinery is concerned. They threw away the detectors and went back to the same old laborious, dangerous way, using local labor to dig, dig, dig. Quite simply, you could show them where to dig and at the same time provide them basic instructions in the care and operation of good detection equipment."

I asked, "What culture?"

"Chimu," John replied, then quickly added, "I can't tell you much more than that until you commit yourself."

I knew a little about the Chimu culture, one of the most sophisticated in the Inca Empire. The Chimu had built extensive cities, but their best-known construction was a series of fortifications along their southern borders. The culture collapsed when they were invaded and conquered from the south.

The Chimu were the first of the gold workers to introduce three-dimensional representations by hammering on wooden molds. They lived in gold-rich country. In the sixteenth century, the Spaniards carried off over 17,000 pounds of the metal. At today's rate, that amounts to over $21 million, unimagined buying power back in those days.

"What kind of a deal are you offering?" I asked.

"I'll buy the detectors and guarantee that you can slip them through Peruvian customs inspection. The people in Peru will show you where to dig and they'll supply the labor. The split goes fifty-fifty. Any gold you receive as your share has to be sold through my office here in Miami." He had laid it all on the line.

Thinking hard, I said, "I don't mind the fifty-fifty split, but I'll sell my gold myself. Also, I don't show anyone how to use the detectors until I'm ready to leave. My knowledge of that is my major life-insurance policy while I'm in Peru."

"Too bad," John said, "but I'm sure the family will not allow the deal to go through if it is not sold through this office."

I couldn't contain myself. "Bullshit, John. Those people don't give a damn how my share is sold. You just want to knock down a commission on my share."

He stood abruptly and repeated himself, "Too bad, Howard. I'll see what the family says, but I don't hold much hope."

"What about that stuff?" I indicated my own treasures sitting on his desk.

"What did I say . . . "

I reminded him, "Twenty-two."

He nodded. He sat at his desk, pulled out a checkbook, and wrote a check for $22,000. Just like that, a personal check. I was slightly awed. This guy was used to dealing in big numbers, numbers I couldn't help but like. I took the check, picked up my silver bars, and we parted with the agreement that he would call me at the Racquet Club if he wanted to talk again.

The next day I went to the Pan American Bank in downtown Miami. I cashed the check, was relieved when it didn't bounce, and placed most of the cash and bars of silver in a safety-deposit box.

After a lunch at the top of the Columbus Hotel on Biscayne Boulevard, I headed back to the Racquet Club for a little siesta, where John Wilson was waiting for me in the lobby. We went out to the poolside bar and sat in the sun.

"The family says okay on the sales aspect. You can sell your gold as you see fit, but you have to show them how to use the equipment."

Now, if he had called me or waited a couple of days I might have reacted differently. But because he had come to see me, I knew he was in trouble. I tried a bluff.

"Sorry, John," I said, "if I can't have it my way, I don't go. I've made other plans."

Now he was squirming a bit.

"Suppose you explain it to them sometime after you get there?"

"Agreed," I replied. "But I'm not going to Peru with orders to show how to use the gear."

John nodded.

"Then I'll go," I said. "Now fill me in."

The family's name was Batres. There were eight brothers who lived with their mother on a huge ranch in the far north of Peru. Because of slovenly agricultural practices, the farm was not profitable; in fact, the only thing that kept them really solvent was the illegal sale of gold. The first treasure had been found by their grandfather, and the whole family had been digging and selling ever since.

John left the two detectors with me, and I packed them in suitcases with a superficial camouflage of dirty clothes. He had also handed me an airline ticket for Lima, Peru, on a flight leaving the next morning.

That evening, I did some fast research on Inca culture in the Miami Public Library. Next morning, I caught the plane for Lima.


In spite of assurances that arrangements had been made to clear the metal detectors through customs in Lima, I was somewhat apprehensive as I stood in the inspection hall, waiting for the baggage to be brought in from the Miami flight. I ran through various cock-and-bull stories I could use if I were challenged by the inspectors, but none of them seemed convincing. Just as the baggage carts began arriving at the counters, I noticed a tall, slim, slightly stooped man with a prominent nose coming toward me. Men over six feet are distinctive in that part of the world, as are prominent noses—he must have spotted me because we were so similar. As he approached I saw that he was followed by a porter with a hand cart.

"Señor Jennings?"

"Yes," I replied. The long diagonal scar from the cheekbone up to the temple, plus the right hand with its missing fingers, told me a lot about him. Attempts to bring the down-turned corners of his mouth into a smile were wasted, for the story was in his eyes—hard and black—the eyes of a man without limits.

"*Bueno,* my name is Cadalzo. I speak not so very good English, but I try. Your luggage here now?"

"This is it," I said, as I pulled my bag off the receiving counter and handed it to the waiting porter.

"*Bueno,*" said Cadalzo. He grasped my arm with his hard left hand and steered me toward the exit. "We not see *aduana,* you call customs—walk out the door—is all arranged."

We walked past the two guards at the door who ignored us as though we were invisible. Outside the terminal building, a car was waiting in the ever-hazy Peruvian coastal sunlight.

"How much does the arrangement with customs cost you?" I asked, as we started toward Lima in the almost-new Mercedes. Hopefully I would have a valuable load of artifacts when I left the country—any information would be useful.

"Not good ask many questions, Señor Jennings," Cadalzo replied. "But it is old arrangement for bringing things in and taking things out of country."

"You must be very proud to be working for such a wealthy and powerful family as the Batres."

His hard, dark features came as close to a smile as possible.

"*Si, Si,*" he replied. "They are best in *todo el mundo*—I am

103

almost one of family for many years—I go to many parties with brothers here in Lima. Is great honor for me to find the young girls for them."

As the car headed toward downtown Lima, I pulled my flight bag from the back seat and took out a bottle of Scotch. After swallowing a long swig, I handed the bottle to Cadalzo. Maybe with a little booze in him I might get a better picture of the Batres family.

"*Gracias, señor.*"

He must have had a throat of leather. He tilted the bottle back and at least one-fourth of the quart disappeared before the gurgling stopped. Up to now, his driving with one and a half hands had been sure and faultless—maybe the Scotch had been a mistake.

"*Muchos gracias,*" he said, handing the bottle back. "You like girl for tonight in hotel? I get young *muy lindo señorita* for you. Is okay you do anything you like to her."

"What do you mean—'anything'?" I asked.

"Anything you want—same as brothers. They have much games with young girls. They do anything they want, but sometimes bad I think."

"How do you mean, bad?"

The alcohol was beginning to work. He was loosening up, and what I was hearing I didn't like.

"Little while ago they take girl to room, six of the eight brothers, and she very beautiful Indian girl and not want to go. She very small for thirteen years and maybe nervous and frightened. It is very sad and embarrassing for brothers. Girl dead."

"They killed her?"

"They not mean kill her on purpose. But they were six men. It was accident."

"What about the police? Didn't they object to the accident?"

"*Si, señor.* This is civilized country. Big investigation, but judge *muy simpático*—good friend of Batres family."

"How much does that cost?"

"More than customs, naturally," he laughed a nasty laugh.

Naturally, I thought. Maybe I should have brought a machine gun instead of the .38 Special in my baggage.

That evening in my hotel room, I thought of backing out of the venture. Obviously, the only law at that ranch six hundred miles north of here would be Batres brothers' law. The thought was not comforting. I had no desire to join all those dead Incas in a communal grave in northern Peru.

I went to bed early, couldn't sleep, got up, dressed, and took a walk in the busy streets of Lima. The fashionable dinner hour for the wealthy is ten to eleven each evening, so that by twelve, most restaurants and *cantinas* are still crowded. The main streets have beautiful and sometimes magnificent buildings, good shops, and well-dressed people. One doesn't see the poverty until turning off into the side streets. There, only a few feet away, is destitution in its most dire form. Lying in their vermin-ridden, tattered clothing, young and old, diseased, despondent and totally defeated, are the descendants of the Inca Empire. The slums and filth are pathetic remnants of the once proud, sophisticated, and cultured civilization.

As I walked through the streets, beset not by professional beggars but by people asking for something to sustain life, I thought of the Spanish conquistadors of the sixteenth and seventeenth centuries. Wherever in the Western Hemisphere they established rule for any length of time, one finds misery and poverty among the descendants of former noble Indian cultures. Maltreatment of 100,000 American Indians has been a popular theme around the world for years, but nothing is heard of the millions of forgotten Indians throughout all of Central and South America. The land now belongs to the likes of the Batres family, with its wealth, its vast, lush acres, and its Spanish heritage of cruelty.

Cadalzo arrived on time next morning for the drive to the airport, where we were to catch a plane for Chiclayo. Cadalzo was much more restrained in his conversation, possibly irritated at my refusal to accept his offer of a young girl, or perhaps because he sensed he had said enough the day before.

The 600-mile flight north from Lima to Chiclayo, on the

ubiquitous surplus C-47 of the feeder airline, passes over one of the most desolate deserts I have ever seen. Between the deep blue of the Pacific off the left wing and the snowcapped Andes towering to the right, lies the coastal plain of Peru—one of the most arid in the world, with an annual rainfall of less than a half inch in some parts. Looking carefully, one can still see evidence of the Inca civilization in the sands—the ancient highway running straight from north to south and the intricate network of lines showing the remains of the once-enormous irrigation system. Formerly green and productive from the industry of the Indians, it is now a wasteland of blowing, shifting sand.

At the small Chiclayo airport we were met by a Land Rover and its Indian driver from the Batres' hacienda. Heading eastward toward the Andes, we began the tortuous four-hour drive that would get us to the ranch late in the afternoon. The road was primitive, and the landscape around us was like a sea of sand, with the mountains in the distance resembling islands rising from it.

This was the area in which the Chavin, Mochica, and Chimu Indian cultures had flourished, reaching astonishing intellectual and artistic heights at the time Europe was sinking in the Dark Ages. From about 300 B.C., the Chavin culture dominated northern and central Peru for centuries, slowly giving way to several diverse cultures. Of these, the Mochica, which dominated the north, left the most extensive artifacts, including pottery, textiles, and realistic effigies depicting everyday life. In about A.D. 1000, the Mochica culture was overcome by the highly sophisticated Chimu Indians, who produced vast symmetrical cities and sophisticated irrigation systems that were copied by the Incas. The Chimu area formed the northernmost extension of the Inca Empire after 1400, including the coastal region as far north as Tumbes.

The art work of these cultures is probably the most prized of any in the Americas, yet an incalculable wealth of their decorated pottery and beautifully fashioned gold lies in many still undisturbed burial grounds throughout northern Peru.

106

Archaeologists will be a thousand years locating, excavating, and examining the millions of graves under the sands of this desert.

For more than a hundred years, many of the Spanish-descendant landowners have made more than a good living from excavation of the tombs, using local Indians as labor at twenty cents per day. The fact that it is illegal has not unduly concerned them; however, prosecutions are becoming more frequent each year as surveillance of this vast area becomes more advanced. It would take the whole ramshackle Peruvian army to stop the digging completely, but the low-flying Air Force planes, working with ground patrols, are making the work much more hazardous.

The only two Batres brothers I ever met were at least as bad as their advance press notices. So was their hacienda—I've seen more stately homes on the wrong side of the tracks in Texarkana. We arrived to find that Gonzalo and Rodriques Batres had certainly not postponed their nightly drinking session out out deference to an expected guest. They were both more than slightly bent out of shape.

I was shown to a room in the large rambling house which promised an interesting variety of animal and insect life. The plumbing facilities were the usual arrangement for this part of the world—a chamber pot, occasionally washed.

I handed a tin bowl to the small boy who had carried my baggage, and shortly he returned it filled with water. Obviously, it would be some weeks before my next bath or shower. After a quick wash and a shot of my whisky, I joined the Batres brothers in what, at one time, must have been an attractive courtyard. Now it was a few square yards of dust and dirt, populated with chickens and starving dogs and surrounded by crumbling adobe walls. Whatever they did with their money, they weren't spending any of it on subscriptions to *House Beautiful*.

The matriarch of the family was about seventy-five, leathery and silent. Surely, I thought, life for her couldn't have been any worse if her ancestors had never left Spain for the glories of the new world.

As Rodriques Batres made the introductions, I was pleased to discover that his command of English was reasonably good. Later, I learned that he had been sent away to school in Lima during his youth.

Aside from the old lady and Cadalzo, there were Rodriques and Gonzalo, both in their forties, and a very tired-looking young woman whom Rodriques introduced as his wife. Gonzalo was single. Around us and in and out of the courtyard were many children, from crawlers to young teen-agers.

"How many children do you have, Rodriques?" I asked.

"Six are mine," he said. "Gonzalo has six or seven." Gonzalo, it seemed, amused himself with the various female servants who passed through the house.

The drink was raw white rum. Gonzalo, who appeared to function as general flunky for the house, was sent inside to get orange juice. On his return with a large jug of juice, one of the children stuck out a leg. Gonzalo went down hard on one elbow, desperately trying not to spill the contents of the jug; it smashed to the ground and juice splattered everywhere.

The hilarity was unrestrained. Without a word, Gonzalo rose to his feet, his elbow bleeding. He left, expressionless, and we didn't see him until the next morning. If that was what passed for fun, I thought, how side-splitting it would be to put a bullet in a gullible *gringo*.

I was ready to get down to business.

"Rodriques, tell me about the conditions where we'll be working."

"We will start," he said, "in a burial ground that my grand-father first discovered many years ago. Some of the graves are as much as thirty feet deep in the sand, but with your equipment we can see if there is anything we missed."

Thirty feet deep, I thought. That was bad news. My equipment would not be effective anywhere near that depth, and I explained this to Rodriques. He didn't seem to be disappointed. Obviously, he had something in mind that would not require us to go that far down.

"Señor Jennings, I want to see your equipment and how well it works. If you will get it, I will lay out some of our recent finds to test it."

When I returned with one of the detectors, Rodriques was placing six or seven gold and copper artifacts of various sizes around the courtyard.

"Now show me," he demanded.

In order to make the adjustment of the controls appear more difficult, I spent a great deal more time than was necessary tuning them, then I placed the earphones on him. As he passed the head of the device over the bits of metal, his reaction assured me that he was satisfied with the performance of the equipment.

Taking off the headphones, he said, "Show me how to set the controls."

"I will show you in time, but you must understand that it takes a great deal of practice to operate these things," I said. "Also, here you have been using the detector under ideal conditions, with the metal only a few inches from the head of the device and lying on the surface. In the field, I'll show you that even a change in the composition of the soil can easily confuse the inexperienced operator." This was quite true, but in any case I felt that one expert on this trip was enough. Withholding the knowledge of how to use this equipment was my only protection.

In spite of my statement, Rodriques put the earphones back on and began to experiment with the controls. Knowing that he would soon discover how easy the adjustment was, I picked up the detector. "It's been a long day for me and I've got to get some sleep," I said.

He wasn't pleased with this, but apparently decided not to make it an issue.

"Later then," he said, and added, "We will eat in about an hour. In the morning I have necessary things to do here. You can come along and see some of the *ranchero.*"

I was tired after the long day and not looking forward to a two-hour meal of questionable quality, so I told Rodriques I would prefer rest to food. He shrugged.

"By the way," I said, just before retiring, "I want to be certain that our agreement is clear before we leave in the morning. It was my understanding from John Wilson that we will split any gold we find fifty-fifty and that I can take my part and leave when I wish. Is that correct?"

"*Sí, sí*, fifty-fifty. *Hasta mañana.*"

In my room, I discovered that someone had taken the opportunity to give my gear the once over. They had been kind enough to unpack and stack everything neatly for me. There was a large bundle of my U.S. dollars piled on the dresser, under my pistol. The pile of money was a little less fat than it should have been—a service fee, no doubt—but what I was worried about was the gun. Checking it over, I was relieved to find that the firing pin was still in place. I was going to have to make sure that that didn't change.

Breakfast consisted of rice and beans covered in pork fat, and it tasted better than it sounds. Afterward, we set out in a jeep to see the ranch, Rodriques driving and the brooding Gonzalo sitting in the back. Rodriques said he had to give instructions to some of his foremen before setting out the next day for our trip further into the desert.

Since the supply of gold had been drying up, the brothers had decided to go back into agriculture. Evidence of their industry and foresight was easy to detect: rusting piles of burnt out pumps and engines. The Batres family had invested in drilling equipment and heavy-duty pumps powered by diesel engines for the water that is in abundance—150 feet down. Professional engineers found the water, dug the system of irrigation canals, and the desert was ready to bloom again.

Then the family turned the operation over to Rodriques, who in turn handed it over to his various Indian foremen, who didn't know a diesel engine from a can opener. The foremen had been told about the importance of oil and water in the engines, but without supervision they soon forgot. The result was $90,000 worth of equipment turned to scrap metal. In one or two places where new machinery had been installed—and kept at least temporarily in operation—there were beautiful crops of sugarcane and corn.

Rodriques announced that the *huaca* which his grandfather had worked would be our first project the next day. The word *huaca* has many meanings, all having to do with something holy or mysterious. A *huaca* can be a religious object of pottery or gold, it can be a shrine or building used for worship, or it can be a mound supporting a building or containing graves. The local Indians use the word to describe many things—from lucky charms to the massive adobe pyramids in the northern deserts. A *huaca* may or may not have graves in or near it. A *tola,* on the other hand, is a mound used only for burials.

The *huaca* chosen by Rodriques for my attention had been a rich source of gold in the past. With the metal detectors, he thought we had a good chance of finding gold that had been missed in previous digs. We had thirty Indian laborers to do the dirty work.

That night I packed my bags for a few weeks in the desert. In Lima I had stocked up on canned food. Healthier systems than mine have cracked up under the strain of what the Batres fed on. I threw in a jacket and a sweater for the cool nights, two blankets, a flashlight, and a small plastic tent. I didn't want to leave much at the house. It was a wise decision, because I was never to see the house again—and some Peruvian bum ended up with two new suits made by Benson and Clegg of London.

In the chill air of sunup we set out eastward across the desert toward the majestic Andes. Rodriques drove the Land Rover, with Gonzalo sitting beside him. I followed in the jeep, which I had insisted upon driving, much to the consternation and irritation of both Gonzalo and the Indian foreman sitting beside me.

As the sun worked its way up and out of our eyes, we could see in the distance, some fifteen miles away, the huge *huaca* toward which we were heading. After seven or eight more

111

miles of the rough and uneven road, the Land Rover stopped by a low mound. It looked much the same as the many sand dunes all around us. When I pulled up behind, Rodriques walked back to tell me that some years before they had found that this mound covered an ancient building.

"We didn't find anything here," Rodriques said. "The Indians are afraid of the place, so we didn't do much digging. Get out and look at it."

"We'll try one of the detectors," I said, getting out of the jeep. I didn't expect to find any metal, but the mineral content of the building material would probably be different from the covering sand, so I might determine the size of the buried building by use of the Fisher M-Scope detector.

Walking around to the other side of the mound, I could see a corner of the finely made adobe building jutting out of the sand. A portion of exposed wall showed what appeared to be an opening.

"Is that a door, Rodriques, or possibly a window?"

"No, I will show you."

Calling the Indian to bring a shovel, Rodriques quickly cleared the drifted sand out of the opening and told me to have a look. It was a rectangular recess in the wall, two feet in width, three feet high, and about two feet deep. I was amazed to find that the two sides and back wall of the recess had been painted with the most beautifully preserved colors in designs and figures that were the same in form and color as found on the pottery from this area. Archaeologists would have a lot of fun with this someday, I thought.

"When we dug here years ago, we found eight of these holes in this wall of the building—all with pictures," Rodriques said.

"Why didn't you dig into it?" I asked.

"The Indians will not dig."

"Afraid of dead ancestors?"

"This is not a grave. It is a palace," he said.

"Then maybe it's a good place to look."

"Even I don't want to go in," Rodriques replied.

An abandoned building, whether it was a palace or not,

probably wouldn't contain anything of value, and it would have been a massive job to remove the tons of sand covering it and filling the interior. Besides, apparently the Batres brothers and Indians could not have been persuaded to dig. Adjusting the controls of the detector to distinguish between the adobe and the surrounding sand, I did a quick, very rough survey of the building. My readings indicated it was about 100 feet long by 40 feet wide, and had at least three partitions.

We reached the *huaca* near midday. There was a solitary figure perched on the massive bulk of the adobe structure.

"He watches for the observation plane and army patrols," said Rodriques.

The size of the mound was staggering. It had once been pyramid-shaped, but now was badly eroded. All during the morning drive it had appeared to be a hill on the horizon, but now, close at hand, it was apparent that the entire 250-foot-high structure was completely artificial, constructed of many hundreds of thousands of large, square adobe bricks. The man-hours of work required to build such a pyramid were almost beyond imagination.

Nearby and on the west side of the *huaca* were great terraced holes partially filled with drifting sand. Covering fifteen to twenty acres, they were the most extensive excavations I had ever seen.

"Isn't it a little dangerous working in these holes?" I asked, noting that the sides of many of the holes had caved in.

"*Sí.* It's very dangerous," said Rodriques.

"Has anyone been killed?"

"Many," he said, "but only Indians."

Our Indian laborers had arrived during the night on horses and burros, and they were waiting patiently in the shade of the *huaca*. Rodriques quickly put them to work constructing our camp, which consisted of a large tarpaulin staked out between two mounds of sand and supported in the middle with center poles. With a sprinkling of sand on top of the tarp and the vehicles pulled up underneath, we were hidden from the air.

After lunch Rodriques ordered the Indians to clean out

three of the larger holes, which had either caved in or drifted in. I had a look around the sites and quickly saw that it would not be necessary for the detectors to function as deep as thirty feet. Because of the previous excavations, I would be able to work to that depth simply by electronically surveying the sides of an excavation.

That evening Rodriques became curious about the metal detectors again. The equipment is simple; though you do need a practiced ear for soil changes, metal rings out loud and clear.

"It's very difficult, as I told you," I said. "If the gold is deep, it takes many years of experience to be able to find it."

"I will try it anyway," Rodriques replied in a somewhat aggressive tone.

"The equipment is sensitive and fragile. I haven't come all this way to have you ruin it in the same way you did the detectors John Wilson sent to you." Rodriques frowned, but there was a sheepish look there as well. "Now let's get this straight once and for all," I said emphatically. "The detectors belong to me and I don't want anyone to touch them until I have the time to teach you to use them. Is that understood?"

He wasn't convinced, but short of shooting it out then and there he could do nothing about it.

The next morning, I chose an Indian from the work force to help carry the equipment and to assist me getting in and out of the holes. His name was Chalo, and I'd noticed him the day before because he'd taken the trouble to find out my name. He called me Don Howard.

My Spanish was sketchy, but I was determined to improve it. Between one of those phrase books that tells how to ask the way to the railroad station, and trying to communicate with Chalo during the next few days, I learned a fair amount of Spanish in a very short time.

Chalo was in his mid-twenties, and he lived with his wife and four children in a small Indian village a few miles to the north. Under any circumstances except the ones in which he was living, Chalo would have amounted to something. He was bright and he had a sense of humor uncommon among the Indians.

114

When the going was good and there were crops to be picked or holes to be dug, Chalo got twenty cents a day. The people in his village exist by growing a little corn and raising a few chickens or a pig or two. Malnutrition, tuberculosis, childbirth, and dysentery take such a terrible toll that one seldom sees an Indian in this area over the age of forty.

Chalo and I began work on the terraces in one of the cleared holes. The terraces are necessary as holes are deepened. Indians working at the bottom shovel material to a terrace where other Indians shovel the material to the next terrace, and so on to the top. A very deep hole can have as many as five terraces with a crew working on each, keeping the material from the bottom moving to the top. All of the workers, except possibly those working on the top terrace, are in constant danger of a cave-in of the loose material. The terraces in the hole where we commenced work were about five feet high, four feet wide, and twenty-five feet long.

I began on the third terrace from the top. I had gone along its surface for only a few feet with the detector when I got a strong signal. *Son of a bitch.* I hadn't expected to locate anything so quickly!

Chalo called another Indian to help, and they worked carefully with a pick and shovel in the lightly compacted sand. Only a few inches down they encountered the grey powdery material that often indicates a grave. Then, digging carefully with machetes, the two Indians began cautiously to widen and deepen the hole.

As I pushed my own machete gently into the material, it was stopped by something hard. Using a hand trowel and my fingers, I removed more of the sand until I was able to pull the object from the hole. It was a beautiful pottery figure of a man with a jaguar headdress. Knowing this had not caused a reading on the detector, I again moved it over the spot and was reassured by an even stronger signal than before.

Two more pieces of painted pottery came out. Then, to one side of the hole, still embedded in sand but with one side exposed, was a large gold chalice, nine inches high, gleaming as brightly as when it was buried. After a bit more delicate dirt removal with the trowel, out it came. It was a large vessel, with a diameter of a little more than seven inches at the top, that was embossed on four sides with the upside-down faces of four hawk-nosed warriors, fierce and proud—only with the open end down, as when drinking, would the faces be right side up. It was incredibly heavy.

I handed the cup up to Rodriques, who had joined us. He was impressed.

"Congratulations, Señor Jennings," he said. "With your machines, I think we are going to find a lot of gold."

He watched as I moved the detector over the hole again. The signal wasn't as strong as before, but there was still a definite indication of metal; we hadn't gotten it all yet. Doing the digging myself now, using only my machete and the trowel, I pulled a highly polished polychrome pot from the grave. Carefully emptying the loose material through my fingers, I heard a rattle, and a heavy gold nose-ring dropped into my hand.

Again I passed the detector over the hole and around the immediate area, this time receiving no signal—we had recovered it all. It was very rewarding, considering it had been the first hour of work with the detector.

My heart still pounding from the excitement of the find, I moved the detector with meticulous care further along the same terrace. Nearing its end, I was begining to think I had been lucky as hell to find that cup so easily. Then, suddenly, I had another signal. It was not as strong this time, but still solid and definite.

As in the other hole, we found pottery first; next came fragments of cloth. Rodriques, who had a market for practically everything from a tomb, brought soft brushes to use in clearing the sand from the fragile, colored material. A little farther on, a large gold disk, which the deceased had been wearing, was found on the material just below the skull. The detector indicated that there was still metal in the grave, but it was another hour before we could cautiously clear all the sand from the cloth and lift its fragments onto a sheet of plastic.

116

The extremely dry climate had preserved the fabric and the entire skeleton as well. The fascinating gleam of gold again appeared in the sand, and I saw a heavy gold bracelet still encircling the wristbone. Taking it off the skeleton, rather than finding it lying nearby, was a special sensation, and not altogether pleasant. Passing the detector over the fully exposed skeleton, I heard another signal. We had already found two fine pieces in this grave—could there be more?

It was difficult to break for lunch, but I thought I'd best appear as unconcerned about our finds as the Batres brothers and our Indian workers, who had shown no interest whatever in the craftsmanship required to produce either the gold goblet or the fine pottery now lying all around us.

The desert was hot now with the noonday sun overhead. After lunch, the Batres brothers and all the Indians sought shade for an hour's siesta. As I lay back against the sand dune under the tarp, I thought of the morning's success. Apart from the pottery, some of which was valuable (although too bulky for me to try to smuggle out), we had in the course of half a day recovered three very valuable gold artifacts, and we were still at work on a grave containing more metal. At this rate, I could stay until I collected as much gold as I wanted or until my companions turned nasty.

In the afternoon, the grave turned up two more metal objects. One was a copper medallion or possibly some sort of buckle found near the waist of the skeleton, and the other was a gold "toomie," a ceremonial knife shaped like a half-moon. It was plain, but very beautiful and marvelously heavy. Nothing more was indicated on that terrace, so I spent the remainder of the afternoon electronically surveying the other terraces leading to the bottom, while all the Indians were put to work cleaning out other old digs.

On the fourth terrace from the top, I received a single strong signal near one end, and on the fifth, the detector indicated metal in two places. In the bottom of the hole, some 25 feet from the surface, I received a good signal in one of the sides of the hole. Despite the tremendous amount of gold taken by

117

several generations in the past, it began to appear that they had left as much or more than they took.

In camp that evening, guns began to appear. I had idly wondered what sort of weaponry the brothers would go in for. Rodriques strapped on a heavy .38 Colt Police Special, a formidable gun.

"Sometimes these Indians steal," he said. "Sometimes I have to shoot them and then they stop."

"Good thinking," I said.

Gonzalo didn't strike me as being bright enough to be trusted with a gun, but he was strapping on a huge U.S. Army .45 automatic anyway. About the only positive thing in this sudden appearance of weapons was that it meant I could wear my own Smith and Wesson .38 Special.

In order to see where we all stood regarding guns, I casually suggested some target practice next morning while breakfast was being prepared. We set up some tin cans at ten paces. I hit seven out of eight. Gonzalo turned out to be a little lacking in coordination, and hit nothing. Rodriques wasn't too bad, but I was pleased to see that he wasn't too good either. He hit two out of the eight.

"You shoot good," he said, not sounding too happy about it.

"Sometimes I have to."

For the next ten days Chalo and I worked side by side. We found a lot of gold. My Spanish developed and our friendship warmed. The Batres brothers should have been cheered by what we were finding, but they weren't. Gonzalo remained his same depressed and depressing self, and now Rodriques was becoming sullen and uncommunicative. Chalo began to use the word *cuidado* every time he referred to them. *Cuidado* means careful, and I was.

As long as the workmen were around, I couldn't imagine that Rodriques would try anything. Murder with that many witnesses, regardless of how far away the law was, would be ridiculous.

Rodriques' increasing irritation was becoming more apparent

118

as I continued to refuse him use of the detectors. Finally I laid it on the line for him.

"Rodriques," I said, "I don't trust you or your brother a damn bit. As far as I'm concerned, the only thing that's keeping me in one piece is my knowledge of the use of this equipment. If you'll get off my back, I'll not only show you how to use it when we get out of here, but I'll give it to you as well. In the meantime, don't ask me again."

He turned and walked away without replying, but there was hatred in his eyes.

That must have settled it between us, because that afternoon Chalo said, "It's time for you."

"Time for what?" I asked.

"I think they are going to kill you tomorrow," he said with resignation.

"Are you sure, Chalo?" I asked.

The sardonic tone of his voice was unmistakable. "No, Don Howard, I am not sure. Maybe the brothers feel generous. Maybe they give us the day off because they are kind. Maybe the brothers love us workers so much they want us to enjoy our holiday."

"What holiday?"

"Tomorrow is the feast day of the patron saint of the village. Only four of us are from the village, but the brothers are giving every man the day off," he explained. He told me the workers would be leaving the camp at sunrise, and they were not to return until the following morning. The whole schedule added up to trouble for old Howard. I thanked Chalo and told him to go join the others. If he stayed with me too long, our association could cause him trouble.

Just before nightfall, Rodriques came over to my tent and announced, "Tomorrow we work alone. No Indians."

I put on my best poker face and said, "Really? Why is that?"

The cunning look belied the bland answer. "Tomorrow is a very important holy day in the village, and we must give them the day free."

119

"That's very nice of you," I said. "I'd like to go to the village. I've never seen a Peruvian fiesta."

His expression froze. "No!" he snapped. "Tomorrow we do something special. There is a secret site; much gold a few miles north. I think you will want to work it with your detectors."

Rodriques was a poor actor at best, but he blew the whole thing by acting chummy. "We will have a good visit to the old site. Maybe find much gold." His sickly smile was meant to reassure me.

*"Bueno,"* I said. He headed back to his bedroll and I finished my drink.

I didn't sleep that night. My mind drifted back to a similar night near the end of World War II, when I was being held in a German prisoner of war camp. We knew Patton's Third Army was close to rescuing us. We had been badly treated by the Nazis, and somehow the rumor started that all pilots were to be executed before we could be freed. When you are a P.O.W., possibility can become reality. I stayed awake the night before we were freed, waiting for death. That night in Peru I stayed awake again, racking my brain to save my life.

The first step I took was to leave my tent, on the slight chance that Rodriques or Gonzalo might take it into their minds to pop me off during the night. I climbed halfway up the digging site and found a terrace on the *huaca.* I waited and thought.

It was a damn shame they were so greedy. We had uncovered fifty-six pieces of gold in a short period of time, and their half would mean a lot of cash to them. If we stayed a while longer, we could double the take. It was all so stupid. But stupid or not, I believed it. I thought about all of those pompous archae-ology types who accuse treasure hunters of leading a soft life on the money from easy plunder. I'd like to see one of them sitting on the side of a *huaca* on a cold night, figuring out how to stay alive so that people could go and look at Chimu vases and breastplates in a comfortable museum.

By morning, I was strung as tight as a bowstring, just like that morning in the German P.O.W. camp. On that day, we found that our guards had slipped out during the night, and hours later the Third Army tanks of General Patton rolled in to liberate us. Now, in Peru, my enemy was still there. I could see him down below doling out small amounts of money as the workers filed out of our camp. Making my way down to the site, I slipped back into my tent. I checked my .38.

Chalo came by with his belongings slung over one shoulder as most of the other Indians could be seen trailing across the desert toward the village, seven miles away. Chalo did not speak. I guess he didn't know what to say.

Pulling up my friendliest grin, I said, "Don't worry." Then I pressed two $100 bills into the palm of his hand and nodded my head. "Now go. *Adiós, amigo. Gracias.*"

I knew he wanted to help, but I could handle this situation better alone. Just like that morning when I was freed from the P.O.W. camp. I had wanted to go alone into the adjacent town, so I had borrowed a German Luger pistol from a tank commander and gone looking for food.

Here, in Peru, I was looking for a way to get out alive. If I waited for the Batres brothers to make the first move, that move might well be fatal for me. I decided to take the initiative. As soon as the last of the Indians was out of sight, I went over to where the foreman was preparing a skillet of rice and chicken. Rodriques poured coffee while Gonzalo sat nearby, glassy-eyed as usual. I drank two cups, warming my insides and perking me up after being awake all night.

I had had a cup of hot coffee given me by an old German couple after I left the P.O.W. camp foraging for food. The Russians had also been released from a nearby camp, and they were in the process of destroying the town, so the Germans were happy to welcome the protection of an American into their home. They told me of food they had hidden in an underground storage cellar—one much like the old-time spring houses with a wooden door above ground. The German soldiers were still retreating through the village, but I approached the door thinking only of food. I did pull my borrowed Luger, in case someone took a pot shot at me from a building, but food was

121

dominating my mind. Months of eating garbage had put an incredible edge on my hunger.

I pulled the door open and looked down the steep stairs leading to the underground room. Light flooded over my shoulder and splashed on the startled face of a German soldier who had hidden there during the night. He jumped up, planting his feet firmly as he instinctively jerked his rifle into position. I was silhouetted by the sun in back of me. I could see the deadly barrel of his gun just a couple of feet below my face.

Just as the Batres' foreman brought me a plate of food, I saw Gonzalo go for the gun in his holster. Before the German had been able to pull the trigger, I had shot him. And as Gonzalo's gun cleared the holster, I shot him. I could have killed him. But one killing was enough in my lifetime. I aimed the .38 at his right shoulder and squeezed off a shot and then another. His body jerked grotesquely as the first bullet hit him, then spun violently from the force of the second blast.

For an instant, Gonzalo lay still, and the vision of the dead German soldier flooded into my mind. I hadn't wanted to kill—Christ! Why do people have to be greedy? Then Gonzalo moved, and I pointed my gun at Rodriques.

"I'll blow your by-God head off if you go for your gun," I shouted. I motioned for the foreman to go and stand by Rodriques.

Keeping both of the men at bay, I moved near the fire and picked up Gonzalo's gun. I told Rodriques to toss his weapon to me gently.

"You bastards were going to kill me," I said. "I *should* kill you." A groan of pain came from Gonzalo on the ground.

"I'm taking half of the gold; my half," I announced.

*"Bandito!"* Rodriques cried.

"No," I said. "I just feel like leaving. That's what we agreed on." I glared at my would-be killers. "Down on the ground! Move!"

Rodriques and his foreman joined Gonzalo on the ground.

I went to the Land Rover and removed the rotor from the

distributor. I put it into my pocket, then ripped off the distributor cap and several spark-plug leads to be sure. Next, I loaded my share of the gold into the jeep and turned the switch. In my anxiety to get moving, I flooded the carburetor. I tried again and again to start the engine, and with each attempt the battery wound down and grew weaker. Then, suddenly, it caught. I turned and fired one shot into the ground next to Rodriques and dropped the jeep into gear. The wheels spun as I roared away.

Robin once asked me why I didn't take all the gold. The treachery of the Batres brothers might have justified such a move, but I only took my share because it seemed to me that to take more would only have put me in their category, and by now I genuinely loathed them. I earned what I took, and I took only what I earned.

As I sped away, I looked in the rear-view mirror and saw Rodriques rushing toward the Land Rover. After a few seconds, I realized he'd had a hunting rifle hidden in the back of the Rover. The first slug tore through the seat next to me and splattered against the dash of the jeep—Rodriques was a better shot with a rifle than a pistol. I swerved the jeep into a series of evasive maneuvers. The weaving was dangerous but it made me a more difficult target. A second shot sounded close but high. The third hit the windshield and shattered the glass. Then the jeep bounded over a rise and I was safe for the moment—out of the line of fire. I raced the jeep to get out of range.

As I drove back in the direction of the Batres' hacienda, I realized that I had no way of knowing whether Cadalzo or any of the other brothers were there, so when the building came into sight I turned the jeep off the dirt road and headed northwest across the desert. I knew that by traveling in that direction I would eventually intercept the road to Chiclayo. There was a once-daily flight to Lima at 12:30 P.M.

Perhaps old Captain Jennings was once again looking down at his prodigal descendant and working a small miracle on his dirty, unshaven, exhausted behalf. Somehow I made Chiclayo on time. Only one major obstacle now remained in my path: how to slip myself and the contents of my knapsack safely out of the country.

I had left the Batres brothers stranded thirty miles out in the desert; with luck, they could hike to the hacienda in ten hours, but even then there was no telephone at their home. They would have to ride horses or an ancient tractor into Chiclayo to notify the authorities to pick me up. But I had seen their influence at the airport, and I knew they were ruthless people. The charges could be serious. I didn't think Gonzalo would die from the wound, not unless his brother abandoned him in the desert. But they could claim attempted murder. It would be my word against theirs.

During the three-hour flight from Chiclayo to Lima, I washed and shaved in the C-47's head. I sure as hell needed a bath, but it was important that I at least *look* as well-groomed as possible. I put on what clean clothes I had in my pack.

We landed in Lima at five minutes to three. Pan Am informed me that they had one seat open on the flight to Panama at four. That was heartening news, but I still had a long, tense hour. Nervously, I kept looking at my watch. I had two major problems: the customs inspection that the Peruvians sometimes made of out-going luggage which they suspected might contain antiquities, and the possibility of the Batres' getting to a telephone and warning the authorities to pick me up.

I purchased the largest flight bag I could find at the gift counter, large enough to hold my twenty-eight pieces of gold. I made the transfer in the men's room, and then went back out into the airport lobby and placed the flight bag on a seat. In order to appear as unconcerned as possible, I left the bag there and walked back to the gift shop. Acting out the casual routine of souvenir shopping, I purchased a few trinkets and a sterling silver cigarette lighter embossed with Inca figures.

When the flight was called, I sauntered past the departure lounge to see how many, if any, tourists were being searched prior to boarding. Frequently, intensive examinations are made for the very sort of objects I was transporting. I also scanned the unmistakable plainclothes police in the lounge, trying to see if they were on the lookout for me. Things seemed quiet and normal—only one man was asked to open his briefcase for inspection.

Perspiration streamed and my pulse quickened as I picked up my flight bag and opened the door into the lounge. When you are trying to smuggle something past a customs inspection, you develop total paranoia: Everyone is looking right at you—everyone is against you. I forced a friendly smile. The customs man smiled, waved me past, and said: *"Buenas tardes, señor."* My tension dropped, and I felt lightheaded. I said, *"Buenas tardes,"* and meant it. It was a very, very "good afternoon."

The Pan Am clerk passed me through the door. I climbed up into the plane, flopped into my seat and then asked the stewardess for a drink, presto pronto.

That night, I landed in Panama and caught a Braniff flight to New Orleans. By mid-morning of the next day, I finally collapsed into a bed in the Hilton Hotel near the international airport. My body was dirty, but it was not stuck in a Lima prison cell or an Indian grave. At last I could sleep.

I dreamed a troubled dream of the Batres chasing me, of John Wilson with some gun-wielding thugs, and finally of a U.S. Customs inspector confiscating my gold. Actually, what had really happened did create a major problem for me a year later. On the U.S. Customs form, I had listed the gold as "Indian Artifacts" and in the space marked "Value," I had simply drawn a line. I had no idea of the value of the contents in the bag and at that time was unaware of the necessity for a gold import license. Upon my early morning arrival in New Orleans, I had walked up to a sleepy-looking customs official and handed him my form. He gave it a glance as I opened the bag. Because the gold was dirty and the light dim, it must have looked to him like a canvas flight bag full of junk metal. He passed me through without touching a thing in the bag.

That afternoon I showered, shaved, and ordered pancakes, sausage, and three glasses of milk. As I spread my treasure out on the rumpled bed, I began planning the next move. Miami was out. New York was a market, but I quickly discarded the idea—too many dangers there. Besides, I hate that city. Suddenly some quirk of memory produced the name of Beauregard Morton, the lawyer I had met with his wife on Roatán. The meeting had been short, but he had seemed to be well-connected. Perhaps I might sell the gold in Atlanta.

I placed a call. His wife, Gail, answered, and I had visions of those lovely legs, and it suddenly dawned on me that I had been out of touch with reality for much too long. She told me that Beau was in Birmingham, Alabama, and gave me a number there to call. In ten minutes, I had him on the telephone.

"How'd you make out in Roatán?" he asked.

I filled him in on the recent past. Then, "Beau, I've got some pre-Columbian artifacts—gold. Do you have any idea where I could sell them?"

He told me that he was in Birmingham talking to some businessmen about land development in Roatán. Some of them might know of a quick market. While I was at it, he suggested I could help him pitch potential land investors.

I caught an early evening Delta flight and Beau met me at Municipal Airport. We went right to a meeting at the huge home of a major building contractor. Three other wealthy citizens were also there. Over drinks, I supported and expanded on Beau's description of the property on Roatán and confirmed his projections for the future. Then I introduced the subject of gold. In a few minutes, I had the gold sitting out on the floor for them to view. They stared for a minute, then one man said, "That's prettier than cornsilk in a cob pipe."

To my surprise, two of the men in the room were on the advisory council and board of directors of a large southern museum.

They arranged a meeting with the curator of the museum. He was impressed with the collection, and we settled down to business quickly. We agreed to a figure of fifteen times each object's weight in gold, and I offered to let him select as many pieces as the museum could afford.

That afternoon, the curator of the museum started calling

126

Howard Jennings

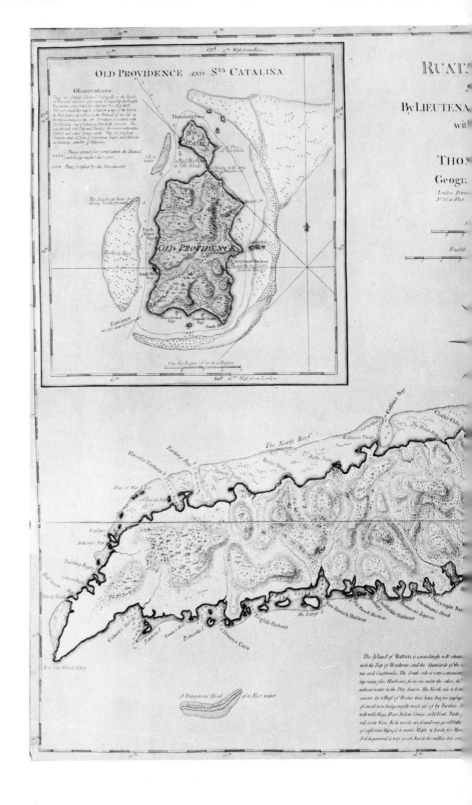

OLD PROVIDENCE AND Sᵗᵃ CATALINA

Observations

Mansfield Point

Sᵗᵃ CATALINA

OLD PROVIDENCE

Western Reef

One Sea League of 20 in a Degree

RUATT

By LIEUTENA

wit

THO

Geog:

The North Reef

Collins Bay

Chalky Bay

Firefly Harbour

Turtling Bay

Man of War

Anthony's Bay

Turtling Beach

West End

SOUTH WEST END

English Harbour

the Large I.

New French Harbour

A Dangerous Shoal of 30 Foot water

The Island of Rattan is exceedingly well situate
with the Bay of Honduras, and the Spaniards of the
ras and Guatimala, The South side is very
ing many fine Harbours, from one end to the
without water in the Dry Season. The North side
a Reef of Rocks that have
of small rocks being mostly made
with wild Hogs, Deer, Indian Conies, wild Fowl, Turtle
ral sorts Nets. In its woods are found very good Oaks
of sufficient bigness to make Masts & Yards for Merc
Soil in general is very good, but in the valleys the

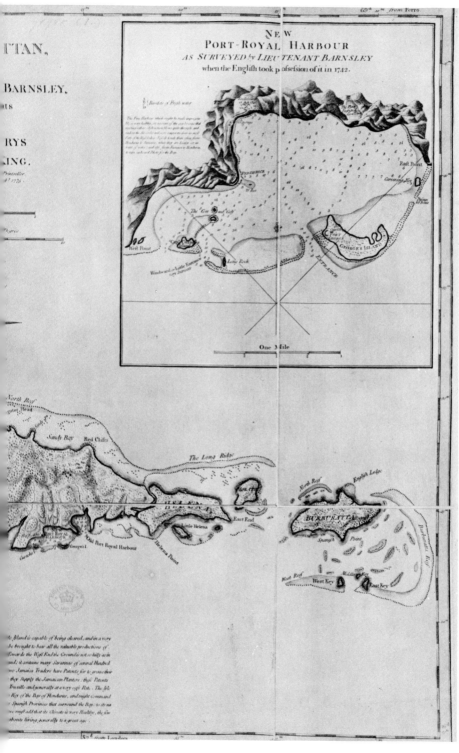

Roatan Island, from the 1775 map by Thomas Jeffreys now
in the British Museum collection.

Old Port Royal Harbor on Roatan Island.

The Cow, the island on which we found the pirate treasure chest.

Some of the pirate debris which we uncovered in our
excavations around Port Royal Harbor.

One of the Pulse Induction's
P.I.-type metal detectors: handy
and versatile.

For depth-penetration, the big
Fisher M-Scope metal detector
is a useful piece of equipment.

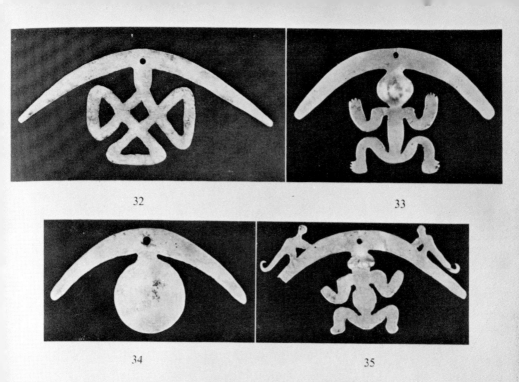

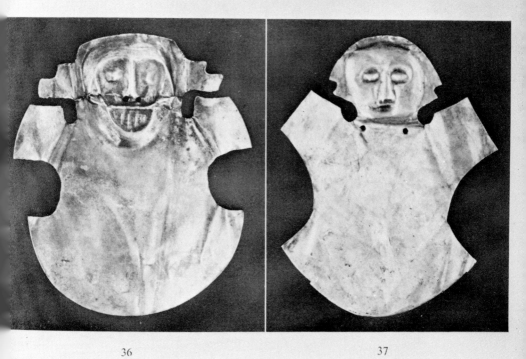

Some of Howard's Inca gold artifacts, as they appeared on a
page of a gallery catalogue in 1965.

Bed and bath: Howard in the jungle.

An Inca grave.

47

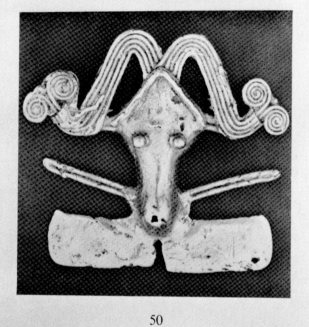

49

50

51

52

More Jennings gold from a gallery catalogue. Howard's
"horny Indian" is lower left.

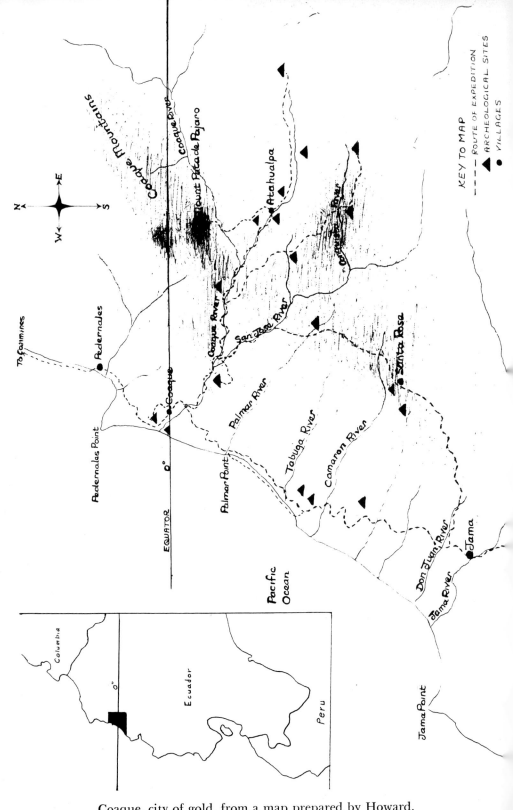

Coaque, city of gold, from a map prepared by Howard.

A comparatively deep excavation at Coaque.

Pretty girls are standard features of Howard's adventures: one of the team members on the second Coaque expedition.

Ancient artifacts recovered from two graves excavated at the lower camp in Coaque.

Howard won't part with this delightful little piece of statuary brought back from Coaque.

Howard, examining an emerald.

A gold Inca sun disc.

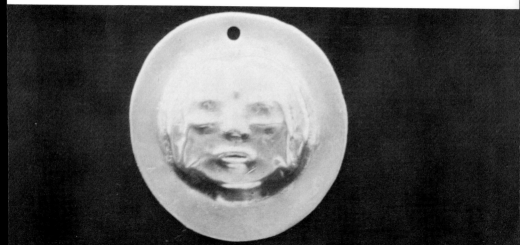

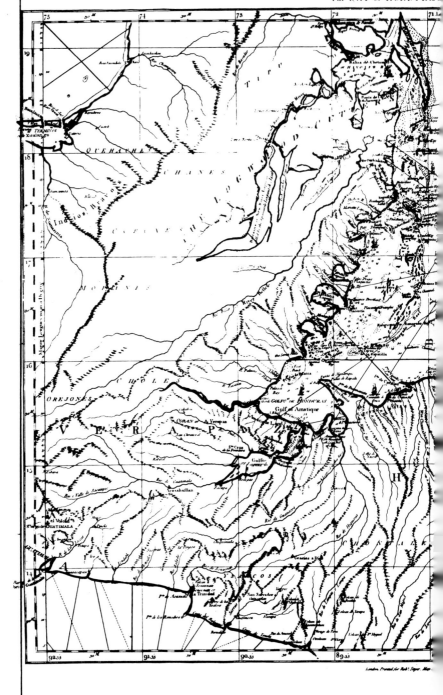

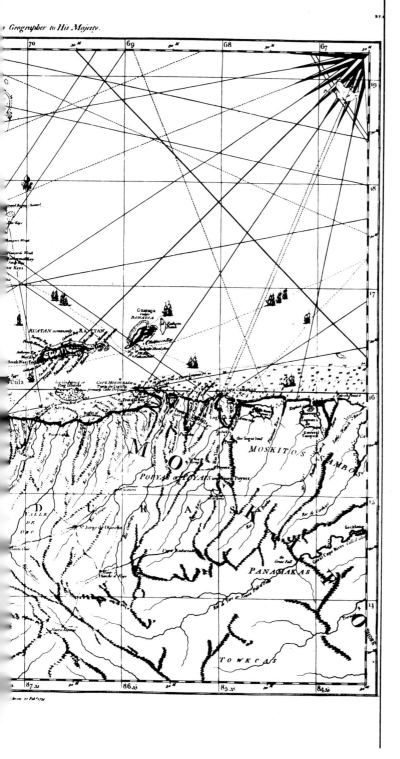

Thomas Jeffreys' 1775 map of the Bay of Honduras not only shows the location of treasure-laden Glover Reef and Four Keys Reef, but pinpoints some of the sunken wrecks.

Treasure: a single day's find at Coaque included gold, platinum and emeralds.

prominent and wealthy men who helped support the museum. Further phone calls were made the next day, and a luncheon was arranged at a venerable local men's club.

Six of the museum's staunch patrons attended the luncheon. Although most of my gold was being held in the museum, I had a few smaller pieces along to show. I told them about treasure hunting and gave them a frank account of the entire affair with the Batres brothers in Peru.

That afternoon the supporters of the museum went over individually to view the gold artifacts and make their own evaluation. By that evening I was informed that the museum had received $26,000 in contributions for the purchase of some of the gold artifacts.

The following morning I went back to the museum and the curator took me down to the vault in the basement. A balance scale was sitting on a work bench, and he picked the pieces he wanted, one by one, and weighed them. He chose the three large cups—two with the stylized heads upside down, one with the heads right side up. Since these were the bulkiest objects, I was glad he chose them.

Finally he made his selection—eleven pieces in all. After handing me back the remainder in my canvas flight bag along with a check for $26,000, he accompanied me to the bank in order to expedite the cashing of the check. Within an hour, I had picked up five packets of $100 bills. I dropped them in the bag with the remaining gold.

Beau took me out to the airport, where I caught a flight to Abilene, Texas, to visit my parents.

Abilene was fine for about two days, but then the old restlessness returned. Within a week, I found myself sitting in a first-class seat of a Northwest-Orient jet bound for Hong Kong. Nestled down at my feet was the canvas bag containing both the cash and the gold.

# 5 GOLD OF THE ANDES

ROBIN MOORE
HQUSASFVN
NHA–TRANG, RVN

ARRIVING TAN SON NHUT 1600 PAN AM FLIGHT
201 FROM HONG KONG WEDNESDAY 21. HAVE
RESERVATION AT CARAVELLE HOTEL AND GREAT
IDEA FOR NEW FIND. JENNINGS.

The sergeant major of Headquarters United States Army Special Forces Vietnam at Nha-Trang, Republic of Vietnam, handed me the telegram when I returned from the Green Beret operation in Tay Ninh. It was the first time I had been able to smile since the somber experience of seeing Lieutenant Perkings blown up in front of me when he stepped on a North Vietnamese mine two days before.

The cable had been waiting for me for two days, which meant that Howard would be hitting Saigon the next day. I wondered if he was really coming just to see me. I knew that the Indians who ran Vietnam's currency black market sent couriers down from Hong Kong every few days, preferably Caucasians. They wore vests lined with gold for sale to rich Vietnamese anxious to convert their wealth into something more stable than 1964 piastres. And, of course, anything that had to do with gold would be of interest to Howard.

In Saigon I stopped by the Special Forces Command Liaison Detachment, wrangled a jeep and driver from my friend Colonel Lanyard, and headed for Tan Son Nhut International Airport.

Howard was the first man off the plane, standing tall and looking heavier than I had ever seen him, as I had suspected he might. I didn't ask any questions.

"If you can hold out for half an hour, we'll be through this

129

damn traffic and at the Caravelle," I told him in the jeep. "There's a fine air-conditioned bar on the top floor."

"The stewardess was generous," Howard said. "I'm sure glad you could get out to meet me, Robin."

"So am I," I replied. "When you get out in the boonies, there's no telling when you'll make it back to Nha-Trang. It's lucky I got your cable. By the way, have you got time to come up? We've got the most beautiful beach in Vietnam, and it's covered with girls."

A momentary light showed in his eyes, and then he shook his head. "I just dropped in to say hello, and then I'm on my way."

I stole a glance at the suspiciously full chest and stomach my lean friend was sporting. He caught my look but said nothing.

At the Caravelle Hotel, Howard showed his passport and registered. "You go on up to the bar," he said. "I'll drop in my room and wash up and change." I watched his glance sweep the lobby of the Caravelle and pause as it fell on the dark-skinned Indian sitting across from the registration desk. The Indian stood up and put down the copy of *Newsweek* he had been reading.

"I won't be long, Robin."

"No sweat. The waitresses are beauties."

We rode up in the elevator and Howard got off on the fifth floor. I went on to the top and made for the cocktail lounge. True to his word, Howard showed up in about fifteen minutes. He had changed clothes, and he looked considerably slimmer and more relaxed.

We sat for a couple of hours nursing our drinks while Howard brought me up to date. He filled me in on his adventures and his troubles with the Batres brothers in Peru, then, motioning for another round, he filled me in on Hong Kong. He had arrived there with the remaining Peruvian gold still in the flight bag he had purchased at the Lima airport. The manager of the President Hotel in Hong Kong had previously managed a hotel in Montego Bay, and he and Howard were old acquaintances. When Howard explained that he had some valuable gold artifacts to sell, the manager arranged a meeting with a Chinese gentleman who happened to be connected with the cultural department of the People's Republic of China.

Howard had been somewhat reluctant to do business with the Red Chinese, but he knew that over half the commercial businesses in Hong Kong are owned and controlled by Chinese Communist representatives and that contact with them would be inevitable. He met with the man, and with a minimum of haggling, they agreed on £10,300 sterling for the remaining pieces.

The next morning he dropped off the gold and picked up the check, then immediately cashed it for one thousand English £10 notes. And then he'd sent me the cable.

That night Howard and I went through one of those all-night bull-sessions, and somewhere between the first drink and dawn it became clear that Howard was now totally committed to treasure hunting. He studied, planned, evaluated, and dedicated himself to the labors, both physical and mental, with the attitude of a professional.

He told me about his new idea, born out of study and plain old East Texas horse sense.

"You know what a wealth of gold there is in northern Peru," he said. "And when I was in Bogotá, looking for the emeralds, I visited the Banco Republico Gold Museum. It's the largest collection of its kind—14,000 pieces. All other museum and private collections together amount to about one-fifth of that figure."

I waited.

He said, "Well, don't you see?"

"See what?"

"Dammit, Robin," he said impatiently. "Struck right in between southern Colombia, where they've found a lot of gold, and northern Peru, where they've found a lot of gold, is Ecuador. There has only been one major dig in Ecuador. That's where I'm heading." He paused. "I wish to hell you'd come along."

But I couldn't leave Vietnam then, and he knew it. So, after a few more days looking around Saigon with me, he boarded Pan Am One, the "round-the-world" flight that starts on the west coast of the U.S. and ends up in New York, the hard way.

The next day Howard deplaned in London for a session with civilization.

Robin knows that my stint in London was not entirely fun and games. I had work to do.

Sandwiched in between long sessions at the British Museum and the Royal Geographical Society, I did enjoy the good food and a couple of months of high living. But research was my primary objective, and I squeezed my academic sources until they were wrung dry. I've always felt that what makes the difference between a professional treasure hunter and a mere thrill-seeker is the amount of preparation one is willing to invest. I invest heavily.

Once I had absorbed all the information available, I headed for Ecuador.

I stopped off in Miami in order to re-equip myself with the latest metal detection equipment, and then caught a flight to Quito. The capital of Ecuador sits on a 9,000-foot plateau, and is therefore blessed with a mild year-round climate even though it is only 15 miles south of the equator. The city is a hodgepodge of architectural styles, with ancient Indian adobe buildings sprinkled among early Spanish churches and starkly modern structures.

The elegant Hotel Quito was my first stop. I rented a suite for two months, and then decided to do something sensible about the large amount of cash I was carrying. Soon I was sitting across a desk from a pretty young girl who handled *gringos* for the Banco Popular. By the time I had opened a checking account, I also had talked the young lady into having dinner. And by the time dinner was through, she had agreed to accompany me on a preliminary search for possible burial areas east of Quito. She had some vacation time due her, and she felt sure she could get away. We decided to leave the next day, as soon as she had called the bank.

Anita was the bright, emancipated daughter of a well-to-do family, but her parents, who lived in another town, were never aware that their daughter had become so liberated as to go flitting off into the back country with a *gringo*. But there were practical reasons for taking her along—in addition to being beautiful, Anita spoke Spanish, and if I would be venturing into head-hunting territory it was vital for me to be able to communicate quickly.

I rented a Land Rover and bought a tent, sleeping bags, and other basic equipment necessary for a short trip into the rugged high country. We headed east from Quito into the mountainous area, which is breathtaking both in beauty and in its lack of oxygen. The snowcapped ranges push up eighteen or nineteen thousand feet into the clear blue sky. Our first stop was to be in the small city of Cayambe.

On our first evening in Cayambe, Anita found an old man who knew many tales and legends about the area. We met him in the front part of his general store, a setting typical of so many I had seen in my travels. The shelves were stocked meagerly with cans of Heinz's Baked Beans and boxes of Kellogg's Corn Flakes, alongside the customary kerosene lamps, coils of rope, and spools of thread. Behind one counter was an incredible sight—a dust-covered rack half stocked with a couple of dozen ViewMaster stereo slides. I've often wondered who sold them to the poor, unsuspecting store owner. I've also wondered who the hell bought the other half of the stock. The sales abilities of both suppliers and retailers throughout the world never fail to amaze me.

After the old man attended to my purchase of three cans of beans, he invited us into his office in the back of the store. The room was musty and cluttered with eons of carelessness. We sat down at a rickety old desk, and he pulled open a drawer. There, neatly organized, were fifteen tennis-ball-size human heads. The old man handled each offering with a casualness

133

that made his sales pitch seem even more ghoulish. I was fascinated by one head, which was topped with red hair and ringed with a tiny red beard. I remembered that shrunken heads compress skin pigments so that Indian heads look ebony and white ones seem brown. I realized I was looking at the head of a white man. As I held the miniature redhead in my hands, I was told—on good authority—that the head was that of a treasure hunter. It seems the poor chap had come from Canada to buy art antiquities and managed to get himself caught by the notorious Jivaros Indians, who did their art work on his head.

I found out later that the story was entirely a figment of the old man's imagination—that the head had really belonged on the body of a free-lance missionary who had allowed his Messianic zeal to overrule his prudence. Several months after I saw the head, it turned up in Quito, in the British Embassy. The embassy, following the rules, packed up the "remains" and shipped them off in a diplomatic pouch to the deceased man's relatives in England—which must have been a hell of a shock for the family.

I didn't buy any heads, but I did manage, through Anita, to learn about a route that would take us near to where I felt there might be burial mounds. After some joking about how the Jivaros Indians would love working on my head and especially my long nose, the old man advised us that *banditos* were known to be active in the area I was planning to visit. That was unwelcome news indeed, but I decided to do some exploring anyway.

The next day, we struck off toward the mountain pass that led into the interior. The road—if it could be called that—headed southeast over a twisting, climbing course that required eleven hours to travel. Some of the route was so dangerous that I made Anita walk while I drove the Land Rover with one foot hanging out the door, ready to jump to safety if the road collapsed. It was nearly dark when we arrived in the village of Oyacachi.

Anita proved her worth again when she was able to borrow a small hut for us to sleep in. The owner was in the hospital, recovering from the loss of an arm in a machete fight. Oyacachi was situated eleven thousand feet up in the Andes, so our physical activities were accompanied by a chest-aching breathlessness.

Anita and I made friends with the inhabitants, and one afternoon I sketched a rough representation of a burial mound— a *tola* or *huaca*. Most of the people looked blank, but then Anita showed the drawing to an old man named Segundo, and I saw nods of recognition. Yes, there were such structures, but the local natives considered them to be the work of nature. Yes, they were accessible, but they were in a valley, three days travel to the east. Yes, there had been some old pottery seen in the area, and there was a small river which had produced gold nuggets.

That night I told Anita I was going into the area. To my surprise, she said: "You are wrong, Howard."

"Dammit, I know there's gold there," I said. "What do you mean, wrong?"

I was mistaken about her objections. "I know you are right about the gold," she said seriously. "But you are wrong to take such treasures from the graves."

One of the disconcerting aspects of treasure hunting is the constant wrangle you face with people who think you are defiling holy places.

"Anita," I said, mustering up my most convincing tone of voice, "the graves I dig belong to a civilization long gone from this earth. No semblance of their beliefs or faith exists in the world today. I do not desecrate the tombs; I honor them by letting posterity know what kind of men lived back in those days."

"It is wrong to disturb the sleep of the dead," Anita said doggedly.

Many Latin Americans feel this way. Perhaps it is because they are the end product of Roman Catholic missionary efforts to convert the mystical beliefs of a sophisticated multi-god civilization to an essentially alien monotheism. The priests of Spain were backed up with a tough army which felt it was functioning with a mandate from Rome—convert or kill. The Indians realized they must change in order to survive, and they cloaked themselves in the thin mantle of Christianity. But a reverence for the old ways has persisted.

I tried to reason: "Look at it this way. Those graves were the easiest place for the living to place the dead in order to expedite their trip to the 'other world.' That's why they put in treasures, to make the afterlife rich. We Christians feel we will pass on into a spiritual life after our soul has gone to God. Material possessions are of no use in the afterlife."

She listened, then thought about it. Then she changed her tack. "You have no right to take *any* treasure from my country," she said. "My country is poor, not rich like your almighty United States."

I sighed. "Anita, just answer me this: What has Ecuador done to explore its national heritage?"

It was an exercise in rhetoric. Only Mexico has made any major effort to discover and share its pre-Columbian ancestry. That's one of the main reasons I've stayed away from the Aztec ruins; the field is too competitive and the restrictions too tightly maintained.

"These are our national treasures," she argued.

"These treasures belong to all mankind. Your government should encourage people like me to discover these artifacts instead of leaving them buried in the ground and withholding them from the world."

This was my major point of contention. I believe that any government that knows there are relics of the past hidden from view is wrong in not trying to share those relics.

"What the hell right has Ecuador or Italy or Turkey or Peru or any other nation to withhold such treasures from the world? Dammit, more people visit the Metropolitan Museum in New York or the British Museum in London than *live* in most of the places where treasure is found. Talk about *fair,*

136

what the hell do the Inca or Maya or Aztec civilizations owe to the people who just happen to live in those countries today? I say nothing."

"You have no right to decide such a matter."

"Well, then, tell me who does have the right?"

No answer.

"Does the right belong to your government, which doesn't have the resources to finance proper programs of excavation?" No reply. "Or does it belong to your historians, who sit around in your university, not anxious to get off their fat duffs? Or maybe the pompous archaeologists, who wrap themselves in academic praise, spending years writing scholarly papers before sharing the fruits of efforts financed with other people's money?"

"Well, *you* still have no right to make such a decision," she said.

I saw I wasn't going to win this argument, so clearly it was time to quit. "Look, Anita," I said, "would it make you feel better if I worked with your government?"

She smiled and nodded.

"Okay," I said. "If I find anything, I'll take it to your government and let them decide what I can keep. They can pay me for whatever they want."

That seemed to pacify her. I knew I couldn't do any such thing, but I would have to continue her education another time.

The next day Anita helped me negotiate with Segundo. I arranged for him to be my guide and foreman for the expedition, and we worked out a financial deal for the hiring of twenty workers, along with a few horses and enough pack mules to carry provisions for two months. The men hired on for forty cents a day, but the animals cost me fifty cents a day—a commentary on the state of values in that part of the world.

We spent another two days buying provisions, then I drove Anita back to Quito and purchased the additional equipment I felt would be needed: medical supplies, digging tools, and a large quantity of canvas to use for making tents and packs. Because old Segundo had delivered such a stern warning about *banditos,* I picked up a used Winchester .30.30 lever-action rifle and enough ammunition to carry on a private war. The manager of the Hotel Quito agreed to store my "city clothes" while I was in the bush. Finally, I said goodbye to Anita and headed back to join up with Segundo at Oyacachi.

Segundo was ready with the men, animals, and food. I transferred my heavy load of metal detectors and personal supplies from the Land Rover to mule packs, and we set off the next morning in a drizzling rain, with the temperature near the freezing mark. The dampness promoted a heavy, slick growth of grass right up to the snow line, which made the footing treacherous for man and beast.

The second day out two of our pack mules slipped on the slick grass, then rolled five hundred feet down the side of the mountain to their death. I left four Indians and two mules behind to recover those grain sacks that had not split open. The rest of us moved on, climbing higher and higher into a weird world of snowcapped mountaintops blanketed in cold, wet, silent clouds.

On the third day we crested the mountain range at sixteen thousand feet, and suddenly we were on the east flank of the Andes, with an incredible view. Segundo was in the lead, and he halted the march a few hours later. Calling me to his side, he pointed in the direction of several valleys stretching away to the east.

"*Tolas,*" he said.

I strained to see. Either Segundo had a vivid imagination or damned good eyes: I could see no sign. I lifted my binoculars from the horn of the saddle. Then I saw them. Columbus may have erred when he identified the North American natives as Indians, and Balboa was certainly wrong when he tagged the Pacific Ocean as "peaceful." But as I studied the shape of the mounds off in the distant valley, I felt pretty safe in concluding that I was indeed looking at pre-Columbian *tolas.* There were seven mounds of various sizes, all situated along a fast-running river, and all in the classical shape of the *tola,* with smooth sides and flattened tops. There had to be gold there.

Using a combination of broken Spanish and sign language, I asked, "How long to get there?"

"Three, four hours," Segundo replied in Spanish.

"Then let's get moving."

We arrived at the first mound about an hour before nightfall. I spurred my tired horse to the river bank, looking for the telltale signs of ancient habitation. Suddenly I was no longer weary. Hundreds of pieces of broken pottery littered the edge of the river.

That first night was miserable. There had been no time to construct a solid camp, so I joined the Indians, who were huddled on the ground, wrapped in blankets or pieces of canvas. I used a poncho to keep out the wetness, and by morning, a thin covering of ice sparkled on the ground and on everyone's bedding.

I supervised breakfast for the workers, and then assigned all of them to begin digging into the bases of two of the mounds. It was vital to prove that they really were man-made mounds before pitching a permanent base camp. Within an hour, there was a pile of highly polished potsherds in front of the campfire. Convinced, I asked Segundo to assign half of the workers to building adequate semi-permanent shelters. This was going to be our home for the next two months.

When the conquistadors came to South America in the 1500's, the god-emperor Atahualpa ruled a realm that ran three thousand miles along the Andes—the Kingdom of Quito. There was enormous wealth here, but Pizarro's brutality resulted in Atahualpa's death by the most hideous form of execution that the Spanish had devised, the *garrote,* which is still in use today.

During my research in London I had come to realize that Ecuador holds no major niche in the annals of Inca history. At the time of Pizarro's conquest, Ecuador had been occupied by the Inca for only about fifty years, and was a poorer outpost of the empire. Pizarro first landed on the coast of Ecuador, but he soon determined that the center of the sprawling Inca Empire lay to the south, in Peru. After Atahualpa's capture, great treasures were sent from all parts of the realm to form part of his ransom—the famous "room full of gold as high as a man could reach"—and one such shipment, out of the northern city of Quito, was supposedly lost in the rugged Llanganati Mountain region. But as far as the Spanish were concerned, the great centers of Inca wealth, and of Spanish plunder, were not in Ecuador. And this view has been held ever since.

Yet all research and logic pointed to a pre-Columbian Ecuador as rich as the more famous areas, and it still seemed possible to me that I might discover something that had been overlooked by the rapacious Spanish. After all, the trip from Quito had been arduous and dangerous. It seemed possible that the natural barriers of the snowcapped mountains would have been enough to prevent the Castilian plunder of the area.

"Work . . . work . . . work," I silently urged the men who were hacking at the grass at the base of one of the mounds. I was eager to see the foliage trimmed back, anxious to start my search.

In the camp, Segundo was guiding the construction of sod houses. I decided a hut would be warmer and less confining than my tent, so I marked out a twelve-foot square for myself. In a few hours the workers had dug down into the mushy soil, erected four walls made from squares of sod, and covered the top with sticks and more sod. Pieces of burlap sacking were hung as a door, and a kerosene lantern provided sufficient light, although the smoke from the wick stung my eyes and nostrils. By the end of the day the base camp was fully in operation, and the digging party had recovered quite a few more potsherds. After a few shots of whisky, I crawled into my sleeping bag in peaceful contentment.

The next day the heavy digging began. After much explanation and instruction to Segundo, I divided the crew. Picks and shovels went into action at two of the mounds, one more than 30 feet high and the second about 25 feet. I wanted an exploratory trench cut through all the way to the ground level, which meant the removal of literally tons of earth. This would take many days, so I took off on my horse to hunt for some game which would provide fresh meat for the camp.

During the journey into the valley I had noticed plenty of deer, and sure enough I spotted a large herd of deer less than a mile east of the camp. I picked out a dry doe and dropped her with one shot from the .30.30 Winchester. (A dry doe is a deer that is not suckling its young. It tastes a lot less gamey than a mother and is more tender than a buck. Some hunters will come across a herd and blast away at the biggest buck they can see, but they'd better have teeth like a shark.) I spotted a second dry doe and dropped her with another shot, then dressed the carcasses and slung them across the rear end of my horse. The workers, who had heard only the two shots fired, seemed to be impressed as much with my marksmanship as they were with the venison.

The first grave was uncovered late that first morning.

There was no gold in the grave, and the pottery arranged ritualistically around the skeleton was rather crude. It did not, alas, represent a wealthy community or advanced culture. By nightfall more graves were exposed, and the quality of pottery was improving, but we discovered only one very plain gold nose ring. Nevertheless, I still had faith in my theory. I ordered two more trenches cut into the mounds, hoping that the quality of the graves would improve as the digging went deeper.

The next morning I left Segundo in charge of the dig and took a shovel and large frying pan to the nearby river. The day was cold, and a freezing drizzle added to my discomfort as I began the back-breaking work of washing a pan of sand and gravel.

"Panning" falls into the category known as "placer mining" and is primarily a process called "sifting"; that is, using gravity to separate the heavier metal from the surrounding matter. In 1848 the old sourdough panners discovered gold at Sutter's Mill, California, and the resultant rush created a city out of the tiny village of San Francisco. Colorado's "Pikes Peak or Bust" rush happened two decades later, and the famous Klondike finds occurred at the turn of the century. Gold panning made men rich overnight and produced instant inflation: Eggs sold for $1 apiece and a shack rented for $100 a week.

It takes a lot of practice and a hell of a strong back to pan for gold. First, the material to be panned must be obtained from as deep as possible—down to bedrock, if you can manage it—because the heavy particles of gold settle downward during movement of the sand and gravel. Normally, a large pan specially designed for the purpose is shoveled brimful of the material to be panned; then, squatting in the shallow water near the bank, one begins the tedious job of washing the forty or so pounds of mud and gravel, holding the pan between the knees. After first pulverizing any clods of clay, the pan is dipped into the water and a swirling motion is commenced that gradually washes clean the material at the top. As the water in the pan absorbs the clay, dirty water is carefully spilled out and clean water dipped in. This is repeated until the water remains clean, even after the material is swirled and scrubbed with one's hands. Then the larger rocks are removed, and a sloshing, side-to-side motion replaces the swirling, allowing the lighter material to "float" to the top and be spilled over the side—gradually and very carefully. The water is replenished and the sloshing is repeated over and over again, until finally nothing will be left in the pan but a crescent-shaped residue of black material around the edge.

If the material is very rich or the gold in the stream very coarse, it is possible that gold might now be visible, when the black material is spread out on the bottom. Since most methods of separating the "color" from the black residue are rather complicated, most miners collect the material at this point and save it up for reworking later, back at camp. I'm told that a practiced hand can wash a pan to this point in twenty to thirty minutes. It takes me about an hour, and after two pans I am usually done for the day, with half the muscles in my body complaining.

But this time all I wanted was confirmation that there was

142

gold in the region. It came within an hour, as I washed the first pan down to the black residue. As I swirled the pan, dots of gold gradually began to appear. I had seen gold panned in Colorado and Wyoming by professionals, but I had never before seen so much "color" in a pan. The river was rich in gold.

Of course, that didn't really prove that the natives had used the plentiful gold for their own jewelry or ceremonial objects. In fact, my research in London had indicated a strong probability that the mountain Indians had bartered gold with the tribes along the coast, who used it to produce the artifacts found in tombs throughout the coastal plains areas of Colombia and Peru. Still, it was encouraging to find the raw material available in such abundance—surely some of it would have remained in the area.

From six laborious pans I netted nearly two ounces of high-grade gold. I was tempted to call off the burial digging and put my work force to the task of panning, but there were not enough pans, and there were no trees around from which to make sluice boxes. I went back to the mound and waited for graves to be uncovered.

My anxious and frustrating wait ended on the sixth day. One trench had been deepened, and I moved in for a sweep with my detector. A strong signal indicated a substantial amount of metal. The grave was cleared in three hours, and my patience was rewarded. We had removed two ceremonial gold knives and several animal figures representing monkeys and jaguars. But the major find was a beautifully crafted gold statue of a little man wearing an elaborate headdress and sporting an erect penis. My theory was solidly confirmed, and I ordered the dig to go forward.

Over the next four weeks the Indians cut trenches through four of the seven mounds. It was heavy work: The mounds ranged in height from fifteen to thirty feet, and a lot of earth had to be moved to cut a trench from top to ground level.

After a trench was dug, I always set the Indians to digging a trench in a new mound while I investigated the one at hand

143

privately. The graves were widely scattered in the mound, and I was increasingly disappointed by the artifacts I recovered. There was gold, but not nearly as much as I had hoped. Except for the horny little gold Indian, the artifacts were crudely made and far between. I had recovered a total of eighteen gold objects, including discs, animal figures, and two plain ceremonial knives. Not bad, but I'd hoped for more.

I was prepared to continue excavating new digs until food supplies made it necessary to leave, but our activities had begun to draw a crowd. For several days, Indians had been appearing on the hills overlooking the valley, and although my people told me they were probably the head-hunting Jivaros, I wasn't particularly concerned. They had blow guns and spears, but I had a Winchester .30.30. However, a second crowd had come from downstream, setting up camp about two miles below us. Through the binoculars, I counted at least thirty armed men.

*"Qui están los hombres?"* I asked Segundo.

He looked down into the valley. *"Banditos, señor,"* he said without expression.

Bandits were a different proposition. Although they had no way of knowing what we were doing, from what I had heard and read I knew they would kill us merely for our camping equipment. I had a strong hunch they intended to raid us, so I decided we would leave the next morning before dawn.

Right after our evening meal we buried the picks and shovels. I knew where to find them in case I should return, and I didn't want our animals to have to carry anything unnecessary. We were going to have to travel light and fast.

We were on our way before daybreak, and by the time it was light we were climbing the mountain. The Indians were grumbling about not having a good night's sleep, and I began to wonder if my concern had been unwarranted. None of the Indians seemed at all worried about the *banditos*.

Then the morning mist cleared. We were about a thousand feet above the camp and some four miles away, but I could easily see men on horseback milling about our sod houses. As

144

we watched, smoke spiraled up into the sky from the grass roofs. At last the Indians seemed to realize that their lives might be in danger, and they quickly picked up the pace, heading westward up into the Andes. I stayed behind for a few minutes and watched through my binoculars as the bandits formed around their leader, who was pointing up into the hills, directly at me. Then, kicking their horses into action, they galloped across the valley after us.

I waited until they were only a mile from my vantage point, and then rattled off a fusillade of shots with the .30.30. The bandits pulled to a sudden halt as I reloaded and fired another volley; then I jumped on my horse and followed after the Indians. The bullets were not intended to hit the *banditos,* but hopefully the shots would cause them to slow down out of respect for my rifle.

The journey into the valley had taken three days, but we made the trip back to Oyacachi in two. If the *banditos* did follow us, they never caught up. In Oyacachi I paid off the crew, adding a bonus of two weeks' salary. I said goodbye to Segundo, telling him I would be back in a year or so for another dig.

The Quito Hotel—now called the Hotel Intercontinental Quito—is a plush hostelry with a casino, a ballroom, three bars, two good restaurants, and a large swimming pool. After those cold, wet weeks in the Andes, these creature comforts drew me like El Dorado. I arrived in the lobby unshaven, filthy with road dust, and followed by a couple of bellboys carrying my muddy gear. If the manager disapproved, he was kind enough never to indicate it. In fact, we later became good friends, and he was always interested in hearing about my trips.

Shortly after I arrived, I learned that another friend, who was also interested in my treasure-hunting trips, was practically on his way to Quito to meet me. Beauregard Morton from Atlanta was just waiting for the cable to hop onto a jet and join an expedition. Ever since Beau had helped me sell the gold artifacts from the Batres brothers adventure, he had been cajoling me to take him out after Inca gold.

145

It was against my better judgment, but I sent off a cable inviting Beauregard to join me. Everybody thinks treasure hunting is romantic until they get out in the bush. Still, Beau might be useful to me in disposing of gold artifacts. I decided I would give him as uneventful a treasure hunt as possible, just to get it out of his system.

In fact, there was someplace I wanted to go. Two Oyacachi Indians had told me of some ruins in another valley on the Amazon side of the Andes. Each of them, independently, had described the ruins of a very large stone building constructed against a cliff. They were afraid to go near it, but they spoke of huge round stone columns that had fallen to the ground. I had never heard or read of any pre-Columbian architecture with round columns, so the ruins fascinated me, and I was determined to have a look.

Beau finally arrived, eager to find and share treasure.

"I'm an excellent horseman, Howard," he assured me.

"But have you ever ridden steep mountain trails? This kind of riding is pretty dangerous. You can fall down a mountain and break your neck."

"Don't worry, it won't happen."

We bought supplies, rented another Land Rover, and left the next morning for Oyacachi. There I hired twenty-five Indians and rented about thirty horses and mules. With provisions for a two-month stay, we set out on a trail leading southeast into the Andes.

Three days out, as we were entering the high mountains, Beau's nervousness began to increase. "Would you like me to carry the rifle, Howard?" he asked.

"Something wrong with your revolver?"

"No . . ." He paused a minute and then said, "But I should have bought a rifle back in Quito." He stopped his horse to let me come alongside.

"You'd better go on, Beau, the trail isn't wide enough here."

He started on again and talked over his shoulder. "Did you hear those cats almost in our camp last night? Must have been a bunch of jaguars or pumas." He looked around worriedly.

"You know, they could jump us anywhere along the trail here."

"They won't attack people unless it's an old animal and can't hunt, or unless it's a female with a cub she's protecting."

"Just the same," Beau said nervously, "I'd feel better with a gun in my hand."

A few minutes later I noticed he was carrying his revolver in his right hand. He would jerk it up to sight and aim at almost any noise he heard, and spent more time peering into the trees alongside the trail than he did watching the path ahead.

At last, the inevitable happened. Rounding a bend in the narrow trail, Beau heard a noise in the bush and spun to point his gun. The sudden motion startled the horse, which sidestepped off the trail, slipped, and went down heavily. Beau was thrown clear, but he crashed into the dense undergrowth and disappeared.

I slid down from my horse and ran to where Beau had fallen. His horse was up and stamping around, so I quieted the animal and tied it to a tree. Then I ran to Beau, who was pulling himself up out of a tangle of growth, cursing and groaning.

I couldn't find much wrong on examination, but Beau complained of sore ligaments in one leg, and he worried about possible internal injuries. So we turned back. It had been a mistake to let him come, I knew, but what really hurt was that we were within one day's ride of those strange columned ruins.

I left all of my gear with Segundo in Oyacachi, intending to return. By the time we reached Quito, Beau had made a miraculous recovery and decided he would wait until he got back to Atlanta to see a doctor. He took the evening flight out. I suspect he is still telling the story of his narrow escapes in the wild Andes.


After seeing Beau off I returned to the hotel and asked for my key at the desk.

"Señor Jennings," the clerk said, "the manager would like to see you as soon as possible."

I went directly to the manager's office, and found him there.

147

He asked if I had a good trip, and we talked about generalities for a minute or two. Then he said, "I am somewhat concerned about a Peruvian who checked into the hotel a few days ago. He has questioned several members of the staff about you and asked when you would return to Quito. He has been sitting in the lobby every day, waiting. Wait a moment and I'll check."

He looked into the lobby, and then returned and described where the man was sitting. I asked if he knew the man's name and was surprised it was not Batres. I assured him it was nothing important, but thanked him for his concern.

I only glanced at the man on the way to the elevator to avoid letting him know that I had been tipped off. After I had showered and changed, I returned to the lobby and bought an American newspaper, then sat down to have a closer look at this Peruvian. He was quite a large man for a South American. His clothes were cheap and rumpled, and he looked out of place here in the hotel, but he also looked dangerous. I had the distinct feeling that I was in trouble.

The man was apparently unaware that I had been tipped off because, though he ignored me during the day, he followed me everywhere I went that night. I guessed he was trying to catch me in the right circumstance, at night, when I would be easy to take. I decided it was time that we met.

In those days the old Hotel Colon had one of the best restaurants in the city. The hotel faced onto a well-lighted street, but the side streets beside it were dark, and on one side of the hotel was an L-shaped alleyway leading to the service entrance. This alleyway, I thought, was as good a place as any for our confrontation.

That night I parked my car on the dark side of the street, and I noticed he was not far behind. I waited in the Land Rover for a few moments to give him time to catch up, then I walked casually into the unlighted alleyway. As soon as I was out of his line of sight, I hurried around the corner, stopping with my back against the wall and my gun in hand. He didn't appear. After a few minutes I walked back out to the street. I

148

didn't see him anywhere, so I had dinner and returned to the hotel.

The next night I did exactly as I had done the night before, and this time as I stopped around the corner I heard him running up the alley. He slowed as he came around the corner. In the dim light I could just see the gun in his hand. He didn't see me until my gun smashed down on his arm. He cursed in pain and anger as his gun clattered on the pavement.

In spite of his pain, he grabbed for me with his left hand. I whipped my gun hand up and caught him across the jaw. He yelped once, and then dropped to the pavement. He was obviously stunned, and I decided not to wait around to find out what he would do when he recovered his senses.

I drove straight back to the hotel and telephoned a lawyer I knew in Quito. I told him the whole story, and ended by asking him to send an ambulance for the Peruvian. He came to the hotel later with an affidavit he had prepared for my signature, but he also advised me to leave the country immediately, before I got caught up in the ponderous Ecuadorian legal system.

There would be no outbound flights until late the next morning, so I took my gold from the hotel safe, loaded up the Land Rover, and drove off for Cali, Colombia, four hundred miles to the north. I had no trouble crossing the border at Tulcán, and checked into the Bolivar Hotel in Cali with the intention of relaxing for a few days.

I was now faced with the inevitable problem of how to smuggle Ecuadorian gold artifacts out of antiquities-conscious Colombia. This was back in the days before the rash of skyjackings, so the use of electronic devices for baggage inspection was not a problem. I finally came up with a technique I was to use many times. I tied the pieces of gold from different lengths of cord to the top of my plastic suit bag, making sure they were evenly distributed from top to bottom. Since most of the pieces were flat, there were no major bulges when the bag was packed with my suits, and I could carry the bag over my arm onto the airplane and hang it in a coat rack that was easily visible from the seat.

I passed through Colombian customs unchallenged and connected with a BOAC flight from Panama to London. The day after my arrival, I took eighteen artifacts to the prestigious Bond Street auction gallery, Sotheby's. Their pre-Columbian expert selected ten pieces, including my small man with the out-sized erection, paying a total of £3,700. The little man brought £1,500 all by himself, enough to offset all of the expenses for the Ecuadorian adventure. Through a friend associated with the gallery, I met a pre-Columbian art buyer from Cologne, Germany, and he paid $4,200 U.S. for another eight pieces.

I had telephoned my lawyer friend in Quito to have the Land Rover picked up where I had left it in Cali. Later, in a letter, he informed me that during the Peruvian's first day in the hospital the police had persuaded him to confess that he had entered Ecuador for a criminal purpose—which meant that my testimony would not be necessary at any time. The Peruvian was in the hospital for two weeks before his trial, at which he was sentenced to prison for three years. He would not admit his intent to kill me, but claimed that the Batres family had paid him $200 plus expenses to work me over—just short of killing.

So, for my effort in Ecuador I realized a healthy profit, the natives of Oyacachi made a pretty good wage, and a sleazy thug hired by the Batres brothers ended up in prison, with a face bent badly out of shape. It had been a satisfying venture, though I still wondered about that ruined building with the round columns.

Someday. . . .

# 6 PAULAYA, RIVER OF GOLD

The postcard, featuring a sultry belly dancer, seemed appropriate for Robin, who was out in the stupid jungles of Vietnam
trying to get his butt shot off. I was in Casablanca at the time,
trying to warm my bones after the cold, wet nights in the mountains of Ecuador.

But after two months of sitting around, wanderlust was
taking hold again. Despite the pleasures Morocco offered, I had
been giving serious thought to the next venture. Ecuador was
still there, with its vast, unexplored, gold-rich burial grounds,
and I would go back someday, but not now. The last trip had
been a bit too chilling.

I found myself remembering the night Robin and I had
slipped out of Roatán Island, and recalling Riley Gough's talk
about a river of gold, the Paulaya River. The notion of scooping virgin nuggets of gold up in my hands was appealing. I had
discovered gold the Indians had found and worked into artifacts, gold the Spanish had taken from the Indians, and gold
the pirates had taken from the Spanish. Now I felt a compulsion
to find some of my own gold.

I invested a couple of days of research in the public libraries

151

of Casablanca, but came up with very little in the way of information. Although the Spanish did at one time run a sizable gold-refining operation in Honduras, the country had never been a world leader in the production of the precious metal. They did have some producing mines, though. Maybe I wouldn't find El Dorado, the gilded city of Spanish and Indian myth, but I would settle for a hoard of gleaming yellow nuggets.

There are two major methods of mining gold. One is by digging out lodes beneath the surface of the earth, much like the mining of coal in deep-shafts; the other is placer mining, used by the old sourdoughs in the Klondike. Most of their nuggets were the size of a pea or smaller, but there were always stories of a stream filled with nuggets the size of walnuts. (Gold nuggets can be big, in fact. The "Welcome Stranger Nugget," which was found in Australia, weighed 2,520 ounces, or close to half a million dollars in today's gold market.)

Dreaming of a riverbed rich with gold, I left my Moroccan pleasure domes and headed back to Honduras by way of Miami.

I had not forgotten the old business with the Peruvian Batres brothers, and I knew their agents might tip them off if they knew I was in town. I was not eager to face another assassination attempt, so I avoided the Racquet Club and checked into a small motel near the airport. By this time, Robin had finished his first tour of duty in Vietnam and was in Jamaica working on his *Green Berets* manuscript. I telephoned him there.

"Hell, no, I won't go up any damn Honduran River," he said. "You think I'm crazy?"

He had already proved that by offering himself as a target to the Viet Cong, but I laughed and suggested we meet in Kingston in a couple of days. Robin gave me the address of a house in the suburbs of Kingston, and two nights later when we met there a large party was in full swing. He filled me in on the Green Berets and I told him about Ecuador. Reluctantly, he introduced me to a five-foot-nine blonde girl whose name was not Pru Potter. Much to my amazement, Pru chattered quite knowledgeably about mining techniques.

"Where the hell did you learn all that?" I asked.

She smiled. "I've been prospecting and potholing for gold since I was fifteen."

"Potholing?" I had never heard the term.

She nodded. "My father bought me the diving equipment," she said vaguely. Then she explained that potholing involves diving into holes of mountain streams at depths the early placer miners couldn't reach.

Damn, I thought to myself, I wonder . . .

"If you're wondering about taking me along on the gold-hunting trip Robin told me about, I'd love to come with you," she said. "I'll pay my share, of course."

I weighed the pluses and minuses: I was heading into a territory of Honduras that is unmapped. There are grisly stories about savage Indians in the area, it would be a grueling trip, and I was planning to be there for several months. It was no place for a girl. A pretty girl. Naturally I invited her along.

"But listen," she said earnestly, "I'm going as your *partner,* not your playmate, okay? Agreed?"

I agreed, not believing a word of it. It took several days for me to accept that we were really to keep things platonic.

When I finished my business in Kingston, Pru accompanied me to Miami. For two days, we shopped for the clothing and equipment necessary for our preliminary inspection trip. Our plan was to make an initial survey, then if things looked promising, we'd mount a major attack on the Paulaya River.

We flew to San Pedro Sula and were pleased to find that the feeder airline in Honduras had started servicing Roatán Island with twice-daily flights. We arrived in Oakridge that same day.

While renewing acquaintances and introducing Pru around to my friends in the village, I kept asking about Riley Gough. At last we heard that Riley was due on the island in two days—maybe.

Honduras' 350-mile coast on the Caribbean is not serviced with any regular schedule. Riley's boat sailed when he wanted it to. It carried whatever he felt could make money, along a route that took him as far west as Puerto Cortes and eastward to the mouth of the Paulaya River, where his family lived in the small village of Plaplaya.

We were at the dock when Riley's boat arrived. While it was being unloaded, I chatted with him and jokingly accused him of getting me hooked on the idea of gold up the river. He regarded me seriously for a few moments and then offered to help in any way possible. "How about a lift to the mouth of the river?" I asked. A few hours later we were sailing east on Riley's boat.

We reached the river the next morning, somewhat wobbly from the rough trip. Riley maneuvered his boat through the entrance channel in the sandbar and docked, then took us to the local store serving Plaplaya. It was owned by Bill Wood and his wife, the only other outsiders in the tiny Sambo town.

I outlined my ideas for the inspection trip. Bill Wood nodded. "Gold is the whole purpose of our store," he said. "The Indians come down river with gold they've panned to trade me for goods."

Pru and I looked at each other happily. "Maybe you know someone we could hire as a guide?"

Bill thought a moment. "There's an old Indian named Concho who lives about forty miles up river. He's spent most of his life panning gold, and he knows the river better than anybody. He's too old to work now so I guess you could hire him."

Pru and I started out with Bill the next morning in his pit-pan, a narrow canoe dug out from the single log of a mahogany tree and powered by an outboard motor. These boats are basically unstable, especially at slow speeds, and they capsize easily. But with a 10-h.p. outboard pushing it along at a speed of 15 to 20 m.p.h., and with a man in the bow using a paddle for quick course changes, the pit-pan can negotiate the rapids with surprising agility. (Coming downstream is trickier, since one must maintain a speed greater than that of the current for stability, which allows for less time to steer around rocks.)

For the first ten miles, the river was deep and slow moving, but as the terrain began to rise, the speed of the water in-

154

creased. Beyond the junction of the Sico River, the Paulaya narrowed considerably, and dense jungle crowded the river on both sides. The current was stronger, and we began to hit stretches of white water. I saw what a job I'd have getting a barge up the river. Aside from the rapids, with their sharp rocks pointing up through the foaming water, there were many places where floods had carried down massive trees and jammed them in the rocks. These often had to be cleared before we could proceed even in the narrow pit-pan.

We finally arrived at Concho's thatched-roof shack. After much ceremonious discussion, the old Indian and I settled on a price for his services. Concho then suggested that the small village of Las Champas, thirty miles farther up river, was the best place for us to see the old Spanish gold workings. Bill agreed, and we got back into the pit-pan and set out shortly after lunch. Darkness caught us ten miles short of the village.

Bill pointed to a sandbar in the middle of the river. "We'd better spend the night there, so the downriver wind will blow away some of the mosquitoes."

On the narrow sandbar Pru seemed a bit nervous, and while Bill and Concho secured the pit-pan she said quietly, "Howard, may I put my sleeping bag next to yours? I'm afraid of the alligators I saw in the river."

"You can sleep *in* my sleeping bag if you want to."

"Then I'd be scared of you."

We spent a very uncomfortable night. Before morning, I had figured out that as the wind blew our mosquitoes down river, it blew new mosquitoes in as replacements.

The next morning, while Bill was putting the gear back in the pit-pan, Concho asked me to watch him work a couple of pans of the sandbar. He was an expert with a gold pan, and in a few minutes he showed me the gleaming flecks of gold that he had separated from the sand.

Concho pointed up the river. "Gold there much heavier. But find color all along river."

As we approached Las Champas, Concho pointed out large mounds along the river bank, the tailings of early Spanish workings. Because of the depth of the river at this point, the Spanish had only been able to work the river banks. In some places, using slave labor, they had been able to divert the river by digging canals.

Pru and I agreed: If the river *banks* had been productive, the untouched deeper parts of the river should be doubly rich.

Las Champas is a town of six Indian families living in four thatched-roof shacks high on a steep bank overlooking the river. Except for Bill Woods, who had been this far up river once before, most of the Indians had never seen white people, and tall, blonde Pru received great attention.

The next day, with Concho and two Indians along to do the digging, we began working our way up the bank of the river. The Indians dug down about four feet to bedrock, then Concho panned the material just above the bedrock. The material from the bottom of each hole produced rich color. We spent three days at Las Champas making tests. I worked right alongside Concho, and I learned again what I already knew: Panning is back-breaking work. I couldn't help but think about those old forty-niners who panned gold all day. Either they were a sturdy breed, or there were lots of rich hunchbacks around Sutter's Mill.

By the time we finished the testing, I was convinced we would recover a lot of gold if our dredge could remove the overburden from the base rocks in the riverbed. I selected a camp site a few hundred yards upstream from Las Champas and hired two of the Indians to clear the land during the next six or seven weeks before our return.

On the way down river to Plaplaya, we stopped to examine several of the sections that were clogged with trees. Bill agreed to hire a crew of Sambos from the coast to clear the logjams.

The rapids remained the most serious problem. It was going to be extremely difficult to tow a huge, equipment-laden barge that far up the river over those treacherous rocks—we'd be lucky if they didn't rip the bottom out of it.

With our preliminary survey completed, we hitched a ride back to Roatán Island with Riley Gough. After indulging ourselves with a few days of relaxation, we then flew to Miami, where the next two weeks were spent shopping for supplies and studying dredging techniques in the landfill capital of America. Most visitors are unaware that ninety percent of glittering Miami Beach was a swamp at the turn of the century, and that there are still dozens of land reclamation operations in progress in the vicinity of the city.

At one major dredging location in North Miami, we made friends with the project engineer, an amiable man who enjoyed adventure vicariously. No jungles for him, but he was fascinated with the project, and he helped me design a functional, durable, dependable barge which would draw no more than ten inches of water, even when fully loaded. He also guided me in the selection of a very expensive, eight-inch, heavy-duty gravel pump and a General Motors 471 diesel engine to power it.

Pru and I had grown closer during the weeks together, so it was no real surprise when the platonic phase of our relationship ended one balmy night in a Miami hotel room. By morning, our partnership had moved to a new and infinitely more satisfying plateau.

We completed arrangements to have the pump and engine shipped to Honduras, and flew to San Pedro Sula to have the barge built.

For the next three weeks I supervised the construction of the vessel, working with the German owner of a Honduran steel-fabricating plant. Although I made some minor changes in the barge plans, by the middle of the fifth week it was complete and I arranged to have it shipped overland to the port city of Puerto Cortes while I went on ahead. The barge arrived just as the diesel and gravel pump were being uncrated. Setting the operating equipment in place was tricky and had to be handled by welders from the local steel plant, since alignment was critical.

The barge was 15 feet wide and 35 feet long, made entirely of heavy-gauge steel, with four large hand winches carrying reels of one-half-inch steel cable for pulling it up river and for holding it in place while we were dredging. The gravel pump and engine were welded carefully into place, and two 25-foot sluice boxes were lashed to the deck, along with twenty-five 55-gallon drums of diesel fuel. We were ready to go.

Early on a Tuesday morning Riley Gough arrived with his boat. We took the barge in tow, and Pru and I joined Riley on his boat for the 200-mile trip in the open sea to the Paulaya River. It was a memorable journey. The barge slewed about wildly, its shallow draft making it dangerously unstable in the rough seas. I spent the day running from one tow line to another as the weight shifted and the hitches creaked and snapped. Several times I was certain my $20,000 investment and all our dreams of gold would end up on the bottom of the Gulf of Honduras—next to a Spanish galleon, no doubt. The first night out, I summoned up enough energy to keep a flashlight playing on the lines, but finally I had to sleep. Pru took over while I fell into a bunk fully clothed.

During the middle of the third morning out, we sighted the mouth of the Paulaya River coming up on our starboard bow. Riley waited for high tide before crossing the sandbar; then, incredibly, we were back in the lagoon at the coastal village of Plaplaya. When we were docked, I climbed onto the barge and performed a thorough inspection. It was bone dry; the design and construction were perfect. In a surge of euphoric relief, I did a flying swan dive into the lagoon.

We paused for three days in Plaplaya, laying in our last-minute provisions and buying a large dug-out canoe, which I fitted with an outboard engine. I hired four oxen for pulling the barge through difficult rapids and shallows and recruited twenty local blacks as a labor force. (These blacks, called "Sambos" along the Mosquito Coast and "Caribs" on the Bay Islands, are descendants of 4,000 rebellious Carib-Negro slaves taken from the island of St. Vincent at the end of the eighteenth century and dumped on Roatán Island. They speak both English and Spanish, and remain in villages along the coast, rarely venturing inland.) We installed two 60-h.p. outboards on the stern of the barge, and with Bill's dugout in the lead and mine at the rear, we began plowing our way up the river.

For the first ten miles the water was deep and the river wide, and we chugged along easily. Then, after passing the junction of the Paulaya and Sico rivers, we ran into the first of the rapids and logjams we had seen on our inspection trip. For the next sixty miles the outboard motors were virtually useless because of the shallow water. For several days we traveled less than a hundred yards, at the expense of sweat, cuts, bruises, and occasionally, a broken bone. At one point, the pressure that the water against the front of the dredge was so strong that the cables pulled a huge tree out by the roots, causing the barge to swing wildly and then tilt sideways, throwing one of the men overboard. He disappeared under the barge just as I leaped for the winch on the other side and slapped the release lever. The dredge dropped back downstream with a hell of a grating and scraping noise, then ran smack into two large boulders. As it bounced to a stop, the submerged man popped to the surface in front of us, unharmed except for a bruised leg and a few scrapes on his arms and back.

Luckily the sharp stones of the riverbed had not punctured the hull. Now we had to get the damn thing off the boulders and floating again. We spent two whole days unloading everything and making an overland portage of our equipment and supplies and then were forced to use all four winches, the four oxen, and all of my hired help to free the barge and pull it over the rapids.

The incident had cost us more than time and bruises. Our powerful radio transmitter, which I had planned to use to call for a charter plane if there were an emergency, had been ruined by water that had poured over the decks.

We picked up old Concho at his shack, and then returned to our grueling battle up the river.

We were more than pleased to see the tiny Indian village of Las Champas two weeks later. The strain had been incredible, but at last we were there. As we began the laborious unloading process, Pru found a quiet spot high up on the bank and sat down to relax for a moment.

Suddenly I heard a piercing scream. I ran to Pru, who was holding her arm. Her face was pale with fright.

"It was a snake—a big one," she cried.

I moved her hand. The two fang marks were oozing blood. I jerked out my shirttail, tore off a strip, and put a tight tourniquet above the wound. The workers and villagers beat the bush looking for the snake so we could identify the type of poison to combat, but it was gone into the dense undergrowth. I had Pru lie quietly on the ground while I strung a hammock in a small shack; as I carried her there, Concho brought my medical supplies from the dredge.

Whether or not to use serum for snake bite is always a difficult decision. It is a horse-serum base, and the allergic reaction it may produce can be as severe as the bite, sometimes causing death. In a hospital, where respirators, oxygen, and antihistamines are available, the reaction can be controlled—but we were five days away from a hospital, and without our transmitter, we were totally isolated.

It seemed likely that the snake was poisonous, probably a pit viper called a barbamarilla, judging from the wound and Pru's fleeting glimpse. Within an hour my fears were confirmed. Pru's arm began to swell painfully. I began releasing the pressure of the tourniquet every twenty minutes, which unfortunately allowed minute amounts of the poison to filter into her system along with her blood. She soon began developing stomach spasms. I administered a full injection of serum from the Wyeth Snakebite Kit, then an antispasmodic shot. In another hour, her pain was so great that I gave her a shot of morphine to ease the torture. I could do no more now than pray.

By midnight Pru was in a coma, her breathing shallow. I thought I was going to lose her. Then, toward morning, her breathing and color improved and she regained consciousness. Because she was still in terrible pain, I gave her another injection of morphine and she drifted off into a heavy but more normal sleep.

For several days Pru was very ill and only able to retain liquids. In some cases a snake bite can leave a person a permanent invalid, but Pru proved to have a strong constitution and an even stronger determination. She refused to consider returning down river to a hospital. Though she had to relearn some of her coordination, in three weeks she was walking around normally; and except for a loss of weight, she was fully recovered.

During Pru's illness I supervised the construction of a permanent camp. Our sleeping quarters would be a large tent, but the kitchen was built of bamboo with a thatched roof, to keep animals out of our food supplies. We made gravel walkways and hung kerosene lights within the camp, then we strung barbed wire fences to discourage strangers and animals who were attracted by the lights. I had acquired a vicious-looking mongrel named Jep back in Plaplaya, so I was not too worried about Indian interlopers.

However, once the local people learned that I possessed a medical kit and some skill, we began to hate Sunday mornings. Saturday night meant homemade rum, and the resultant booze-brawls produced a collection of wounds that would have delighted any medical student. My initial venture into surgery was on a boy of about seventeen who had been sliced with a machete from his left collarbone down across his chest and stomach to his right hip bone. For three hours, sweat poured from my forehead as I labored through sew and tie, sew and tie, sew and tie. When the last suture was tied off, I injected him with a massive dose of antibiotics. He was on his feet the next day and working for me within two weeks.

Concho selected the spot to begin our dredging operation. It was a deep hole and we found it covered with about four feet of overburden—mud, stones, and silt. We probed with steel rods. Below the mass of natural debris was solid bedrock—gold would have settled there.

For the next week I trained the laborers in the operation of the equipment and handling of the barge. We pushed and shoved, we handled and coaxed, and finally we attached the steel cables to sturdy trees, and the barge was anchored. The work was backbreaking, and I began to understand why the Incas, who associated gold with their gods, called gold "The Sweat of the Sun."

I spent a considerable time in the water under the barge,

wrestling the suction pipe into the hole. At last we began pumping. As we went deeper the rocks were bigger, and someone had to remove them from the opening of the intake pipe. The Sambos were fearful of working underwater where the alligators lived, so that task fell to me. Using a hookah diving rig, I would lash a rope around the rock, and then use the winch to pull the obstruction free.

Our two sluice boxes were fitted together and floated on the downstream side on buoys of empty fuel drums. All along the bottom of the sluice were a series of riffles, or traps, about two inches high. As the material ran down the long ten-degree slope of the sluice, the heavier materials would be caught behind the riffles while the useless gravel and sand were washed on out the end. The procedure was critical: If the pump dredged too fast, the gold would be washed away along with the sand and gravel. If the pumping action was too slow, the gold would not be picked up from the riverbed. When I was not in the water directing the scoop of the suction tube, I stationed myself at the pump engine with my hand on the power lever, monitoring the speed of the water flow.

At the end of the first full week of operation, we were delighted to find that we had twelve ounces of gold. Not a fortune, but a major encouragement. It was late October—if the annual rains held off another month we would easily recover our investment.

During the next three weeks we pumped up four hundred and eighty ounces of gold. While Pru and I were weighing out the nuggets, a splash of water dropped on my head. Then I looked at Pru and noticed tiny droplets bouncing off her khaki shirt. The first rains had begun to fall.

That night we heard thunder far up the river in the mountains. In the morning the Indians insisted we should not work. I was tempted to order the pumps started, but old Concho pleaded with such conviction that I agreed to move the dredge around a bend in the river, where the current eddied. As I surveyed the temporary anchorage, I wished that we could shelter our valuable barge in some safe backwater, but this was the best we could do.

That afternoon the water level began to rise and trees started coming down the river. Massive trunks of mahogany came roaring down on us like lomomotives, some of them preceded by roots that reached 25 feet across. If the barge had been in the channel, any one of those trees could have capsized it.

By evening the river level had risen five feet and was still climbing. I slackened the mooring lines as the water rose, which it continued to do all through the night.

The rains finally stopped the next day, but the flood waters stayed with us for the next week, bringing our operation to a halt. During the enforced lull, Pru and I took horses and explored the surrounding jungle. There was abundant game—deer, ocelot, jaguar, wild boar, and endless varieties of tropical birds, including a very edible wild turkey—and we saw much evidence of old Spanish activities, particularly the piles of tailings along the river from their mining operations. There are few Indians left in the area, thanks to the Spanish cruelty in handling slave labor and to the snakes, tuberculosis, and intestinal parasites that cut so many Indian lives short. There is a small tribe of Paya Indians (closely related to the Maya) living a few miles east of the Paulaya, but their numbers are diminishing fast. We saw no substantial old ruins, though the forests are littered with potsherds and some of the Indians claim to have found gold artifacts. We did dig into three man-made mounds, but found only crude pottery fragments that weren't encouraging.

When the flood waters receded, we found that they had carried silt and gravel fill into our working area under the surface of the river. In effect, we had to start from scratch, frustrated by the knowledge that another heavy rain could set us right back to the start again. Even so, by the end of November we had collected eight hundred ounces of gold, despite several interruptions by torrential rains. We had reached our break-even mark, and work would be nearly impossible from that point on.

163

The river was twelve feet over normal, and we were forced to man the securing lines day and night. Our graveled camp area was surrounded by a sea of mud. I had to face the depressing truth: We were confronted with sitting out the two-month rainy season.

Every two weeks Bill Woods traveled upstream in his pit-pan with supplies and mail. On one of his trips in early December, he delivered a letter, mailed six weeks before, from the United States Bureau of Customs. According to the letter, I had been found in violation of Public Law 19, US Code 1592, PL 31 CFR 54.8, and a whole wrath of other numbers and references and declarations which all boiled down to the charge that the gold I had brought in from Peru and sold to the Southern museum had not been declared as gold, and that I did not have a license to import gold.

As I remembered the situation, I *had* declared the gold as artifacts, but I had not placed a value on it because I had no way of knowing the value. As for the license, I had not known that such a permit was necessary. (Incidentally, a license *is* required by law, but it is the easiest free permit you can obtain. All you have to do is apply to a United States embassy or consulate, and it will be issued immediately.) The shocker was that penalties totaling $270,000 had been imposed on me. I couldn't believe it—over a quarter of a million dollars!

I felt that the Batres brothers had won at last—they were the only ones I could think of who could have tipped off customs. I wrote an explanatory letter to U.S. Customs, adding that I would be out of the country for several months, but that I would arrange a meeting as soon as I returned. The mental burden of this legal problem began weighing on my mind.

The rains continued and tension built between Pru and me. I had become a rotten companion, so when I suggested she go home for the Christmas holidays, she agreed. We also agreed that she could come back if she wanted to, but I privately guessed that I'd never see her again. I took her down river to Plaplaya the next day, and she went on alone to La Ceiba to catch a plane for civilization and home. I returned upstream, the journey made far easier by the swollen flood waters that covered the treacherous rocks of the rapids.

In a few days I was regretting that I had let her go. Except for the Indians and our work crew, I had no one to talk to, and, besides, everything in the tent reminded me of the girl. Depression deepened. For the next six weeks, I was never entirely sober and kept feeling more sorry for myself every day. Loneliness, anger at the Batres brothers, and concern over my government's claim for a quarter of a million dollars, all preyed on my thoughts constantly. At one horrible time during that period I seriously considered never leaving the peace of the jungle, where problems were simple and basic. Then another problem developed.

I had been doing a considerable amount of diving while we were dredging, and apparently I had swallowed a large quantity of river water. Suddenly I was hit with the unmistakable symptoms of intestinal parasites and amoebic dysentery. Although I had been strict about chlorinating and purifying our drinking water, rivers and lakes in tropical lands are notorious for their dangerous infections, and within days I was a very sick man. The best of my medication had been used up in treating the Indians. What I had left was ineffective. I began dropping weight and losing strength rapidly.

By mid-February the rains stopped, and we cranked up the dredge. I was weak from my illness, but I still kept the pumps going twelve hours a day. Then other smaller annoyances began to crop up.

Opossums started raiding the cook shack. Jep would bark at night, and I'd clamp a flashlight onto the barrel of the rifle and blast away. I killed nearly thirty scavenging animals, which I threw into the river.

Then one night the dog barked, and I pulled my weak frame out of bed, grabbed the rifle, and pushed open the cook shack door. There on the floor of the shack stood a huge alligator, at least twelve feet long, staring at me. The .22 was too small for such a brute, but I emptied the magazine into him. He casually finished tearing out the rear wall and departed. Evidently he had developed an appetite for the opossums I had thrown into the river and had dropped in to see where his supply was coming from.

Bill Woods had brought us twenty-five chickens to supply some meat and eggs, and I had built a pen to keep them safe from marauding animals. One night I heard a commotion in the pen. I taped my flashlight to my twelve gauge, double-barreled shotgun and ran out of my tent. The gun light framed a large jaguar in the pen with a chicken in his mouth. I fired both barrels. Everything went quiet. I had killed the jag, but I had also killed all except two of the chickens.

I was losing my battle against the jungle.

By mid-March I had claimed more than thirteen hundred ounces of gold, but I was so ill that I could only sit or lie on the dredge and watch the operation. I even required help in climbing the river bank up to the camp. Realizing that I was a sitting duck for anyone who decided to steal my gold hoard, which I kept buried under the plastic floor of the tent, I also began to feel that the dysentery could easily kill me if I did not get medical attention soon.

A late storm up river finally decided me. We could hear the thunder and see the lightning. Before the high water could reach Las Champas, I ordered the camp struck and the gear loaded onto the dredge. We cut loose the sluice box and pulled the support pipes from the river, then released the cables and started downstream. I took my gold and went alone in my dug-out canoe, ostensibly to spot any logjams in the river, but also to keep on my guard against theft.

We had spent more than two weeks fighting our way up river. Sliding down on the flood crest, the trip to Plaplaya required only two and a half days. I arrived at the mouth of the river a six-foot three-inch 140-pound skeleton, barely able to lift my eighty-two pounds of gold. In fact, I could barely walk.

After a few days of rest, I decided to take the dredge back to Roatán, where I could perhaps sell it. I hired Riley Gough to tow it up the gulf to Oakridge, and once again spent the night watching my barge as it bounced in the sea. Mooring lines broke twice during the night, and both times I was forced to jump aboard to relash the lines. I have seldom pushed myself so close to the absolute limits.

We spent nine hours on a crossing that normally required five, approaching the dock at Oakridge shortly after dawn. As we reached the mooring, I had a delirious vision of Pru standing on the dock waiting for me. There she was, pretty as a picture. But it was no vision. She had returned the day before and was trying to find a boat that would take her to Plaplaya.

Pru tried to nurse me back to health, but with little success. After a few days we chartered a plane to fly us to the hospital in La Ceiba. On arriving in the city, I took Pru and my heavy duffle bag to the Banco Centrale, where I maintained a current account. Walking up to the manager, I plopped the bag on his desk.

His greeting was cordial. "Señor Jennings, what can we do for you?"

"You can buy this gold."

He looked confused, but smiled. "Of course."

". . . about eighty-two pounds worth," I added.

When he'd recovered from the shock, he sent for a clerk with a set of scales. The bank was used to the Indians coming in with a few ounces to sell, but he had never seen this much at one time. In an hour, I walked out of the bank with $45,000 deposited in my account. Pru helped me check into the local hospital, but then I urged her to go home. We made plans to meet in London as soon as I could travel, and I weakly kissed her goodbye.

# 7 THE GOLDEN FROG OF THE JIMINEZ

☙

FOR TREATMENT OF AMOEBIC DYSENTERY . . . £1 2s.

As I looked at the list of charges, I thought about what a remarkable thing the British National Health program was—less than five bucks for an examination, treatment, and medicine for Howard's amoebic dysentery. Still, the poor bastard looked awful. He was thin, his face drawn, and there were dark rings under his eyes. Although the attention he had received in the Honduran hospital had arrested the ailment, a total cure is long-range. When you get hit with the *endamoeba histolytica,* the parasite has a way of staying with you. The only cure is intensive medication, and probably the best place for this treatment is in the London Clinic's world-renowned tropical disease center. So far, Howard's cure had been going on for nearly a month. The one bright spot in his otherwise tortuous recuperation was that the U.S. Government's absurd $270,000 claim against him had been dropped in favor of a nominal settlement.

I had found Howard in London shortly after his return from the Paulaya River venture. I had arrived at his flat on Marlborough Hill, intending to spend a week meeting with my London publishers and relaxing away from New York. I had just completed my second tour in Vietnam, and I was ready for some good living, but not quite prepared to plunge back into the whirl of Fun City. London seemed like the place to go. I ended up being a field medic for Howard, who was weak in body and spirit.

As we walked outside the London Clinic one lovely spring afternoon, he said, "How about drinks at the Royal Court?" I agreed that a visit to our old hangout might perk him up.

169

As we settled ourselves on bar stools, Howard suddenly said, "Ever hear of Coaque?"

"No," I said. "And I suspect I should keep it that way."

Howard persisted. "Come on, Robin, this is the big one, the lost City of Gold. I've been researching it for a long time. Take a crack at it with me."

I replied, "Howard, I can't. I've got two books in production and two more to get started. I don't even want to hear about it."

I heard about it.

Coaque was an ancient city in Ecuador, reportedly rich beyond imagination before the Spanish conquistador, Francisco Pizarro, plundered the west coast of South America. Howard had first heard stories, then had done some research, and finally had decided that he would go and try to find the lost city. Those words contain the dream of every treasure hunter—the Lost City. To an adventurer, it is not the painstaking, meticulous reconstruction and excavation of a site that is attractive—finding the first treasure and establishing the validity of the theory is the goal. The detail work is left to the archaeologist with his crews of dedicated college students, who devote their time and youth to operating a dig.

I listened, but was distracted by a tall, attractive woman using the telephone booth at the end of the lounge. Howard finished his pitch, saw that I was not interested, and followed my eyes. He was off the bar stool like a horse out of a starting gate, and I knew that he was well on the road to recovery.

The girl, whose name was not Jane, joined us for a drink. Five feet eleven, thin, with long dark hair and a very English accent, she had recently separated from her husband and was in the process of obtaining a divorce. Howard's stories of treasure hunting found an interested audience in Jane, and another drink soon led to dinner. At about ten o'clock, I discreetly offered to check into a hotel for the night. Neither Howard nor Jane demurred. I sensed that Jane was about to become a factor in our lives.

The next morning I dropped around to his flat and found

that Jane was still there, doing her best to learn how to cook pancakes. From the contented grin on his face, I could see that Howard was not all that sick any more, and I felt sure that Jane could fill the bill as a nurse, so I packed up my clothes and headed back to New York.

They became more involved with each other, and at some point he told her about his plans to search for the lost city of Coaque. But it was the island of Roatán, off Honduras, where Howard and I had first discovered an honest-to-God treasure, that really captured her imagination.

His affection for Jane grew, and so he decided to take her to Roatán for a visit while she was awaiting her divorce. Before they even arrived, they had decided to make their home on the island. Working from Howard's rough sketch, they built a lovely, Tudor-style house on the property that Howard had bought during our first trip to Roatán, right there in Port Royal Harbor.

Before they were completely moved in, a man from Chicago appeared and offered to buy the building. Howard sold at a profit and decided to build another. He did, and the same thing happened again. A wealthy rice grower from Arkansas bought the second home, and Howard started a third.

This diversion from treasure hunting occupied the next three years of their lives. By the end of the second year, in 1969, I paid them a visit. I was astonished when I saw the tiny Tudor village Howard had carved out of the jungle. There were three large and lovely homes, all most civilized, and the whole thing ran as gracefully as any hamlet in England. Daytime was spent in hiking, swimming, or fishing, and night was crowned with nearly formal dinners, good wine, and pleasant music. It was a far cry from my memories of machetes and Kool-Aid.

One night when I asked Howard why he wasn't digging up the rest of Port Royal Harbor for treasure, he explained that he and Jane were very much in love with the life they had going for them and he did not want to jeopardize their tranquility. He had often looked out toward little Careening Cay, where he was convinced that that third Mitchell-Hedges chest still waited. He was tempted, especially since advances in metal detection equipment made it possible to search near saltwater, but the island was still tied up in an estate with fourteen heirs, and he had given up any hope of getting permission from all of them. As for the temptation to try a clandestine search, that was ruled out by the heavy growth of mangrove trees on the island, the exposed roots of which would make use of the detectors almost impossible. Any attempt to clear sizable areas would be noticed and reported, and Howard had no intention of risking his home and investments on the island by angering the authorities.

But he *had* been thinking of treasure again, it seemed. He had heard of still another treasure from the rice grower who had bought the second house. The grower had been investigating rice farming possibilities in Costa Rica when he noticed some extensive excavations on a large farm near the village of Gaupiles in the eastern part of the country. Apparently, the digging had been considerable—and quite old, too, because trees had grown up in some of the unfilled holes. The local story was that tomb robbers had uncovered many gold objects.

Over the years, Howard had collected an impressive library on pre-Columbian artifacts. He showed me a tattered book by a Swedish archaeologist named Carl Hartman, who had conducted sizable digs in Costa Rica in 1896, 1897, and 1903. Hartman had opened hundreds of tombs in that part of the country, and his large collections had ended up in museums in Stockholm and Pittsburgh. The man seemed to be more of a treasure hunter than archaeologist—he paid little attention to cataloging or chronology, but he dug up one hell of a lot of gold.

"Another exploration?" I asked.

"No," Howard said. "It seems there was an old Indian who worked for Hartman. The Indian stole some gold from the sites and buried it near his home. He promised it to his daughter, but died in a 1919 flood before telling the location. The daughter died in 1930, and her son, Ignacio, moved out of the jungle and into the village of Guapiles. He is still alive and claims the gold was never found, even though he and his mother dug up a considerable portion of their property looking for it."

The bug had its teeth in me again. I was between books, and Howard assured me we could make a quick trip, without weeks in the bush. We packed up Howard's detectors, left Jane to her housework, and flew to San José, Costa Rica.

We invested an hour at the airport, watching the baggage inspections in the departure area, and were pleased to see that they were nominal. If we found the gold, it looked as though we would have little difficulty getting it out.

By noon the next day we had driven our rented car to the village of Guapiles, where we checked into the better of two horrible hotels. After lunch we drove a harrowing ten miles over punishing roads to the farm where the old Indian was working. We met Don Pablo de Meza, who owned the farm, an arrogant man whose work clothes were spotless and whose shiny boots seemed never to have touched the ground. He was mounted on a beautiful palomino, and his soft pink hand rested on a .45 revolver. We asked for Ignacio.

"Why you want the old man?" Don Pablo asked. "You think you find his gold?"

Howard made no effort to hide his irritation. "Maybe," he said. "Where can we find him?"

Don Pablo replied, "He is fired."

"Why? Because he wouldn't tell you where the gold was?"

The man on the horse smirked. *"Sí, hombre,* and also because he is too old to work."

"Where did he go?" Howard asked.

"Who knows?" Don Pablo said. He spurred the palomino into a trot, leaving us standing there in the hot sun.

We decided to do some asking around, and the first man we met on the road to town told us that Ignacio had moved back into Guapiles with his widowed daughter. He directed us to a shack at the edge of town. When we arrived, Ignacio was sitting in the shade feeding coconut to some scrawny chickens and small pigs. We introduced ourselves, and in a few minutes

173

the old man warmed up. Perhaps he was lonely, or maybe he could tell that we were not there to steal from him. He agreed to take us to the ruins of the house where he grew up. The trip would be rough, he warned: a full day on horseback and a half a day down a river by canoe. To be willing to make that trek, old Ignacio had to be sure of the gold, we felt: He was seventy-four years old.

"How about buying him a decent meal," I suggested.

"Great idea," Howard agreed. "If we can *find* a decent one in this town."

It was unlikely that Ignacio had ever been in a hotel dining room before. We seated him at a table, and even though the place was awful, he maintained an impressive dignity.

During the meal, we offered the old man his choice of two ways of splitting whatever gold we might find. He could either take half of the gold when we dug it up, but receive nothing if nothing was found, or he could be paid a flat $500 and then only claim one-third of what we found. We were both a little disappointed when the old man elected to take the money, but we had to admit that $500 would mean a significantly higher standard of living for this poor man.

The next morning we picked up Ignacio at dawn and found out that Don Pablo de Meza had learned of our meeting with the Indian while we had been dining at the hotel. He had visited Ignacio's daughter, who had told the Don that we were leaving in the morning for the Jiminez River.

We talked as we drove to the spot where we would leave the car, and found that Ignacio had no fear, but a great hatred for Don Pablo. The old man explained that we were heading into an area where he would find friends and relatives, but he cautioned us to remain on our guard: Don Pablo was a bad *hombre*.

We arrived where the horses were waiting in time for a second breakfast, and politely accepted an unwanted plate of red beans cooked with pork. The "horses" turned out to be one mangy nag, a mule, and two burros. We loaded the mule, Howard took the horse, and Ignacio and I mounted the burros.

Then we set out along the banks of the sluggish, muddy Jiminez River.

There was impenetrable jungle on our left, and the first three hours were shaded. Then the morning sun turned into the noon sun and we were hot and sweaty. As we passed small groups of shacks along the river, people waved and shouted to Ignacio. By mid-afternoon, we had arrived at the shack of Ignacio's cousin, also a very old man. We turned down an offer to sleep in the tiny house; we strung hammocks outside, started a campfire, and settled down to an exhausted, dreamless sleep.

The next morning, we set off in the cousin's two canoes, accompanied by Ignacio's two 40-year-old nephews who were to do the heavy work of clearing the site of the old house. Within a few minutes, the gentle rocking motion of the boat coaxed Ignacio into sleep. The river was quiet and smooth, and the canoes glided under green branches that spread out beautifully over the water. After a time, I too began to doze in the sun and awoke with a start three hours later, as the canoe bumped into shore.

"Here we are," one of the nephews announced, jumping ashore.

"Where the hell is 'here'?" I called to Howard in the other canoe.

"I guess over there," he shouted, pointing to the thick undergrowth. "I see some posts that might have been a foundation."

Then I spotted the erect piles of green foliage. Like the other houses we had seen along the river, this house must have been built on stilts in defense against floods. Nothing was left except the stilts.

The two nephews began clearing a wide path to the site of the building while Howard and I unloaded the equipment and old Ignacio.

We set up a camp very close to the river. The rainy season was only beginning, and we felt that the threat of floods was minimal. The slight breeze from the river was as valuable as air conditioning. If we had gone further inland, the heat would have been stifling.

175

We investigated the house site. As the workmen chopped away the superficial growth, it was easy to see the results of the back-breaking work which Ignacio and his mother must have put into their own search for the gold. The entire area under the house had been dug up to a depth of about three feet. They had been so thorough that some of the underpinnings of the house had been weakened and eroded by floods. The house must have simply collapsed and washed away.

By noon the next day, the area that had been under and around the house was cleared sufficiently for Howard to begin operating his metal detector. As he had predicted, there were immediate results: door hinges, nails, broken machetes, and a pile of junk metal. But every signal had to be investigated, and by the end of the first day we were dismayed to find that we had recovered all the metal that the detector indicated in the area where the house had stood.

"What now?" I asked.

Howard said, "Well, hell, we've come this far. We'll just have to extend the search area."

He ordered the workers to begin cutting, and we wandered down to the river to talk over the situation. Just then we saw a small canoe approaching, and recognized the passengers as the two sons of one of our workers. Ignacio joined us at the river bank as the canoe was beached. The youths were perspiring heavily, and it was easy to see they had come down the river in haste. We helped pull in their boat and listened as they told Ignacio that Don Pablo and four other men had set up a camp near where we had parked our car and loaded our pack animals. They were all armed and appeared to be waiting for us.

"They're waiting to steal all our rusty hinges," I said.

Howard was more sober about the situation. "Well at least they're staying put. That gives us an advantage."

We fed the young boys and dispatched them back up the river to keep an eye on Don Pablo's camp.

That night Howard and I both had a hard time sleeping. Mentally, I rehearsed a Vietnam-type counter ambush, but we were really too undergunned for that. At about three in the morning, while I was hunched down over the fire and sipping a cup of coffee laced with brandy, Howard came from his hammock and joined me. "Is it always like this, Howard?" I asked him. "This is as bad as a jungle operation across the Cambodian border."

A grin crossed his face. "More or less. Somehow my trips seem like a piece of cake when I'm planning them, but more often than not they end up sticky as hell. Gold seems to attract trouble."

We found the gold the next morning.

Howard had taken the detector down to one of the boats to change the batteries. He turned the machine on and zeroed it in on a hunk of iron in the boat. Without really meaning to, he left it on when he carried it back up the bank to the house site. Halfway up he picked up a strong signal. We dug into the soft earth of the bank and discovered a layer of river stones.

On seeing the stones Ignacio suddenly exclaimed, *"Madre mia!"* Apparently, his grandfather had built these stone steps up the muddy river bank to the house. Ignacio remembered that after each flood season the steps had to be carefully cleaned of mud. That had been one of Ignacio's chores as a child. Until now he had entirely forgotten the steps.

The covering debris was removed in less than an hour, and Howard picked up a strong signal over the largest stone. The workmen pried the rock up, and there, embedded in soft clay, was a large rough pottery jar, about 12 inches in diameter and 18 inches deep. When we got it out, it appeared to be filled with earth.

Howard handed me a trowel, and I dug into the mouth of the jar. Moments later I pulled out a large gold frog. When I'd cleaned away the coating of dirt, the frog squatted there, nearly filling the palm of my hand. It was incredibly heavy for its size and it gleamed with the unmistakable yellow luster of gold. The detector had proven its worth.

The frog had been near the mouth of the jar, and I started to dig deeper. Howard stopped me. Then he asked the nephews to go up and continue clearing the area away from the house.

"Why?" I asked. "If this is it, let's go."

Howard shook his head. "The gold concerns only Ignacio, you, and me. Why get those two men's minds all filled with gold lust?" I had to admit he was dead right—we already had a bunch of greedy nuts trying to kill us off for booty they weren't even sure we had.

I was elected to empty the jar. Ignacio and Howard cleaned each piece as I pulled it out. We worked for an hour. When it was finally empty, there were 103 pieces of gold, each one a treasure in itself. There were more frogs, bracelets, butterflies, some human figures, and several golden buzzard coins, more frequently described as "eagles."

I flipped one to Ignacio, and he seemed stunned as he stared at it. I could see him considering the years of discouraging toil that he and his mother had invested in finding his grandfather's trove.

Howard separated the hoard into three piles as equal as it was possible to make them out there on the bank of a river. He told Ignacio to choose the pile he wanted. He picked the one closest to him. His trust was touching. The old man took off his shirt and began wrapping up his share in it. I went up to the camp and returned with a small overnight bag I had used to bring extra clothing. We loaded the remaining piles of gold into it.

"We've done it, Howard," I said, zipping up the bag. "Now let's get the hell out of here."

"I'm with you, Robin," he said. "I think we should head on down river to the coast."

"What about the rental car?"

"Hell, we can pay the car agency to pick it up. That's better than getting shot at by old Don Pablo."

Right.

Howard tried to talk Ignacio into coming with us to the mouth of the river, but the old man was tired and felt he would be safer staying with his relatives. He told us to take one of the canoes and travel down river to the village of Parismina, where the Jiminez emptied into the Caribbean. He felt sure we could find transportation there to take us to safety.

We were not happy about leaving the old man. I have often wondered if he lived to enjoy his grandfather's treasure, or, if he did, whether it came too late in life.

The coast was much nearer than we expected—we were there within two hours of leaving Ignacio. At Parismina we noticed a large fiberglass speedboat with two big outboard engines. We discovered it belonged to a local store owner, who offered to take us to the large port city of Limon, 25 miles down the coast, for $50. Well, what the hell, we'd be safe and back in civilization for only $2 per mile. It seemed like a bargain.

The sea was calm, the boat was fast, and by mid-afternoon we were in Limon where we caught the afternoon plane to San José. We were showered, shaved, and dressed in time for cocktails, with sixty-nine pieces of gold stashed in the hotel safe-deposit box. We drank a toast to Don Pablo, sitting out in the jungle waiting to ambush us. The next day we hid the gold in suit bags and flew to Panama, where we connected with a flight to London.

Howard cabled Jane to fly over, and we had a short, happy holiday together. I left them in London, but because of some problems with the English auction rooms, Howard eventually arranged to have our gold sold by Parke-Bernet in New York. The sale, handled through a friend, brought $68,000.

Howard and I kept in touch, but did not see each other over the next year or so. He and Jane returned to their exotic life on the island of Roatán, and he again became involved in land development there. But deep down, I knew he was still obsessed with treasure.

So I wasn't too surprised when one day he turned up in London, pounding together an expedition to Coaque.

# 8 COAQUE, THE GOLDEN CITY

"It is said that the chief Indian gave
D. Francisco Pizzaro an emerald as big as
a pigeon's egg used for grinding wheat,
in exchange for seventeen Indian women . . . "

FERNANDO DE HERRERA,
*Sixteenth-century historian*

If you ask almost anyone, even most Ecuadorians, how to get to Coaque, you will probably receive a blank look for your trouble. As I had pointed out to Robin, if you study most current maps, even the most expensive, highly detailed ones, I doubt that you will find Coaque pinpointed.

I myself was forced to refer to Marshall H. Saville's 1910 map to find the present city and river of Coaque. That map was drawn as a result of the George G. Heye Expedition, which was one of the most elaborate of several early twentieth century explorations of the west coast of Latin America. Finding Marshall Saville's name led me to a highly informative article by him in *Contributions to South American Archaeology*. Everything sounds so simple when I say: "I found a map" or "It led me to an article." Let me state right now, productive research on lost treasures is damned hard work. One must dig through dusty archives for long hours, which grow into days, and often into weeks.

In the stacks of the British Museum and the Royal Geographical Society, I built a picture of the great Spanish conquistador, Francisco Pizarro. The story of his march along the west coast of South America was chronicled by his cousin, Pedro Pizarro, whose journal refers to Coaque, the City of Gold. Pizarro was born in the 1470's and was with Balboa in 1513 when he discovered the Pacific Ocean. In 1532 he encountered the famous Inca leader, Atahualpa, high in the Andes. Pizarro first professed friendship; then, after kidnapping and holding the Indian emperor-god for ransom, Pizarro had him killed.

But before Pizarro even dreamed of the wealth he would find in Peru, he ventured into what is now known as Ecuador. His ship's pilot had first seen Coaque in 1526, during their second voyage down the west coast of South America. Subsequently, in January 1531, Pizarro sailed out of Panama on a voyage of thirteen days, landing most of his men and horses at the mouth of the Esmeraldas River. There he began a march southward along the shoreline with his ships kept close in for supply and support.

Pedro Pizarro's journal relates that the highlight of the adventure was the sacking of the town of Coaque. He wrote that the town was near large and high mountains, and that the neighboring farm land was extensively cultivated. The plunder taken from the Indians was mainly in gold, silver, and emeralds. Diarists seem to disagree on the actual amount of booty taken, but Pizarro placed the value at 200,000 castellanos. Considering the recent rise in the value of gold and allowing for inflation, that figure would convert to somewhere between $4 million and $6 million in raw gold value today. That is not taking into account the unique value of antiquities, which can run ten to fifteen times the value of the gold they contain.

Another record keeper, a secretary named Xerez, stated: "They marched along the shore, finding all the inhabitants in arms against them. They continued their march until they reached the village called Coaque which they entered, for the inhabitants had not risen as in the other villages." Pizarro, true to form, finding the local people non-hostile, proceeded to take their wealth. He shipped out the loot on three of his ships to Panama and Nicaragua, then ordered more troops. Two of the ships came back with 26 horsemen and 30 foot soldiers.

Pizarro then headed southward toward Peru and history, but the records contend that the plunder of Coaque was his greatest up to that time. And if that were true, there had to be some gold left in the burial mounds. The area around Coaque was ripe. I needed to know more.

Many of the accounts I had found kept referring to documents located in Spanish archives. I decided to go to Seville to see the actual records.

The Spaniards who conquered Latin America not only kept most of the gold they found, they also kept astonishingly complete records. The Archivos des Indios in Seville are overwhelming. In my travels, I had so improved my Spanish that I was able to perform most of my preliminary research alone in the dusty rooms filled with huge, incredibly neat records and diaries and reports. Among the discoveries was a vivid account by the Spanish poet Fernando de Herrera, who, three hundred years ago, apparently wrote on mundane historical subjects before turning to sonnets. Here is the crude translation I obtained:

> One morning they reached Quaque, a town
> surrounded by big mountains, and there they created
> panic among the Indians. Indians could have
> encountered and resisted them, but they didn't because
> they thought that by doing no harm to those men, they
> were not going to receive injuries from them also, but
> they, the Indians, were wrong. The Indians only ran
> into the woods taking weights of gold, silver, and
> emeralds, little emeralds that in those days were
> considered precious, but many of those emeralds were
> lost. According to the priest Reginaldo de Pedraça,
> Order of Saint Domonique, "Those emeralds were said
> to be even harder than iron, and that nothing could
> break them. Trying to prove this, many emeralds were
> destroyed by hammer." Some did say that the priest lied,
> and that he himself was hiding the emeralds somewhere.
> A few others did hide some emeralds.
>
> The treasures were gathered for the King's Treasure,
> some of which was to be distributed among them. If
> somebody kept some part of the treasures hidden, he had
> to pay with his life for such a treason. This order was
> kept all along the journey. The Indians were afraid.
> They were astonished looking at the horses. They even
> believed that the Spaniards were immortals. One of the
> Indians returned from the woods and took refuge in

his own house. He was taken in front of Don Francisco Pizarro, and the Indian said to him: "I was hidden in my own house, not in someone else's house, and you, against our own will came to our land to frighten us. My people left because they were afraid." D. Francisco Pizarro answered: "Tell your people to come back, my intention is not to harm them, you are wrong, you should have come to make peace instead of running away as you did." The Indians (children, women and men) came back from the woods, but soon afterwards, seeing that they were not considered but only treated as servants, they decided to return to the woods, where they could not easily be found.

With the gold and precious stones, D. Francisco Pizarro decided to send two ships to Panama and a third one to Nicaragua. Bartolemé de Aguilar was in charge of them. Those ships also carried passengers, horses, and letters to his friends on which he wrote about the richness of the land, and also that it only was governed by one man, from whom he could expect a lot of good. Those who remained in Quarte, land on the Equinoccial Line (Equator), had to suffer several diseases during those seven months. Some went to bed and woke up with swollen members; others with contracted members; others never woke up, and some others with inflammations that took twenty days to cure, and warts on their eyes, all over their bodies, and great pains that did not allow them to walk, and made them look like monsters. Those who cured that very infectious disease, tried to cut off those warts they had, but most who did, bled themselves to death. Some of them had minor symptoms, and they thought that the reason of the disease was that they had eaten a poisonous fish given to them by the Indians, so they ate fruits, corns and roots and did not touch meat or fish. The were all longing for the return of the ships. . . . Diseases continued, food started to become scarce, so they decided to move to another land. Just about to move, they met another ship with supplies on which were travelling Alfonso Riquelme, Treasurer; Garcia de Sancedo, merchant; Antonio Navarro, accountant; Geronimo de Aliago; Gonzalo de Farfan; Melchor de Verdugo; Pedro Diaz, and many others. They informed D. Francisco Pizarro that due to his rapid departure from Seville, some officials who were left behind asked in a Requisition presented to the authorities in Panama, to have his journey stopped, but that the King, in spite of (Pizarro's) having left behind Royal Officials, was not prepared to stop his voyage, but granted him (Pizarro) the Right to choose officials among his crew while the Royal Officials did not reach him. . . .

Indians by then had changed their mind about the Castilians. Their opinion was not quite the same they had before. They thought that Castilians were cruel, thieves of lands, able to do harm to those who were not causing them any, and that they had big horses that flew as the wind, long spears and sharp swords which cut anything they touched. . . . News of all this reached the Inca governors at Cuzco.

They arrived to another town named Paffao, and there, the peace maker Don Francisco Pizarro said: "Our people won't offend those who abide by the King of Castilla, we offer true Peace, a peace that comes from our will, not a false one." It was then that Indians started serving the Castilians to their best, because indeed they were used to serve their masters well. It is said that the chief Indian gave D. Francisco Pizarro an emerald as big as a pigeon's egg used for grinding wheat, in exchange for seventeen Indian women they had from other towns. The chief Indian did not know it was a valuable stone, he thought that it was worthless. After that they left Paffao, in very good harmony with the Indians.

After several days of intensive digging in the archives, I headed back to London to wrap up my affairs before Jane and I headed off for Coaque.

This was to be no small jaunt. We were searching out one of the great treasure areas of the world. Coaque was once inhabited by Indians who kept domesticated animals, wove wool and cotton, and were accomplished artists in gold and silver. They had developed agricultural tools of copper and other metals, had tended advanced gardens, and had planned city streets. Marshall Saville, writing of his 1908 expedition, said: ". . . it is not at all improbable that [burial] mounds marking the sites of ancient cities lie buried in the jungle." He also observed that ". . . in ancient times this beautiful region contained one of the most important and populous cities of the entire northwest coast of South America. . . . Many of the flat-topped hills appear to have been artificially leveled and this spot is undoubtedly the site of ancient Coaque. All along the southern banks of the river we find innumerable traces of ancient remains. . . . Along the beach from the mouth of the river to Pedernales Point, a distance of little over a mile, we saw potsherds strewn along the shore."

On October 25, 1971, Jane and I left London to begin our search. Our first stop was Miami, my regular jumping-off point in treasure hunting. Even then, I was still wary of the Batres brothers from Peru, so we made our Miami stop as short as possible. I went shopping for a couple of .38 caliber revolvers, a .30.30 rifle, and sufficient ammunition to sustain us for an extended jungle trip. Then I outfitted Jane with jeans, heavy shirts, rain gear, and good, stout boots to protect her legs from snake bites.

Back in Quito, we purchased our major provisions—hammocks, machetes, tinned foods, coffee, whisky, and the like—and after two hectic days of negotiations, I rented a Land Rover. Car-hire agencies want an Inca king's ransom when you are asking for a vehicle for two months, and after all that haggling I still ended up leaving a deposit of $1,000.

Finally, one morning we drove west out to Quito in the direction of Bahía de Caráquez, which is 300 miles away on the Pacific Coast. We had our equipment and supplies, and we had brand-new detection paraphernalia that would help me wrestle some of that gold away from the earthen vaults of Coaque's burial mounds—I hoped.

The first two hundred miles of the road west were reasonably easy, but as we came down the mountains toward the coastline, the going got perilous at times. Occasionally, we would hear the roar of a landslide in front or in back of us. I was skirting one such pile of rubble when Jane asked, "How far below this road is that valley, Howard?"

I gave a quick glance out her window and replied, "About a thousand feet, more or less."

"That's what I thought," she said with a twinge of nervousness in her voice. The wheels of the car were only a foot away from a nonstop plunge to the bottom.

"If it worries you, I'll go faster 'til we pass this landslide," I suggested cheerfully.

Her silence was deafening.

Ninety miles south of our target, we hit the coastline at Bahía de Caráquez and discovered that a Land Rover is excellent transport on a beach at low tide. Dry riverbeds are also easy, and there were more than twenty rivers and streams to cross before we arrived at the Coaque River. In a few weeks those dry riverbeds would be so swollen that crossing them would be impossible.

Our Land Rover purred along on the hard-packed sand, but at several points on our journey north to the equator we were forced to travel inland to avoid rocky stretches of coastline. Many of the inland trails were mountainous. Going down one steep incline, we began to pick up too much speed. I pumped the brakes. My stomach knotted as the vehicle kept going. I pumped harder and faster, but still no braking action. After a jolting, heart-in-throat roller coaster ride down and along a sheer precipice, we finally slowed to a stop at the bottom of the hill.

When I jumped out and raised the hood, I found that the master cylinder was leaking—we were out of brakes. To make the 350-mile trek back to Quito was out of the question. The delay would put us right into the middle of the rainy season. For the rest of the trip, downhill runs were made with the car in low gear and my heart in my mouth.

187

Late the next afternoon, after a harrowing nonstop day of driving, we came over the brow of a hill and looked down into the magnificent valley of the Coaque River, a wide fertile expanse with the broad, swift-flowing river cutting through the jungle. We were exhausted, but we stood perfectly still, taking in one of the most awesome views I have seen in all of my travels. The huge, molten-red ball of the sun floated on the rim of the Pacific Ocean, and on our right the jagged peaks of the Coaque Mountains rose 20 miles away above the dense, green, vine-snarled jungle. We were precisely on the equator.

We pitched a temporary camp and settled in for our first night in Coaque. We slept deeply, too tired to hear the screeching pumas, wild turkeys, monkeys, and birds. In the morning, we trailblazed along the river and came to an Indian village, also called Coaque, which we hoped was near the site of the ancient Coaque.

There were about twenty huts of thatch and bamboo, which should have been filled with naked children, squawking chickens, and barking dogs, but everything that was live disappeared magically when we arrived. Chocolate bars finally restored the children to visibility, and soon after, the grown-ups began to appear. It was a poor-looking village, but the inhabitants had an abundance of natural food: bananas, papaya, citrus fruits, and many types of game and fish.

The Indians were delighted to learn that I was looking for workers and was planning to pay cash. My labor force signed up for the equivalent of forty cents per man per day.

The village women were shy, and too busy to ogle the new visitors anyway. As in most Indian cultures, the men do the fighting and hunting and the women do the work. (We learned that it required eight hours of hard labor for one woman to husk sufficient rice for ten people.) And the Indians marry early. One man who worked for us was twenty-four, his wife, twenty, and they had six children with another on the way. The wife would probably live to be twenty-six or twenty-seven, and then die in childbirth or of dysentery.

Yet the people were friendly and kind, and they shared some

of their odd but tasty meals with us. (We were careful never to ask what exactly it was we were eating.) Jane hit it off quickly with the women. She served them a special lunch of tinned food, which astounded them, and she gave them colored scarves and plastic hair clips.

The village was at sea level, with the hills towering about it on all sides. Here, according to Marshall Saville's assumption, was the probable site of Coaque, the ancient Inca city. We set up a camp on the south bank near the mouth of the river, then reconnoitered the valley and hills on horses hired from the Indians. It was Jane who first spotted the potsherds that were being washed out of the river nearly a mile from its mouth, a certain sign that many people had once lived here. We tethered the horses to examine the pottery. Most fragments were very poor in quality and of crude workmanship.

But Jane was enthusiastic. "We're very lucky to have found evidence so quickly, don't you think, Howard?"

I hated to disillusion her, especially since she had spotted the pottery fragments first. "It was a very good find," I assured her. "But the people who lived here were fishermen, workers, probably in the service of the more sophisticated hierarchy living up there." I pointed to the hills east of the river. "There I think we'll find finer pottery."

"Then let's go there," she said.

For five days we hacked our way through the dense vegetation, paralleling the river's south bank and heading east. We looked for man-made mounds and stopped to make excavations in likely places, but found nothing. Using my meager Spanish, gestures, and drawings, I described to our Indian workmen the kind of mounds I was looking for. One of the Indians said he could take us to such a mound further up river, but when we arrived there I saw it was high and irregular, a natural hill and not a classical South American *tola*.

However, I could see, further to the east, a high, flat area between two hills. It was so level that it seemed unnatural, and there appeared to be several large depressions in a straight line on a part of the ridge leading up to the leveled area.

189

"Do you think that's Coaque?" Jane asked, after surveying the area with the binoculars.

"No, we're too far up river, but I've got a strong hunch it's the site of another town."

"Let's go," she said.

We found nine depressions, equally spaced in a straight line, each one about 18 feet in diameter and 3 feet deep, resembling filled-in wells. Then I made our second discovery. Really excited, I grabbed Jane's arm and pointed to a flat area of about two hundred acres nestled between two hills. As we hurried up to it, we could see that the ground was littered with highly polished polychrome pottery fragments. These were made by true artists, with excellent craftsmanship. All our disappointment dissolved. An ancient city was buried beneath our feet.

I chose a central depression for our excavation, staked the outline of a trench for our initial dig, and ordered the Indians to dig. To a depth of several feet the earth and rock fill was quite loose. It was getting late in the day, so I sent the Indians to carry supplies from the Land Rover and walked Jane back to the new camp site. We had a snack from the small food supply we carried in our saddlebags, and then I headed back to the trench to dig.

It wasn't more than ten minutes before my trowel struck a hard object. Because I was scooping the earth away carefully, it was another five minutes before I could grip the object and cautiously pull it free; but as I brushed the clinging dirt from it, in the fading light I saw a glint of gold.

I shouted for Jane to come, holding the object aloft. It was a magnificent solid gold ornamental headdress. We were filled with excitement.

At a depth of 8 feet in the depression, we encountered a floor of unfired clay, slightly domed in shape, which continued to a vertical wall. What we had found was a chamber cut into solid limestone rock which, perhaps a thousand years ago, had been plastered with the layer of clay. Digging under the dome of clay to a depth of ten feet we found the first remains of a body, a grey powdery material with a few scattered human teeth and a fragment of jawbone. Jane and I, with our gardening trowels, dug under the body remains and found the first group of artifacts: bowls, several pottery lamps, two small pottery figures (one painted, whose vivid colors had lasted all these centuries), a bird-shaped whistle that still worked, human and animal figures, and many smooth green serpentine beads.

We completed the excavation of the burial chamber in two more days, preserving as much as possible the clay-lined and covered chamber walls. It turned out to be a huge bowl hollowed out of the solid rock to a depth of 12 feet. I knew we had not yet found Coaque—we were too far upstream—but the quality of everything we had found proved that the people who had lived here were wealthy and highly artistic.

Early the next morning we were enveloped in the low clouds which often cover the hills in the area. As we were drinking our morning coffee, Jane suddenly said, "Howard, why do I have the feeling we're being watched?"

At almost the same moment, I caught a quick movement in the trees in back of Jane. Quietly I said, "Sit still. There *is* something or somebody in the trees in back of you." I had my gun ready. I stood up and called, "Hey, *amigo?*"

An Indian looked out from behind a tree. I motioned to him and he approached, smiling.

"*Como se llamo?*" I called.

"Anestro," he replied. (I've spelled it phonetically, since he can neither read nor write.)

We talked, after our fashion, and I learned that, as a hunter, Anestro knew the hills and mountains on either side of the Coaque River from its mouth on the Pacific to as far east as the Coaque Mountains. I invited him to join us as a guide and laborer, and he accepted. He was the only Indian we met who seemed to have some awareness of the importance of the artificial mounds he had seen. None of the other Indians had any knowledge of their ancestry or of the Indian Empire that once claimed this land. But Anestro seemed to have an interest in antiquity.

Over the years, as he hunted game to feed his family, Anestro had seen other locations where there were depressions similar to these we were working. Some, he said, were on a long, flat place high in the hills north of where the Coaque River entered the sea. I was delighted. Perhaps this, at last, was the site of ancient Coaque.

We had already dug up several valuable pieces of gold, but this trip was to be exploratory, in preparation for a large, well-manned expedition after the rainy season. The gold had been there for centuries; it could remain a few more months. But I was still anxious to pinpoint the City of Gold. After a discussion with Jane, we decided to take a look at Anestro's suggested site.

The next morning we found a place to cross to the north bank of the Coaque River. With our Indian laborers following and Anestro leading the way, we worked our way north and up into the hills.

As we pushed along the gently rising ridge, I suddenly realized we were traveling on an ancient road. It must have required a huge work force in those forgotten times to accomplish the shaping and filling which provided the even, wide surface to the top of the hill ahead of us.

We climbed higher and entered onto a long, well-formed section of level ground. It had obviously been leveled by man. We rode our horses the half mile to the end of the plateau, which was about the width of a football field, and stared out at the soul-stirring sight of the mouth of the Coaque River, a thousand feet below, pouring its waters into the blue vastness of the Pacific. We stood looking at the sea, as many an Indian chieftain must have centuries ago.

Jane broke the silence. "What happened to the city, Howard? Did the people just die out and the buildings rot away?"

"It was destroyed by the Indians themselves," I answered. "They tried to ruin it so Pizarro couldn't use it. Then they abandoned it and fled, probably to Quito."

"Senseless," she said, half to herself. "Pizarro destroyed an entire culture, a civilization, just for gold."

It was mid-afternoon when we dismounted and began walking around. Sticking out of the eroded soil, and just under its surface, were all manner of ancient objects, obviously from a sophisticated civilization.

We frequently bent over to pick up and examine beautifully made pots, some painted and intact, others broken. Perhaps the most fascinating ancient works in pottery are the Indian whistles resembling one- to four-note ocarinas. These ancestors of our modern-day "sweet potato" were made in the form of birds and all sorts of human and animal figures. I picked up a jaguar, and brushing the dirt off it, located the blow hole in the pottery animal's rear end and two finger holes, one on each flank. When it was thoroughly cleaned, I would have a two-note whistle at least half a millennium old.

Had I really found it? The City of Gold, first seen by Francisco Pizarro and lost for nearly five hundred years? A few days of digging would tell the story, I hoped.

"Howard," Jane said, "Shouldn't we make camp first and then explore this place in the morning?"

Reluctantly I agreed. It is no fun to make camp in the dark. But with an hour or two of daylight left, I couldn't bring myself to leave this burial ground. "You supervise the Indians. I'm going to start probing right here."

Jane left with the Indians, and I walked over to the first of the depressions Anestro had pointed out to me earlier. It was about three feet deep and fifteen to twenty feet across. I stepped down into it, pulled the rifle strap off my shoulder, and laid the gun down. Then I began searching with my metal probe.

Marshall Saville had written that Coaque was on the southern bank of the river. I was about to prove that undisputed authority on pre-Columbian Indian culture to be in error. The mercenary lust for gold was still boiling inside of me, but the thrill of discovery was almost as strong.

I felt the point of my probe make contact with something solid. I pulled the probe out of the dirt and set it on the ground by my side. Then I reached for my spade and started digging. It was late afternoon, but the heat was still intense, even at this altitude.

In an hour I had carefully removed the dirt down to four

feet, where the point of my probe had made contact. I was evidently into a grave; I could tell by the color of the dirt, which was a moldering grey instead of the yellowish texture of the surface soil.

I reached down into the shallow excavation and my fingers wriggled through the dirt and touched metal. I found the edge of the piece of metal and gently pulled it from the earth. Getting to my feet I shook the thin object, and as the dirt of centuries dropped from it, I saw that I was holding a pre-Columbian death mask. The gold gleamed in the setting sun as brilliantly as the day some Indian artisan had pounded the face into the sheet of yellow metal.

The months of planning, the jungle hardships, the researches and theories all fell away. Alone, I stood on what had to be the outskirts of ancient Coaque, clutching the golden mask and looking out over the blue Pacific Ocean.

My thoughts were interrupted when Jane came up behind me, let out a shriek of delight, and snatched the death mask out of my hand.

"I didn't even bother to break out the metal detector," I said, turning from the ocean. "Found it with the probe."

"What a strange-looking face," she said in a hushed voice.

"They actually made these masks look like the face of a dead person."

"Did they put them over the face of the corpse?"

"I've never uncovered a grave and found one over the skull. Usually you find the mask buried on the chest." I took the shining gold mask back from her, turning it to catch the rays of the setting sun. "This could be a thousand years old."

"What did they actually do with those things?" Jane asked.

"No authority has been able to answer that question definitively." I tapped a small hole at the top of the mask. "Most of them have this hole at the top. The theory is that they were worn around the neck on some sort of a cord."

"I don't think I'd like to wear a mask that was supposed to look like somebody's dead face."

I looked at the death mask again. Then, reluctantly, I said, "Let's get back to the camp. It will be dark in minutes. There's no twilight on the equator."

Jane and the Indians had done a good job of making camp. Our hammocks were strung beside each other, the plastic sheets suspended above them to keep off the unpredictable rain. The Indians had chosen a site a hundred yards or more away from ours. They had even gone down to the river below and brought back water buckets for our use.

I stripped off my hot, sweat-soaked clothes and poured a bucket of water over myself. Then I lay down on the bedding roll in my hammock, and instantly plunged into a deep sleep.

Dawn erupts violently on the equator. A big red ball of energy bounces into the sky with such vitality that it is easy to understand why the Incas considered it a deity. To them, the sun was an agent of the creator-god, Viracocha, and because the sun was so important, it was deemed that all Inca rulers were descended from the sun and therefore could do no wrong. And that's the feeling I had as I rolled out of my hammock: Today I could do no wrong.

Pizarro had come to the new world shortly after the death of the Great Inca, Huayna Capac, who was believed to be the direct descendant of the sun. Huayna Capac had left a legacy of confusion, and his empire was torn between his sons. One was Huascar; the other was the man who was destined to be the victim of Pizarro's most ignoble act, Atahualpa, the ruler who provided a ransom of a room filled with gold as high as he could reach, and who was rewarded with death. As Jane and I sipped our morning coffee, I wondered how many of the ancient man-gods of the Incas had ever walked on this exact spot.

I pressed the work crew to the digs by six-thirty in the morning. We went directly to the depression in which I had found the gold death mask. I wasn't sure just what these depressions were, but they were surely some kind of a tomb. I walked over the site with my metal detector but found no signal. This had

195

to mean that the gold, if more was there, was beyond the ten-foot effective range of the instrument. I then directed the Indians to start an excavation, and took Jane for a walk.

As we walked, we talked again of that lurid time in the early 1500's when Pizarro and his 188 men and 26 horses had conquered this land. The Indians never had seen men on horses and for a time believed the men and mounts to be one animal, a horrifying apparition. The Spaniards had firearms, the Incas had only spears. But I think the most fatal aspect of the confrontation was the Inca philosophy of war. Gold had a ceremonial significance to them, but because it was in such abundance, they placed a low value on it. To the Inca and most other pre-Columbian Indians, real wealth was measured in slaves. So when war was conducted and battles fought, killing the opponent was simply throwing away wealth—preferably the enemy was to be captured and enslaved. The Inca had never perfected the art of slaughter. The Spanish had.

"It isn't fair," Jane said.

"No, but it made Spain the wealthiest country in the world at that time." Yet even so, a wealth of artifacts were lost to Pizarro because they were buried.

Most of the Inca statues, pectorals, and toomies that were found were melted down by the Spanish. The statues and pectorals were graven images, which were condemned by the ever-present priest-explorers who accompanied all expeditions. And the toomies, the crescent-shaped ceremonial knives, were used in sacrificial ceremonies, a gross violation of New Testament beliefs. Even if an explorer such as Pizarro wanted to keep a relic intact, he was faced with the wrath of the clerics, who represented themselves as the voice of both God and the King of Spain. It is a sad fact that only three codices of the historic picture writing of pre-Columbian Indians exist today. Once there were thousands, but they were ordered burned by the priests, who looked upon the material as part of pagan worship. I have stood for hours looking at the beautiful Codex of the Mixtex, or Cloud People, in the British Museum. It tells the story of Chief Eight-Deer Ocelot-Claw, of the trials and tribulations and joys of his 52-year life. Every time I dig, I move gently, hoping that I might uncover one of those picture-writing books. That would really be a treasure to bestow on mankind.

We continued to dig and soon uncovered another ancient grave. It had housed a person who was not of great wealth, but I was far from discouraged. The population of the Coaque valley in ancient times was reported in tens of thousands over a period of eight or nine hundred years; therefore, we were in an area that had to contain well over half a million graves, based on the short lifespan of the early Indians. Gold would be there, in great quantities.

After four days of hard labor in the 90° temperatures, we completed digging out two of the depressions to which Anestro had led us. We found them constructed in the same manner as those upstream, and we dug down eight to ten feet, terracing steps to the bottom as we dug. My opinion was reinforced as we worked. These strange tombs could represent only a small part of the burial ground for a city as large as Coaque. But I was more than ever convinced we were on the site; the entire top of the 1,000-foot-high ridge had been completely flattened off for half a mile and was about a hundred yards wide, too large an area for an ordinary Indian village.

In the first depression, at a depth of seven feet, we began to encounter the grey-colored earth, and from then on we dug cautiously as I probed the dirt below us. I was increasingly amazed that I had found the death mask a mere four feet below the surface. Perhaps it had been put that far above the actual grave as a sort of curse, or to stop a superstitious pillager from digging any further.

Below the seven-foot level, Jane found a gold headdress once worn by some Indian prince, or wealthy citizen. At the same depth, we found a second and a third body, curled on their sides in the fetal position. They were equally well-endowed for the afterlife—buried with them were necklaces, bracelets, tiny statuettes, and medallions which were gold. I soon began to realize that my original hopes were being confirmed. But

197

the potentially enormous size of the dig at Coaque was going to require greater organization and a concentrated search for the main burial ground, for here were only a few of the well-like tombs. Jane and I were faced with the impending rainy season, which would either isolate us from civilization or force us to take a long tortuous route inland—and neither prospect seemed attractive to us. Besides, I was eager to put together a major expedition. We had made the initial location of the area; we would leave and come back in June with a full crew of diggers.

But there were two local legends that nagged at me, and I was determined to seek out the foundations of the stories. Through the years, Indians had related a tale of a city which stood atop one of the two high peaks of the Coaque Mountains; Pizarro gave brief mention to it in his journal. The other legend was of an old Indian who had stumbled on more than eighty pounds of gold artifacts. The old man was supposed to have lived on the Conquista River, which runs through the Coaque Mountains.

I found these tales irresistible. With the plan to return firmly established in my mind, I decided we could invest at least a few days in trying to find the city in the mountains. It turned out to be more of a chore than I had anticipated.

Mount Pata de Pajaro is only 2,000 feet high, but it is the highest mountain on the coast between Panama and Peru, and a nearly constant low cloud cover obscures the top from general view. I soon discovered that no one, not even the curious Indians, ever made an attempt to scale the peak. There are reports of ferocious animals on the approaches up the side of Mount Pata de Pajaro, but the Indians were more afraid of the blue lights they claimed to have seen shining at night. This was a sign of ghostly activity. I figured I could handle the animals with my rifle, and I reasoned that the blue lights were probably St. Elmo's fire, a harmless phenomenon caused by buildups of static electricity.

Finding native help who would believe me was another matter. In the end, I had to buy the valor of one little brown Indian named Maximo for $1.60 a day, four times the usual daily

198

rate, in the small village of Atahualpa at the foot of the mountain. (The name of this village—plus one workman with the same name—is the only evidence I have that the Incas were ever in this area.)

Early one morning, we struck out to climb to the city. We carried food and equipment for only three days, plus my revolver and the rifle.

By late afternoon, Jane, Maximo, and I reached an abandoned hunter's hut part way up the mountain. Jane prepared a hot meal with an awesome skill. She turned canned sardines, tuna, carrots, and potatoes into a remarkable combination, which we topped off with tinned cherry cake and coffee.

We had cleaned up our plates and secured our cooking gear just as night and a heavy rainfall slammed down on us. Our evening was spent dodging rain and worrying about the possibility of an early rainy season. The water dripping on us was an ominous reminder that flooding rivers could strand us for several months.

After a hurried breakfast the next morning, we began climbing on foot, hacking out a path with our machetes. Water captured on bushes and trees drenched us, and the wet ground made the going difficult. We reached a small, flat plateau about midway to the top by eleven o'clock. At first I thought this might be the site of a town, but a close inspection provided none of the classic signs of ancient inhabitation. No potsherds, no traces of land leveled by man, no unusual mounds or depressions. Above us, the mountain still loomed, lost into a cloud of mist. Momentarily we were tempted to abandon the rest of the climb.

"If we give up here, we'll always regret not knowing what's at the top," I said, and Jane agreed.

Luckily, the vegetation began to thin out, and we slogged upward with a little less physical difficulty, though the mist of the cloud limited our visibility. At one spot we had to penetrate some heavy, dank vegetation, thick with tree branches. Maximo was leading, Jane second, and I following. The trees hung low, and I spotted a snake just as it uncoiled from a branch. As I yelled a warning, Maximo's machete flashed, and the snake's head was sheared off. It was an enormous monster, as thick as a fat man's thigh and eighteen feet long. It was an anaconda, a sort of Latin American python that can crush the bones of a man's body.

Our nerves were shaken, but pressed by the urgency to complete this exploration and head back to civilization, we continued our climb, fighting to gain three feet only to slide back two on the slippery grass and undergrowth. Three hours later we crested the last obstacle of slimy, moss-covered rocks and reached the summit.

The mountaintop was flat, but only measured about 30 by 75 feet—hardly the site for a city.

Jane said, "Well, at least we've killed a legend. What do we do now, climb the other peak?"

While Jane struggled with a sputtering cook fire, I examined the mountaintop. There was no pottery, but at a depth of eighteen inches the earth was nearly blood-red in color. As a geologist, I recognized the possibility that the soil might contain a valuable mineral, and if so, we were standing on a mountain of it. I took samples in a plastic bag for later analysis.

Jane had produced another miracle: tuna fish and spaghetti with onions, peppers, and hot sauce. It was marvelous, although I suspect that with the bottle of homemade white rum that Anestro had given us before departing, anything would have tasted good.

Next morning, as the first glimmer of dawn lightened the misty cloud enveloping us, we started the descent. Emerging from that blinding cloud halfway down was a great relief. We hurried toward the hut for the warm dry clothes we had left there the day before. The hut was in sight, near a large outcropping of rocks, when we heard the growl from a crevice between two boulders. We froze. Without further warning, a huge jaguar sprang out. It stared at us for a moment, then with two quick steps leaped at us. My rifle came up by reflex and I fired, hitting the cat in mid-air. When it hit the ground, within three feet of us, it was dead.

Maximo examined the big cat. Then he lifted a back leg. *"Mujer,"* he added.

He had his knife out, looking at me. *"Yo quiero?"* he asked.

"Is he mad, Howard? Why does he want it?" Jane asked, moving closer to me.

"She's in her prime and her hide will bring a good price. But they usually don't attack people. Unless—"

There was a faint mewing, and a mini-copy of the big cat came out of the cave on uncertain feet. It was very young, looking for its mother. In an instant, Jane had it in her hands, stroking it. "I'll be your mother," she said softly. And she was, faithfully.

I made a crude nipple from a finger of a rubber glove that Jane produced from her duffle, and stretched it over a bottle full of milk and sugar. The kitten thrived. In a day it followed Jane everywhere, convinced she was its mother. Before we left it had progressed to raw meat and had grown alarmingly. It is now in Miami with friends who already have several unusual animals.

We changed to dry clothes while Maximo finished skinning the big cat, which we estimated to weigh three hundred pounds. It had been a difficult trip up and down the mountain, but at least Maximo had come out ahead. Besides the jaguar skin, he had the skin from the huge snake to take with him to market. All Jane and I had to show for the trip was a plastic bag of red dirt, which later analysis revealed to be only low-grade aluminum ore.

Back in the mountainside village of Atahualpa, the Indians told me of several mounds in the area. They said they were not far, and they were right. Within five miles I saw nine mounds, all large and man-made, and I filed them away mentally for the major expedition which we would mount after the rains.

The downpours had subsided somewhat, but I estimated we had only a few days before we would be trapped. Nevertheless, I decided to let Maximo take us to see if we could find the old man who was supposed to have stumbled upon eighty pounds of gold. Even back in 1971, when gold in the U.S. was only $35 an ounce, that would have amounted to over fifty thousand bucks. The gold might have been washed from graves during the river's flood stages, or a massive earthquake, which supposedly had sheared off the sides of mountains twenty years before, could have ruptured graves and spilled out treasure.

We went looking for the man, who was called Moifus Conforme. Fortunately, we were able to use the Land Rover for a part of the distance. There was a rough trail southeast of the Conquista River, but after three hours of bone-rattling driving, the trail ended at an Indian's house in a narrow valley. The setting was beautiful and peaceful; grassy slopes, grazing cattle, and a sparkling stream.

We left the car and bartered for horses and mules from the Indian. We loaded the metal detection gear and supplies on two mules. The going was still slow and rough. The horses stumbled over logs and boulders hidden in the thick bush. I began to have serious doubts about the sanity of this side trip, but I was determined to find out all I could about the area.

The sun was setting, and I had just about decided to make camp in the next clearing, when we broke out of the jungle and saw not only the Conquista River, but the rude house of Moifus Conforme. It was made of bamboo and thatch like all the others we had seen, though much larger, to accommodate the fourteen children and the innumerable grandchildren, great-grandchildren, and in-laws who were all living a peaceful, simple life out here beyond the reach of civilization.

Moifus Conforme was seventy-four years old, which is incredibly old for an Indian, but he was as active as a man of thirty-five. His face was creased with wrinkles and had the fine, soft, leathery look of well-kept, expensive boots. He was mystified but rather pleased at having such strange guests, and he insisted we stay at his house. He was a simple man, trusting and patient. The flock of children obviously loved and respected him.

I told Moifus the stories we had heard about the "river of gold." He left us, returning two minutes later with a four-inch figure of a man and a two-headed, entwined snake bracelet. Both pieces were solid gold and beautifully made, but I was not really surprised—I had noticed that food was being prepared and served in polychrome pottery that would enhance any museum's pre-Columbian collection.

Moifus told me that he had collected many gold objects in the Conquista River over the years and sold them to a dealer in the city of Chone, forty miles over the mountains to the southeast. When he proudly related that the dealer had paid full value in cash on the basis of weight, I did not have the heart to tell the old man that he had been cheated out of the much greater antiquity value.

As he described his finds, the earthquake theory grew more and more plausible to me. Soil erosion by rains and flooding waters alone should not have produced the artifacts in the locations he related. Innocently, Moifus had never given much thought to Inca burial mounds. He had simply found gold, which provided a slightly higher standard of living for his huge family. He was quite aware that many people had inhabited the valley in ancient times, but the custom of burial mounds had vanished with the early Indian cultures. The "cooking pots decorated with colored pictures" meant nothing to him other than a kitchen utensil. We went to bed with a soft rain falling, a reminder that our time was running out quickly.

Early the next morning, with Moifus as guide, we set out on the journey up the Conquista River to pinpoint the places where the old man had found his gold. With us were Maximo and two of Moifus' sons, who were old men in their own right. Our horses took us part of the way, but the rest of the trip was on foot through the densest jungle we had ever traveled. Huge elephant leaves blocked out the sun, turning the jungle into a streaming, perpetual twilight. Cruel vines and lianas wound around our legs and seemed to be trying to capture us. We sank into bucket-sized holes under the rotting vegetation, and we tripped over fallen tree trunks infested with stinging ants and spiders. It was impossible to stand up straight and see anything more than a foot away. We had to slash and chop our way with machetes.

As we moved slowly through the jungle, monkeys and a noisy variety of birds passed derogatory comments on our presence. From time to time, old Moifus pointed out a spot where he had found gold, but still he urged us on. When we finally arrived at the main location, I was dismayed. The site was at the base of hills that rose four or five hundred feet from the valley.

"Look at that maze of bush," I lamented. "We can't sink a spade in that dense growth, and it will take days to clear the land well enough even to work the detection equipment." I shook my head in despair. Here was a site that could yield a fortune, but we'd have to leave it as we found it.

Jane said, "All right, we'll just hire a work force two or three times the size we've been working with."

I looked at her in amazement. "They still couldn't clear it in time to allow us to get back to Quito by using the Land Rover. We'd have to travel over a hundred miles on horseback, fording rivers by hanging onto horse tails. You wouldn't like that."

She wouldn't give up. "Then there's only one other solution. We'll stay and work right through the rains and to hell with it."

Jane had a family and friends in England. Christmas time was approaching. She was being irrational. I was determined to leave and plan a proper expedition of the size justified by our findings, but I saw I wasn't getting through to her, so I let the subject drop.

As a diversion, I took the men and began searching a dry riverbed. I was looking for pottery that had not been moved downstream, pieces with sharp edges rather than those which were rounded by the eroding process of movement along a riverbed. We spotted one such area, and I guessed there was a burial ground not far up in the hills. A long, thin strip of hammered gold gave credence to my theory. Possibly it had been part of a necklace or bracelet.

As we moved from the riverbed and up the side of the hill, old Moifus came up beside me with excitement in his voice. This was the area in which he had found the heaviest gold pieces. We reached a plateau he had described, and it was everything he had indicated it would be. The area was littered with more potsherds than we had ever seen—plain ones, painted ones, even some completely intact. I stubbed my toe on a gold medallion which was sticking up out of the earth, and immediately performed a superficial sweep of the area with my electronic gear. I was overwhelmed with signals. Before nightfall, I had picked up a copper axe head, a gold nose ring, and a small gold disk, which were all only a few inches under the surface. It was easy to locate building sites by the raised rectangular shapes of earth.

As the size of the site became clear, and as I considered the sophistication of the pottery and other artifacts, I became convinced that this might well be the most important town site I had discovered to date—perhaps even larger and richer than Coaque. It seemed incredible that I could be standing on the ruins of a once-enormous settlement of which no record seemed to exist. However, the entire area is relatively unknown to archaeologists and historians. Since Pizarro's time, only Marshall Saville's 1908 expedition had explored the area, and that party stuck close to the coastline, twenty miles to the west of the Conquista River. The entire province of Manabi was apparently heavily populated by sophisticated cultures in pre-Columbian times, yet little or nothing is known of these civilizations.

We pitched a temporary camp, and the next day I had the men bush a small area. We found more treasure, but my joy of discovery was dampened by the realization that we must leave—the cloud formations indicated that the rains were almost upon us.

While we were working, old Moifus told me about an incident that had occurred about a year before. A treasure hunter from Colombia had discovered a large burial mound about seven miles south of the village of Santa Rosa, a town on our route back to Bahía de Caráquez. The Colombian had located a great deal of gold, but he had run into bad luck. One of his young Indian diggers had been killed when the soft earth of the mound slid into the deep hole in which he was digging. The local Indians were so incensed that they delivered the Colombian to the authorities, and his treasure was confiscated before he was thrown into jail for manslaughter. I decided I would have to check that site on the way out.

One of the hardest things I have ever done in my life was

to begin the hike out from old Moifus' site that afternoon. We had found gold easily, and had left many signals undug; we had only covered a small portion of the area. Only the thought of returning in June allowed me to place one foot in front of the other.

To make the trip out worse, Jane had begun to sulk. She had wanted to stay, and she was angry when I ignored her pleas. We hadn't been getting along well for weeks, and I was beginning to think it might be time for us to part company.

After a mildly hair-raising trip on trails now wet from the nightly showers, we reached Santa Rosa by late morning the next day. Santa Rosa is a small, primitive village of not more than twenty crude shacks, built on about eighty acres of land which had obviously been leveled by man. It was apparent that a much larger city had been there centuries before. Within the center of the present village we saw several burial mounds, and the local people reported that there were many more in the surrounding jungle.

Just as we had been told, we found a partially dug mound alongside a small trail seven miles south of Santa Rosa. We could see where the unfortunate Colombian excavator had worked. He had dug out about one-third of the mound, which was 100 feet long, 30 feet wide, and about 12 feet high. We set up a camp and began to explore. Within forty minutes our detector led us to a beautiful piece of gold, a five-inch-long hammered sheet stylized into a human figure. The small hole in the top indicated it was a pectoral, worn from a string around the neck.

By the end of the second day we had found seven important gold artifacts and several minor ones. The productivity of the site was prompting me to think about hiring a local crew and working right through the rainy season, but that night I gave up the idea.

It wasn't really that hard to give up. Jane and I had one hell of a battle after dinner. Our relationship had been growing more strained day by day, partly because of simple clashes of temperament resulting from the pressures of such close team-work, and partly for deeper problems I needn't go into. In any case, a storm had been brewing for some time, and that night it broke, violently.

Nasty comments were followed by nastier comments, and before I realized it she was yelling, "Oh, you bloody bastard!" and lunging for a folding camp stool. She whipped it at me like a cricket bat. As I reached out to fend off the blow, my finger caught in the folding mechanism of the chair. I let out a yelp of pain, and then looked down to find that the third finger of my left hand was bent at a very odd angle indeed, obviously broken. Half a bottle of whisky and the first-aid kit supplied the anesthetic and equipment required to set and splint the break. But I suspected that nothing could repair the damage that had been done to our personal relationship.

We packed out the next morning and drove all day, fording nine rapidly rising rivers, and we reached Bahía by sundown. In two more days we had driven to Quito and checked into the Hotel Intercontinental Quito, adjusting to civilization and protecting our hoard of gold. Our tempers had calmed enough for us to enjoy the hotel's swimming pool, bars, and casino. The next week seemed almost indecently luxurious to us after the past two months in the bush.

A couple of days before heading back to London, I decided to lay some groundwork for my return trip. I set up an appointment with Ecuador's Minister of Culture, Dr. Jorge Gomez.

The ministry building in Quito is one of those modern-day civil-servant structures designed to leech on the life of a civilization long since dead. The reception area is filled with displays of the national wealth while dozens of spoils-system flunkies collect unearned paychecks without giving one damn about the priceless treasures around them. I was ushered into Doctor Gomez's office, and I shook hands with the short, rather pleasant little man behind the large desk.

During one of my earlier ventures, I had persuaded a Miami printer to run off a bunch of business cards identifying me as a director of archaeology for a nonexistent Texas museum. Business cards always seem to impress Latin American bureaucrats. At the opening of the meeting with Gomez, I explained that I had been exploring the ruins of ancient Indian cultures. Then, after presenting my phony credentials, I gave him a photocopy of a map that Jane and I had drawn showing the location of ancient Coaque. I carefully avoided all mention of digging, and emphasized that we had been on an exploratory mission. The doctor nodded and seemed only politely interested in the map.

I explained that I wanted permission to return next June, after the rainy season, so that I could continue my explorations with the help of others interested in the history and culture of Inca civilizations. He continued nodding in a bored manner. Before he could fall asleep, I got to the point.

"I know that your ministry goes largely unappreciated," I said. "You must have many expenses for which you are not reimbursed by the government. As a token of my appreciation for the cultural aspects of your historic country, I would like to make a contribution to the work of your ministry." With that I handed him a stack of ten $50 bills, and suddenly he was not bored. His smile broadened, and the money vanished into a desk drawer.

"Señor, give me your address. I will mail you the necessary documents for your valuable exploration work."

We chatted for a few more minutes. He reconfirmed that he would expedite the necessary papers, and he also made it clear that it would be possible for me to make an even larger contribution if I really wanted to. I encouraged the impression that I would do so when I returned.

Jane and I carefully hid our gold in suit bags and arrived without incident in London on the morning of Christmas Eve.

We hustled around the city, trying to catch up on the spirit of the holiday, and that night we had a dozen or so friends in for a party. Jane had bought a small Christmas tree and set it up in my flat. She decorated it with $45,000 worth of pre-Columbian gold ornaments.

Just before New Year's Day, after Jane and I had had our inevitable final battle, I took off with the gold for Germany and sold our trove to a collector in Cologne. I sent Jane her share and tried to lose myself for a while. We had been together for six years, but too many things had come between us.

# 9 GIRLS IN BOOTS: COAQUE REVISITED

"We Spaniards suffer from a disease which
can be cured only with gold."

HERNANDO CORTEZ

By mid-February I was back in London, trying to pull together plans for a major expedition to Coaque. Help came from
quite an unexpected source.

Because we had broken up, Jane had tried to find some activity to occupy her time. That activity turned out to be a series
of magazine articles on our Coaque venture. The magazine
she selected was a national weekly publication called *Woman's
Own,* which has one of the largest readerships in England.

Because we had been so close, and because it was difficult to
make a clean break, especially since we had various joint holdings in property, I decided to help her pull the material together for her story—a woman's look at treasure hunting. As
research developed and editorial meetings progressed, someone
suggested I use the press as a means for assembling an expedition. It seemed like a good idea.

The *Evening Standard* is one of the national daily newspapers which enjoys the widest distribution throughout England. At my first meeting with the *Standard's* editors, we
agreed that the story should be printed. It ran as a five-part
series between March 5 and 10. In the last installment, the
final two paragraphs read as follows:

> In retrospect, it had been a hard but most rewarding
> experience. We had discovered the sites of three
> important Inca cities, more than 15 mounds which

209

could be burial mounds, and an untold number of
untouched tombs. There will be easily enough to occupy
us for the five months starting next June.

But most satisfying is the knowledge that we
discovered an area which may prove to be one of the
most important for archaeological study in South
America.

In a box under the concluding article, the editor ran a short
note to the reader. I didn't particularly approve of the headline
wording, but the editor thought it would be good for a laugh:
"WANTED: GIRLS IN BOOTS." It mentioned that I would take a
limited number of interested people on my next trip to Coaque.

Four hundred people were interested.

As a result of the addendum to the article, Jane became
angry as hell at me for trying to get girls for my next trip to
*our* sites. Remembering the difficulties with Jane on the previous trip, and realizing that our relationship had deteriorated
even further, I told her I could not consider taking her with me
on the new expedition. It was going to be difficult enough
supervising the care and feeding of twenty novices without
the distractions that our conflicts would cause. Perhaps I even
hoped that a few weeks' separation might serve to mend the
breaches in our relationship, but this was not to be.

Finally, I sent out a form letter to all the four hundred
people who had inquired about the expedition. In this letter,
I explained that I was planning to select a group of twenty
young women and men and stated that the price would be
£550, or about $1,400. The cost factor eliminated many of the
four hundred, and I rejected many of the applicants who sent
in unstable replies to my form letter. (Four girls addressed me
as "Dear Tarzan," and said they were prepared to go any place
with me and do anything. Some of the men requested photos
and addresses of the girls who would be going along.)

Out of the remaining letters, I picked eighty men and
women. I sent out a second, more detailed form letter request-
ing a great deal of specific, individual information.

I finally interviewed fifty people. Jane had at last accepted

210

the idea that she would not be going on the second expedition and helped conduct the interviews. She was able to answer many of the peculiar questions asked by the girls.


I was well aware of the enormity of the task I was undertaking. We were facing a rough trip into a remote and unexplored area, and for the safety of the whole group I wanted people who would follow every instruction. I deliberately picked young men and women with no prior experience in the jungle or even outdoor living. I felt they would be the most receptive to discipline.

The one exception was 56-year-old Bill Roberts, the only applicant had who experienced jungle living and a man who struck me as steady, calm, and capable. I was sure he would be a great asset to the project.

Two others I picked were not really young. Thirty-nine-year-old Don Mountford had been one of the competitors in a recent transatlantic air race. ("I read that story," he said, "and thought I'd be wasting my time applying, not being a girl in boots. But I wrote anyway.") Peter Johnson owns a small manufacturing company that specializes in electronic eavesdropping and surveillance equipment. One of his products is a powerful light-image magnifier called the "Star Bright," with which one can see up to a hundred and fifty yards away in the pitch black of night. I knew this would be a useful instrument for the military, and I had just read that the government of Ecuador had been overturned by a military junta, which would mean a new man in the Ministry of Culture. My friend Doctor Gomez, who had so cheerfully taken my $500 and who had failed to send the promised permit, could no longer help, but if I could ingratiate myself with the army, maybe I wouldn't have to worry about the new Minister of Culture. Peter was amenable to making his equipment available and promised to help me become the Ecuadorian army's best friend.

During the final interviews I told all applicants there must be no hanky-panky between the sexes. I knew that twenty inexperienced men and women in the jungle could furnish enough problems without conflicts arising between members of the opposite sex. I hoped my warning would keep things low-key as long as possible. Every one of the men unquestioningly agreed that relationships would be platonic, and only in Peter Johnson's eye did I detect a gleam. I made him my deputy expedition commander, hoping this mantle of responsibility would cause him to set a good example for the others.

Without question and with minimal investigation, all twenty of my co-adventurers paid over £220 to me upon committing themselves to the trip. I am authorized to place an F.R.G.S. after my name, as a Fellow of the Royal Geographical Society. The families of a few of the applicants did call the society, and there was a bit of stickiness at first, since the society's Board of Governors wondered whether I was using the society to promote a profitable venture for myself, but happily that confusion was quickly cleared up.

In stating the terms of our agreement, I stipulated that all members of the expedition would share equally in whatever the group found. I planned to stay on at Coaque for at least another two or three months after my twenty stalwarts returned to England, but the main task was to locate, confirm, and clear the burial ground I was seeking.

As preparations were moving along, I received a totally unexpected communication from as unlikely a source as I could imagine. An old boyhood friend, Bill Davidson, sent me a telegram from Galveston, Texas, informing me that he was on the beach, had no prospects, and if I had anything at all he could do, please to include him in.

I had no knowledge of what Bill had been up to or what sort of man he had developed into, but I sent him a telegram telling him to meet me in Miami three weeks hence if he wanted to go on a trip to Ecuador with me. I came to regret sending him that telegram.

At the Carlton Towers Hotel I gave a party for all my explorers and their families. At the party they paid me the balance of the money for the trip, and I handed out the air tickets, London to Quito and return. Altogether it was a pleasant party.

The *Evening Standard* printed a story about our imminent departure, and Jane again began to raise objections about not being included in the trip. But my finger was still painful and misshapen where she had broken it with the camp chair, and I was adamant. I was going to have a tough enough time just keeping the group alive and well.

Two weeks before the group was due to arrive at Quito, I hopped a plane for Jamaica to meet with Robin. I had tried to convince him by phone to come along to Coaque, and I thought maybe my physical presence would persuade him. But he was getting ready to finish up his latest book, and he wanted to be in Miami for the national nominating conventions. I packed up and met with Bill Davidson. He was waiting for me at the "low-profile" motel we had picked to avoid attracting attention. (I was still on guard against the Batres brothers and their local man.)

We bought camping equipment and two guns for Bill—a .270 rifle and a 12-gauge shotgun. My guns were in storage in Quito. We hopped a flight from Miami to Quito and checked into the Hotel Intercontinental Quito. I went alone to the Ministry of Culture to confirm the approval for my expedition. I had not been mailed the promised permission, but I knew that in Latin American bureaucracies *mañana* is a firm way of life and I hoped that the letter had merely been pigeonholed.

I was ushered into the minister's office to meet the man who had replaced Doctor Gomez. I was dismayed by the cold reception given to me by the new minister, Dr. José Samaniego. Before I could utter more than a few words of introduction, he said, "I have no interest in any deal you made with my predecessor, Señor Jennings." Pulling a file from the same desk drawer that had received my $500 contribution, he slid the folder toward me. It contained the articles from the London *Evening Standard* five months before. I felt a sinking sensation in my stomach. The Ecuadorian Embassy in London had probably sent the articles on to Quito.

213

Doctor Samaniego fixed me with a stern stare. "If these articles are to be taken seriously, you have illegally excavated and smuggled gold artifacts out of Ecuador." He paused, drumming long, bony fingers on his desk. "Is there any reason why I shouldn't have you arrested, Señor Jennings?"

"Doctor Samaniego," I began, thinking desperately, "surely you must know that newspapers exaggerate." I managed a confidential smile. "Some English papers will print anything to expand their circulation. That's what happened in this case. The whole series was very distressing to me. Except for the fact that I did discover Coaque, the rest of the story is pure fiction. Not a shred of truth. A pack of li—"

Samaniego broke in on my babbling. "Fiction or not, this kind of report will encourage any number of treasure hunters to go into the area."

This is the classic problem in the comparatively poorer countries of Central and South America: They don't want outsiders digging, but they don't have the money to do the digging themselves. Their biggest fear is that a mass invasion will descend on a particular spot, because they don't have the facilities to protect the wilderness areas from plunder. Well, to hell with it; I have never gone sneaking into a site which was being given proper, professional attention by archaeologists, but I had by-God found Coaque with no help from scholars and I was by-God going to dig it. If I could just get past this arrogant bureaucrat.

With all the theatrical sincerity I could muster, I said, "The purpose of my giving the information to the paper was to encourage archaeologists to study the rich heritage of your country. Do you feel that a secret report of my discoveries should have been circulated only to archaeologists? Had it not been for my years of research and the dangerous, costly expedition I made last year, Ecuador's Ministry of Culture wouldn't even know of the existence of Coaque. Are only archaeologists to be given credit for discoveries?"

"Señor Jennings," he said with finality, "I am not going to argue with you. You are not permitted to return to Coaque."

Well, I thought to myself, I have only one card left to play. Now's the time to throw it on the table.

"Doctor Samaniego," I said, "it should make interesting reading in the world press that you have refused entry into Ecuador to twenty innocent British subjects. Especially since this may be the largest group of British tourists ever to come to this country."

"I said nothing of refusing entry," he said quickly.

"You mean you will refuse them permission to travel freely within your country?" I pressed. "Is that it?"

"If you cable your group that they are not permitted to go to Coaque then they will not come," Doctor Samaniego said hopefully.

"It's too late to stop them, and I wouldn't do it anyway," I said, now feeling more in control of the situation.

"I see." He stared down at his desk, musing on the problem. "Come back in the morning and I will see what is to be done about you and this group."

"Fine," I said, standing up. *"Hasta mañana."*

I left the ministry and proceeded directly to the headquarters of the Ecuadorian army. In my briefcase, I had new brochures on the equipment Peter Johnson manufactures.

Army HQ was a large concrete block building, and I walked in past guards who were somewhat less sloppily attired than most soldiers of Latin American armies. After explaining the wares I wanted to demonstrate, I was shown into the office of the head procurement officer of the Army of Ecuador, a Colonel Lopez.

Colonel Lopez was intensely interested in "Star Bright" and the electronic surveillance equipment. His eyes gleamed at the thought of being able to bug the office of government officials and other army officers. I left Peter Johnson's brochures with the colonel and said that I was having the equipment sent over to Quito from London. I would be pleased to demonstrate it to the army and then, if they liked our devices, we could discuss a sale.

I went back to the hotel, where I found Bill Davidson at the

215

bar fast approaching inebriation. I left him there with the warning that he had better be in good shape for the reconnaissance trip we would be making to Coaque in two days.

That evening, I had dinner with Anita, my old friend at the bank. She was friendly, but my offer of a nightcap in my room was declined. That affair was over.

The following morning when I returned to the Ministry of Culture, Doctor Samaniego seemed to be just a fraction less hostile. The meeting was short and to the point. The twenty Britons of my group would be allowed to make an exploratory expedition to Coaque; however, we would be accompanied by a military escort to insure that no excavations were made and no artifacts removed. Well, this was better than nothing, I thought. Maybe we would be able to buy off the soldiers, especially if the military was pleased with Peter Johnson's equipment.

After taking leave of Doctor Samaniego, I went directly to Army HQ, where I found Colonel Lopez waiting for me with a General Rodrigues, Army Chief of Operations. He, too, was intensely interested in both the electronic surveillance equipment and the light magnification unit. I told the two officers that my group would be arriving from London in ten days, and that they would have the equipment with them. I had one of Peter Johnson's bugging units with me, so I gave the general and colonel a demonstration of how it worked.

On the way in to see them, I had planted the battery-powered transmitter—small enough to be concealed in the palm of my hand—under a pile of papers on a table in a reception area. Now I turned on my FM radio receiver to its highest frequency, and we were hearing the chatter of the clerks in the outer office. Slow smiles spread across their faces.

Before I left Army HQ I explained that I was taking my group to Coaque and would appreciate any assistance and co-operation that the military in Bahía de Caráquez could offer us. The general sent a teletype message to the commander of the Manabi Province, ordering that I be provided with any assistance necessary, even to the extent of loaning me any weapons I might need. The meeting had been cordial, and I headed back to the hotel with a feeling of confidence quite different from the day before. I spent the next day shopping for supplies, then poured Bill onto a flight from Quito to Bahía. His drinking was beginning to worry me.

In Bahía de Caráquez, I rented a Land Rover and searched for a bus I could charter to transport my expedition from Bahía to Coaque. The only vehicle I could find was an old chassis with seats mounted on an open wooden platform, but it would move twenty people.

With that problem solved, Bill and I got into the Land Rover and headed for Coaque. The rainy season should have ended in June, but rains were still falling in August that year, and the car sloshed through muddy trails with wheels spinning. As we splashed through precarious fordings of swollen rivers, I dreaded the thought of moving my group along that route in the rickety, open bus.

At Coaque the Indians greeted me warmly. I employed a young man called Atahualpa as boss-Indian and had him hire a crew to build a large camp. (I asked him about his name, but he was completely ignorant of its origin—or of anything about the Incas, for that matter.) Within two days they had constructed a comfortable camp with two large huts, one for the men and the other for the women. A dining facility was set up between the huts, a primitive shower was built nearby, and Camp Number One was ready for occupation. I left Bill to supervise final preparations and to guard the liquor locker, then headed back to Quito to await the group from London and to gather up the final supplies we would need. I chartered a DC-3 to fly my group to Bahía, but the difficulties of moving a large group into a wilderness were beginning to cause me concern.

I checked in with the Ministry of Culture. The minister was "not available," and I was kept standing around while an officious clerk shuffled papers. While standing there being rudely inspected over the rims of eyeglasses, I suddenly decided to try a new approach. I told the clerk my group would be gathering at the airport at nine in the morning. I had, in fact, arranged for the flight to take off at eight, and I hoped it

217

would take the Latin bureaucrats a while to catch up with us.

Next I visited my friend, Colonel Lopez, and told him that the electronics equipment would be in that afternoon. The colonel assigned a captain to go with me to the airport in order to expedite customs clearance, which was just what I'd been hoping for. In addition to the military gear, the group was also bringing along several metal detectors, and now I'd have no problem getting them in.

As the plane taxied into the parking area, I felt great. Then I watched the passengers descend the stairs, and I began to feel uneasy. I counted eleven girls and nine men. There were supposed to be ten and ten. I recognized Peter Johnson's secretary, but I couldn't spot Peter.

Suspecting trouble, I ran across the ramp toward the group. After hurrying through greetings and handshakes, I cornered Peter's secretary, Helen.

"What happened to Peter?" I asked.

"He couldn't make it at the last minute," she replied cheerfully. "He sent me in his place. His plant manager quit and he has to run it himself until he can get another manager."

"What about the electronic equipment?"

"He wasn't able to get it together," Helen said. "He was just too busy."

"Oh, for Christ's sake," I said, looking over at the waiting captain. "Didn't he know I was counting on the stuff?"

"I'm sorry. All I know is Peter couldn't come, and rather than waste the money he let me have the holiday."

"Now look, Helen," I whispered urgently, "we're in big trouble if the army thinks I've let them down on Star Bright and the other stuff. So I want you to tell the captain that you are Peter's secretary and that there was a factory problem. Tell him any by-God thing, but make it good, or there'll be no trip to Coaque. Try to convince him the devices are coming on the next plane."

"I'll do my best."

Fortunately, Helen did a superlative job on the young captain. Yes, of course, everything was on the way. It would appear any day now. The captain looked at me dubiously. I smiled reassuringly.

"Let's get these people and their things through customs, Captain," I suggested. "Then I'll find out exactly when your shipment is coming through."

With the captain's help we cleared the metal detectors through customs, then went to the hotel and checked the group in. They were so tired they went immediately to bed.

I took the captain up to my room and offered him a drink. He stiffly declined. "O.K., Captain. Until our electronic gear arrives, take this as a gift for the President." I handed him the bugging device which had so fascinated his superiors, and he took it gratefully. At least he would not be returning empty-handed. "We'll have the devices shipped directly to Colonel Lopez," I said as he was leaving.

I called Doctor Samaniego to confirm that our flight would take off promptly at nine the next morning. The military escort would be there, he assured me. Next, I rang Helen's room and told her to cable Peter Johnson to send the equipment immediately to the chief of army procurement in Quito. Then I collapsed.

By eight the following morning, the entire group was aboard the charter plane and the engines were warming up. The plane landed us at Bahía de Caráquez two hours later. I held my breath, but there were no angry officials waiting. Evidently confusion still reigned at Quito.

We transferred to the Land Rover and bus and started up the coast. The rains had finally stopped, so the river crossings were not as bad as I had feared. We reached the mouth of the Coaque River by late afternoon, and pitched camp in a clear area at the river's edge.

The next morning we began the most arduous part of the trip, the exhausting trek up to Camp Number One. The tortuous trail traveled through head-high grass crawling with ticks, and 90° heat scorched down as we climbed up to our camp directly on the equator. There was joking, but no whining, and the group, sweaty and bug-bitten, was still cheerful

219

as they flopped onto the benches on either side of the long dining table.

I announced we would have a briefing before dinner that evening, then gave them the afternoon off to settle in their quarters. I was fascinated by the speed and casual attitude with which the group began to establish their own social structure and living conditions. Their personalities and backgrounds were diverse, and their ages ranged from sixteen to fifty-six, but within hours, friendships formed and the huts were transformed into homes.

The first item I covered in my briefing concerned the military. I knew that the people in the Ministry of Culture would be upset by my trick, and I was sure they would try to dispatch the army to supervise our expedition. I also felt it was very unlikely that the soldiers would find us in the jungle. The *Evening Standard* newspaper articles were more concerned with adventure than factual details, so they would offer little in the way of guidance for any searchers. I was also playing a strong hunch: The Ecuadorian government would be reluctant to toss twenty British subjects into jail.

But, guarding against that possibility, I told the group: "If the military should descend on us, our Indians will give us an advance warning. Be sure that all artifacts are hidden and all digs are concealed. There is nothing they can do to us if they cannot prove that we have been digging up pottery or artifacts from grave sites." I paused to let that concept settle into their minds. Then I said, "Speaking of artifacts, may I remind you of the rules of the last and only other visitor to this city. Five hundred years ago, Francisco Pizarro ordered that any of his men caught taking gold or emeralds for himself would be executed. History records that none of his men ever tried to cheat the King's treasury." There was a nervous titter from the girls, but the point was made.

I outlined camp procedure: Washing of dirty clothes would be done by two Indian women whom I had hired for that purpose; morning and midday meals would be prepared by two Indian cooks; the evening meal would be produced by the group on a rotating basis. I would select the dig sites, then the group would divide up into small cadres to work with the Indian laborers. Patience was to be the paramount guideline— I did not want a priceless artifact damaged or destroyed by impatient hands or shovels. I demonstrated how to use a small garden trowel to work into the soil once the telltale grey dirt of a grave is spotted. Then I demonstrated how a soft paint brush is used to remove dirt from pottery or metal. I capped the meeting off with a talk on how to sift through grave debris and also how to squat and kneel in a dig to avoid cramps or backaches. After dinner they were reluctant to leave the table, so we had an impromptu party around a jug of the locally made white rum. Travel fatigue finally caught up with the group and they began slipping off to their hammocks. By nine o'clock, the camp was asleep.

The next morning began a day of learning how to survive in the jungle and avoid the many hazards of insects, snakes, and poisonous plant life. The use of a machete is essential in the jungle—it not only clears your path of clinging vegetation, but it is the quickest and most accurate weapon against snakes. The weight of a machete, however, can cause serious injury to the novice who misjudges the follow-through and swings the blade into his leg or foot.

I ordered the group to take malaria preventative pills each morning and drink only chlorinated or boiled water. Cuts, abrasions, or illnesses of any kind were to be reported to me immediately. A simple untreated scratch can quickly result in a major medical problem in the jungle. Except for trips to the toilet, the members of the group promised not to walk alone in the jungle.

That afternoon I conducted machete practice. Pretty soon my charges were cutting great swaths through the jungle. One girl was a former fencing enthusiast, and she soon became the women's machete-swinging champion. I gained confidence in my people.

I was particularly worried about poisonous snakes, so I spent some time teaching the group how to apply a tourniquet to

221

stop the poison from getting to the central nervous system. As always, I had a supply of anti-venom serum immediately at hand.

By the following morning we were ready to start the search for the boundaries and burial grounds of the ancient city. I assigned four Indians to watch for army search parties, then divided my group into four sections and sent them out to test holes along the ridge. Each of the test holes dug by the four parties was noted on a large map that Bill Roberts had made of the ridge.

After three days of digging into the ruins, I could see that the old city was much larger than I originally suspected. Evidence from the test holes, in the form of broken pottery, revealed that Coaque had been at least three-fourths of a mile long.

The work pattern was soon established. Each morning, the gold searchers doused their clothing with kerosene to help keep off the mosquitos, sand flies, horseticks, ants, and hornets. They returned each evening muddy and tired, but uncomplaining and still filled with enthusiasm. The pile of potsherds collected in the digging began to grow at one end of the communal dining-room table. In the evening, after showering and putting on clean dry clothing, we sat down to dine on venison, wild boar, or wild turkey—whatever I, as the great white hunter, could shoot that day. Afterward, there was the white rum and speculation about what would be recovered the following day.

It soon became clear that Bill Roberts, senior mentor of the group and Indian Army Veteran, was "the man who had everything." We called him the walking general store. If you wanted to hang something up, he had a ball of string. He had candles, pencils, rubbers, elastic bands, polyethylene bags. He had lighter fuel and flints, which even I had forgotten. He had safety pins, a compass and thermometer, torch batteries, flashcubes, nail-scissors, envelopes, cellophane tape, tissues, an inflatable ball, a chess set, needle and thread, and spare boot laces. "I had to pay a lot of excess baggage on the way out

222

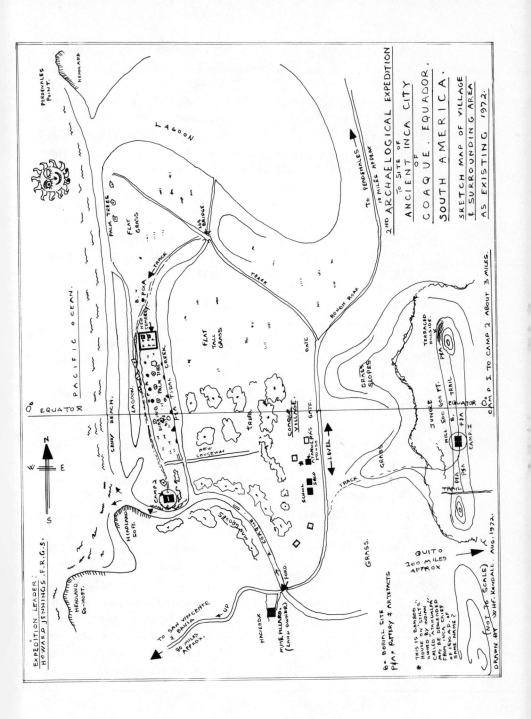

2nd ARCHAELOGICAL EXPEDITION
to SITE of
ANCIENT INCA CITY
of
COAQUE, EQUADOR,
SOUTH AMERICA.

SKETCH MAP OF VILLAGE
& SURROUNDING AREA
AS EXISTING 1972.

EXPEDITION LEADER:
HOWARD JENNINGS. F.R.G.S.

PENDRHALES POINT.

HEADLAND.

LAGOON

PACIFIC OCEAN

EQUATOR

PALM TREES

FLAT GRASS

LOG BRIDGE.

TRACK

B. CREEK PSA PSA

TRACK

ROUGH ROAD

To PENDRHALES
10 MILES APPROX

FLAT TALL GRASS

GATE

GRASS SLOPES

TERRACED HILLSIDE.

JUNGLE

MILL 500 600 FT.

B. EQUATOR TRAIL

PSA

TRAIL PSA CAMP I.

PSA PSA

TRAIL

TRACK

GRASS

LEVEL

Camp P I to Camp 2 about 3 miles.

SANDY BEACH.

LAGOON

DIGGING @ PALM TREE.

B. TIDAL CREEK.

TREES.

NEW CAUSEWAY

COAQUE VILLAGE.

WRANGLER'S GATE.

WRANGLER'S HOUSE

SHOP

SCHOOL

QUITO
200 MILES
APPROX

R. COAQUE

MANGROVES.

HEADLAND 50FT.

CAMP 2

FORD.

KING PILIARD. (LAND OWNER)

HACIENDA

To SAN VINCENTE & BANIA
80 MILES APPROX.

GRASS.

N
W   E
S

B = BURIAL SITE
PSA = POTTERY & ARTEFACTS

* THIS IS BAMBOO
HOUSE ON 'STILTS'
OWNED BY INDIAN
CALLED 'ATAHUALPA'
MAY BE DESCENDED
FROM INCA CHIEF
OF 1530 A.D. OF
SAME NAME?

(NOT TO SCALE)

DRAWN BY W.H. KENDALL. AUG. 1972.

here," Bill reminded the constant succession of borrowers who came to him for their needs.

Though the women were young, attractive, and many were openly receptive to the attentions of the men, I was surprised to see that the men showed little response. It became an almost sexless group in which brother-sister type relationships developed between the sexes, though there were indications that this was not to the liking of all of the women. The open-sided huts afforded no privacy for dressing or undressing, and often the girls lingered over the undressing process, with provocative looks toward the men's quarters. I suspected that night forays between the huts would be encouraged by the girls.

On the fourth day we found our first grave, and by using the metal detector we recovered the first gold of the expedition. It was only a small gold nose ring, but the group was as thrilled as if it had been a jewel-studded crown. The grave had been found only one hundred yards from the camp site on the side of the ridge below the leveled top. A second hole dug nearby confirmed that we had found a burial ground, for here, too, were the remains of a skeleton surrounded by the objects meant to accompany the deceased into the afterlife. There were beautifully painted pots and pottery figures in the second grave, but no gold or emeralds.

Francisco Pizarro had reported that the Indians in Coaque had possessed emeralds, and that he and his men had taken many of the precious green stones from them. We had found Coaque's burial ground and now were eager to prove Pizarro's report. If the Indians had emeralds in 1530, then the graves of their ancestors should contain them as well.

I assigned half of the group to continue exploration for another burial ground while the other half went to work excavating the nearby site. The men of the group worked with the Indian laborers, using picks and shovels in opening the graves, while the women carefully sifted through the remains within. I was amazed at the patience of the women as they sat almost unmoving, hour after hour, carefully examining and sifting the contents. With the help of the electronic equipment, several more gold objects were now added to our trove: a sun disk, a small death mask, beads, and some little animal figures.

Then, on the sixth day, we recovered the first emerald. It had been fashioned into a round bead by an Indian hundreds of years before, but it was a beautiful stone equal in quality to any of the emeralds I had seen from the Muzo Mines in Colombia. The fact that it had been pierced prevented it from being a gem, but I felt that its interest as an antiquity might make it equally valuable. Moreover, I was elated to have verified Pizarro's report.

One day, while excavations continued in the burial ground, I worked with the metal detectors along the old road that runs through the town. I found several copper bells, two copper axe heads, and a gold plaque, but my greatest prize was the recovery of two objects which proved, beyond doubt, that Pizarro had visited the site 443 years before. They were two parts of an iron horse bridle, and I knew the bridle could have only come from one of the twenty-six horses Pizarro had with him during his conquest of the Inca Empire. No white man had been on the hill since that time. Later, London experts confirmed that I had, indeed, unearthed a sixteenth-century Spanish bridle.

That same day, my joy of discovery was dampened by the responsibility of command: dysentery appeared. I needed about five minutes to realize that my old friend, Bill Davidson, had failed me miserably. He had been drinking too much and working too little during the entire venture, and now it was evident that he had even neglected the one important chore I had entrusted to him—he had forgotten to chlorinate the water. So within twenty-four hours, I was saddled with fourteen very sick people in the middle of a jungle. Then, without warning, the rains returned. They were not the heavy, torrential rains of winter, but the camp site turned to mud, hammocks became wet, blankets were sopping, and equipment was damaged. The rain persisted, and soon the trail up from the local village became so slippery that our pack burros could hardly make it uphill with the water for the shower tanks. But despite these trials, the group held together, and after a few days of medication and rest, most were back at work in the cold drizzle.

An interesting but annoying distraction now entered camp life—the mica monkeys. The tiny animals became braver and braver each night, leaping onto the hut roofs, disrupting games of chess, even entering the women's hut and rummaging around. They were amusing and impish little creatures, but I had to remind everyone that they could give a painful and possibly dangerous bite.

The horse-riding novices learned the hard way on scrawny local nags with harnesses held together by bits of old string. One of the girls was flattered to be offered a prize horse belonging to the señora, the local landowner, on the condition that the horse not be used for baggage; but the horse turned out to be terrified of snakes and would shy at any bit of twig in the grass, frequently throwing its rider to the ground.

Despite all the problems, everyone enjoyed the evenings. "You can forget everything," one of the young men used to say, "just sitting quietly and listening to the sounds of birds and crickets and monkeys." Some would wander off and tape sounds, others would watch the hummingbirds hovering, and a few would sit around the hurricane lamp, scribbling in diaries and notebooks or listening to Bill Davidson's guitar.

The swirling mist of the ever-present clouds enveloping the hill created an unhealthy climate, and consequently, more of the group took to their hammocks. Some of the group members were covered with insect bites and were obviously allergic to the bite of the many ticks in the jungle; others had high fevers with chest pains and bad coughs. They responded to treatment with antihistamines and antibiotics and were digging again in a few days, but they were soon replaced in the hammocks by others who had fallen ill. I spent most of my time on horseback, hunting in the early morning, then visiting the exploration parties and the excavating group, and then ministering to the ill in camp. It was maddening to look through the mist down to the white sand beach eight hundred feet below, where the sun shone every day.

At the end of two weeks, we had opened twenty-one graves and had recovered eighteen emeralds and eleven gold objects. We weren't much richer, but we had accomplished my primary objective of locating a massive burial ground. The one we were excavating probably contained several thousand graves.

The thought of leaving such a lucrative area was discouraging, but I had to consider the health and the safety of the group, many of whom were now ill with a variety of complaints. There was also the matter of Bill Davidson: His negligence in not chlorinating the water was still the reason for some of the sickness, and his drinking was becoming a constant irritant.

Actually, moving down to the sunny beach for the last two weeks wouldn't interfere with my overall plan. We would all have a pleasant rest, and after I had seen the group safely off from Quito to England I would return to Coaque. Then I would do a real job on the burial ground. I figured that with the metal detectors and Indian diggers, I could pick up several pieces of gold every day, and if I stayed in Coaque another six weeks, I could take more gold than I could smuggle out of Ecuador. In fact, my best course would be to acquire another Land Rover and drive out of Ecuador as I had a few years before.

My head Indian worker, Atahualpa, had brought me several highly polished potsherds which he said had washed out of the north bank of the Coaque River where it entered the sea. It turned out that there were human bones washing out with the pottery, so I felt there must be another burial ground near the river. The Indians also said that they found green stones in the river at certain times of the year, and I remembered Herrera's history, which I had read in the Archivo General de Indies at Seville, and his description of a gigantic emerald. It would make sense to explore the area around the river's mouth.

But first there was the matter of moving to attend to. I gave my Indians orders to build another camp for us two hundred yards from the Pacific Ocean, behind the magnificent white sand beach where the river empties into the sea.

Before we all moved to the lower camp, I had a quiet chat with Bill Davidson. We were still friends, but both of us realized that it would be the best thing for everyone if he absented himself on moving day. So, as we packed up and started down to the beach, Bill cheerfully said goodbye to the group, telling them he was going to do some deep-sea fishing down south. At the bottom of the hill, he made for the Indian village, where the vehicle which delivered supplies to us from Bahía de Caráquez would return him to civilization.

The difference in weather down at the beach was incredible, considering that we had moved no more than three miles. Here the sun was shining brightly and the cooling breeze blowing across the ocean created a near-perfect climate.

Again, I had specified two buildings, assuming that the group was content with that arrangement. But before we'd moved in, two of the girls approached me with the suggestion that we drop the sex segregation. "Most of the girls would like to sleep in the same hut as the men," one of them said. "Do you have any objection if a vote is taken?"

I had no objection, but I did insist that it be unanimous. "If any member of the group objects to this arrangement, then consider it vetoed," I said.

An hour later, when everyone was assembled, I put the question to them, and much to my surprise there was not one objection to the plan. Within minutes the men and women were dispersed throughout the two huts. Since there were more women than men, many of the men slept with a woman in hammocks on either side. My own hammock, covered over with a plastic sheet, was strung up thirty yards from the camp, since I prefer sleeping in the open.

On our first evening in the lower camp, one of the men spoke these words into his portable tape recorder as he sat on a log alone, looking out over the vast Pacific Ocean:

"Today we have moved camp from the jungle to the Pacific

Coast, where the River Coaque spills out into the sea. Well, we've got the most perfect camping site you could imagine—great rollers coming from the Pacific. The sun is just going into dusk. We've had some pretty miserable weather up in the jungle, raining, sticky, rather English weather really. Here it's different. The temperature is up to ninety degrees, but the cool stream of the Humboldt Current helps to cool it down, so it's cool enough to sleep under blankets at night. There's a lot of driftwood on the shore . . . there are half a dozen cows strolling here, though God knows what they eat."

In the healthy, sunny environment, the insect bites healed quickly and the fevers disappeared. Soon everyone was back to work with enthusiasm. Examination of the river bank confirmed that here indeed was another burial site. Little digging was required before we began to encounter whole pots and pottery figures. I was somewhat disappointed in the quality of the artifacts, since they did not seem to represent a culture as sophisticated as that of the inhabitants of Coaque. I couldn't help looking up to the cloud-covered hill we had left and planning my return for more of the riches I knew were there.

Now that we were down at sea level and close to the Indian village, the group had the opportunity to get to know the natives and study their living style.

"These are marvelous people," one member said into his tape recorder. "They live on next to nothing, but they're very happy, smiling, their children well looked after, and always dressed in their best to come to camp. They seemed thrilled to have us there. We took lots of photographs of them, toothily smiling five-foot-nothing men in straw hats and checked shirts, delighted to be in the picture: Pacifico, Segundo, Doloroso, Banjo, super names."

The natives spoke no English, but one girl in our party was a graduate in Spanish of Trinity, Dublin and she was constantly called upon to translate. She reported that a very classy Spanish is spoken there. "I do try to talk to the women," she told me, "but really, there is very little we can say to each other. None of them has ever had any job or contact outside her home."

Among the natives were two redheaded children with pale, freckled faces, quite possibly further proof of Pizarro's stay at Coaque. There had been parties of explorers since the conquistadors, but no Caucasians had lived among the Indians since Pizarro. The genes producing the redheads could have been influenced by the Spanish adventurers four centuries ago.

I was still convinced that somewhere in the vicinity was located a fabulous emerald source. I never ceased asking about the green stones. The Indians had so little interest in them that it was hard for them to remember specific instances of seeing the stones, but I did learn that they appeared immediately after the torrential rains of the wet season. These were not the emerald beads washed out of the graves; they were stones direct from the source. By elaborate questioning, I ascertained that some of the emeralds were still attached to their shale matrix. And all descriptions indicated that some were the size of the eggs laid by the hens.

What a fabulous discovery was waiting to be made! I prayed that the special equipment from Peter Johnson had arrived while we were out here in Coaque. I expected difficulties with the Minister of Culture, and I knew I would need the support of the military junta to find and claim the source of these emeralds, which could be cut into five-, six-, perhaps even ten-carat gems. All the gold in all the graves in Latin America paled in significance beside the vast wealth that lay in the ground somewhere up river, perhaps within ten to fifteen miles of our camp.

Meanwhile, the digging continued. Fifty test holes were sunk to try to locate burial grounds in the fifteen or twenty acres along the bank of the river. Several skeletons were found and some rather sophisticated artifacts recovered, but we located neither gold nor emeralds.

With only a week to go before we would have to pack up and return to Bahía de Caráquez, I sent some of the sharpest searchers up river to make one major effort at locating the source of the emeralds. If I could only get some idea of where to look, perhaps when I returned I could actually discover the emerald lode and stake out a claim. I patrolled up and down the river as the group probed and dug, but we didn't find a single emerald in the riverbed.

But I was not—and am not—discouraged. Those emeralds are there! If I could just return, with some geologists and a crew of Indians, for a more extensive search between August and December, when the river is at its lowest. . . . I have yet to meet an Indian along the Coaque River who has not seen the emeralds, but since they attach no importance to the green stones, they merely let them wash out into the ocean. Someday . . .

The two weeks by the ocean produced a substantial pile of pottery, utensils, and figures, but only a few gold trinkets. Every member of the group expressed a desire to remain, but it was time to pack them out and send them back to England. I announced we would strike camp.

While the group was packing, I removed the spare tire from the Land Rover and carefully taped our gold objects and emeralds inside the casing. I was anticipating some trouble from the Ministry of Culture.

I called a meeting of the group and supervised the distribution of pottery artifacts among the members. I explained that we might be met by the authorities, but that everyone would be quite safe if no one admitted to digging. We agreed to claim that all of the pottery had been purchased from the Indians living along the Coaque River. Export of the pieces could hardly be denied.

The trip down from Coaque was exhausting. There had been little rain by the coastline, and dust covered us as we drove along the bone-shaking route. I was not surprised when we were met by four policemen and six soldiers at the outskirts of Bahía de Caráquez. We were arrested immediately and taken to the police station in the center of town. Predictably, Doctor Samaniego from the Ministry of Culture was there to greet us. He was in a foul mood. He had made two attempts to find us in the jungle, but his men couldn't even find the Coaque River.

"Well, Señor Jennings, what do you have to say?" he asked.

"I hope you have sufficient grounds for arresting my group," I said angrily.

"Let us call it a slight detention, Señor Jennings." Then, after a deliberate pause to gaze at the group, "Until we have made a thorough search of you and your people."

He moved away from me and addressed the group: "I want you nice English people to understand that it is Señor Jennings who has put you in this trouble," he told them. "We do not wish to disturb your holiday here, but if we find any valuables which you have dug up, Señor Jennings will not be returning to London with you."

Their painstaking search lasted for seven hours. Doctor Samaniego and an assistant made a list describing in detail each artifact as it was produced from the baggage. The same question was asked as each member brought his baggage forward for inspection. "Did you do any digging in the jungle?" The reply was always the same: "No, I bought my pottery from the Indians."

At the end of the search, Doctor Samaniego was obviously disconcerted. He also began to appear somewhat embarrassed. He had been responsible for mounting an operation that had netted nothing more interesting than pottery artifacts, and he could not even prove that we had not purchased those. The Land Rover, with the spare tire mounted prominently on the hood, stood outside. It was not searched.

When the last member had been searched and released with an apology, I said to Doctor Samaniego, "I'm sorry to have caused you all this trouble; however, we have been inconvenienced as well. I'd like to ask a favor."

"What is it?"

"So that we don't have this same problem at the airport in

Quito when we leave for England, I'd like a permit from you to export the artifacts you have examined."

"All right," he said irritably. "I'll have it for you in the morning before your plane leaves."

The primitive plumbing in the small local hotel made no provision for baths or showers, but by now the group was too tired to care. We were all asleep within minutes, caked with dirt. I was up before sunup next morning to remove the gold and emeralds from the tire on the Land Rover and pack them into my luggage. Now I was ready to head for Quito.

Our prearranged, chartered plane arrived on time in the morning. Doctor Samaniego handed me the export permit as I was boarding.

"Goodbye," I said to him. "I hope you'll have a different perspective on this affair someday and realize that what I found at Coaque is more important than how I found it."

"Maybe you are right." There was an air of defeat about him. *"Adiós, Señor Jennings."*

I am sure that the immaculate Hotel Intercontinental Quito had never seen the arrival of such a tattered, dirty group as ours. In obvious confusion, the desk clerk called the manager, whom I had known so well from other trips.

"Welcome back," the manager said as he came out of his office. "You look as if you've been in the center of a disaster." I laughed and nodded. "I'm sure you would prefer to register after you have changed," he suggested diplomatically.

I dispatched the group to their assigned rooms, then turned back. "I don't suppose anyone has been asking for me?" I asked the manager.

He smiled, remembering that incident from an earlier trip, when the Batres brothers had sent me a visitor. "I think you must have convinced someone that vengeance doesn't pay."

As we all gathered for drinks before dinner that night, I doubt if anyone could have recognized us as the group that had arrived earlier in the afternoon. My group of adventurers had returned to civilization. The girls had visited the hotel

233

beauty salon, and most of them had on nail polish for the first time in a month. Some of the men had grown beards in the jungle, but they were now shaved and neatly dressed in suits, ready for a night in the hotel casino.

Peter Johnson's secretary and I spent several hours checking with various air-freight operations at the airport. There was no indication that Peter had shipped the electronics samples for the army.

"Your boss really screwed me this time," I said wearily. I had hoped to go back to Coaque and dig up a huge load of gold—now, any such plan was out of the question. The army would not offer any assistance; I had failed them. My only hope was to stick close to the group and to exit with them. They were now *my* only protection. I was convinced that if I allowed those Englishmen on that plane without me, Doctor Samaniego would have me in the pokey on some charge or another within minutes.

The next morning I shepherded my charges out to the airport and checked them in for the flight to London. I collected together all of the gold and presented it to the customs inspector, along with the export permit from Doctor Samaniego. There was a bit of confusion because the permit identified no gold artifacts, but the Minister of Culture was an important man and his name carried weight. We made it out of Ecuador with everything.

By mutual consent, we entrusted the valuables to one of the girls in the group, and at the time of this writing the pieces are at Parke-Bernet's in New York awaiting auction. We are all eager to learn what sort of prices the ancient emerald beads will bring, since none such as these have ever appeared at auction before. I'm sure there will be no major hesitation on the part of the museums to bid on the stones which were "plundered" from graves and "smuggled" out of the country of origin. As usual, they'll just look the other way as they raise their hands to bid.

We all arrived in London safely and rather sadly took our leave of each other. We did get back together for a post-expedition party some time later, though, and they presented me with a lovely silver cigarette case. I guess they had forgotten the tick bites and the dysentery and the cold rain. But I haven't forgotten, and I never will. I still think about those untouched burial mounds in ancient Coaque, and I often daydream about that mysterious source of emeralds up the Coaque River. But I am also a practical man, and I realize that other people will have to attack those treasures, at least until there is another revolution in Ecuador and I can possibly figure out how to buy off a new Minister of Culture. I sure as hell can't go back there as long as Doctor Samaniego is in office.

# Afterword ─────────

## THE TREASURE HUNTER

That, with many thanks to Robin, brings my personal narrative up-to-date. As you will have gathered, several chapters—the best ones, I hope—remain to be written. But first I shall have to live them. For the present, I'd like to close this part of my story with a few words about what it means to be a treasure hunter—why I do it, how I do it, and what I plan to do next.

Perhaps the very first point I should make is that I don't flatter myself that I do things other people couldn't do. If there is anything special about the life I lead, it consists primarily in one thing: choice. To be a treasure hunter, you have only to *want* to be a treasure hunter. The rest—the skills, the luck, the adventures, the discoveries, and, yes, the disappointments—will follow in due course. But first you must choose.

If you think you would like to be a treasure hunter but aren't sure your wife would approve, or doubt that you could afford to take so long away from your job, or are afraid that, as a woman, you might be compromising your femininity, then in effect you have already made your choice. Because treasure hunting isn't so much a vocation as it is a life style. It isn't enough just to want treasure, or even to want to hunt for treasure. You have to want *all* the things that go along with treasure hunting: utter freedom, a certain rootlessness, a willingness to take great risks, a readiness to stretch your capacities to their limits, an aceptance of self-discipline, and much, much more. If your primary motive in wanting to be a treasure hunter is to get rich, you are better advised to go to work for a large corporation.

Sometimes people ask me quite directly how much money I've made on this or that venture. I always find this reasonable

237

question difficult to answer. At a cocktail party it is easy to impress people with figures—$27,000 on this trip or $51,000 on another—but if one examines those figures from the point of view of simple investment, considering the capital in, the profit out, and the return on the time and money invested, the numbers can be much less impressive. A C.P.A. would look at such things as "tied-up capital" (those monies that are earning no interest) or "continuing overhead factors" (such as the cost of maintaining a full-time flat in London) and might give a depressing verdict on treasure hunting as a career. If you have an accountant's mind, you really shouldn't consider spending your life in search of lost gold.

But, for me, the life of the treasure hunter brings intangible rewards that cannot be measured on a profit and loss statement: the thrill of the hunt and the pride of being your own man in a world where personal freedom seems to shrink, and governmental interference to expand, with each passing year. Millions of people in the world have sacrificed their individual choice of behavior in exchange for third-class "cradle-to-grave" security. Security is something the treasure hunter does not have. In fact, it is precisely the thing he does not want. I think *living*—that vivid sense of being really alive—must be equated with challenge. And challenge is the denial of security.

There are, of course, many sorts of challenge that men can face. There are still remote frontiers waiting for man to attack, even if they are becoming more and more difficult to find. And for those so inclined, there are still places left in the world where fortunes wait to be found, even if it becomes increasingly difficult to hold on to them.

Your neighborhood library is probably full of books on lost treasure, legendary gold mines, sunken galleons, rivers where gold and precious stones may be found by the bushel. Many of these stories are folklore worth no more than a passing daydream. But some are authentic, and they have captured the imaginations—and sometimes even the time, money, and sweat—of many substantial citizens. Among those who have tackled the mysterious "money pit" of Oak Island was a future president

238

of the United States, Franklin D. Roosevelt. And in the very recent past, one legendary treasure cache has involved an Attorney General, a Senate committee, New Mexico's governor, the Army, the Air Force, several Congressmen, and platoons of lawyers, including such familiar names as F. Lee Bailey and John Dean. This gold hoard, supposedly totaling several million dollars, is believed to be hidden in caverns on Victoria Peak in the San Andres Mountains of New Mexico, about 25 miles from Las Cruces. Victoria Peak is on land belonging to the White Sands Missile Range; and so far the Army has succeeded in keeping treasure hunters out, despite law suits and pleas at the highest levels of government.

Many governments treat the idea of buried or sunken treasure with utmost seriousness, as I've pointed out elsewhere. Some discourage treasure hunting; others license hunters and claim a share of whatever is found; all of them know quite well that vast fortunes remain undiscovered in all the oceans and lands of this planet. My own ventures into the business of treasure hunting happen to have centered mainly on the lost cities of the Inca and pre-Inca cultures in the area from the Yucatán down through central Peru. Here and elsewhere there are many rich sites still unexplored. I'll mention some of these later in this chapter. But first I'd like to return to the theme of challenge for a moment. The rigors that I faced in quest of treasure were, for the most part, neither trivial nor terrible. They were simply problems of various magnitudes that had to be confronted with as much intelligence and technique as I could supply.

Survival in the hostile jungle, for example, is not quite like camping out in a national park, but many of the dangers have been exaggerated. The large jungle animals rarely attack humans, except in defense of their young, and the mighty anaconda, bone-crushing villain of the jungle films, is generally much too lazy to attack anything. (This huge snake spends most of its time dozing on tree limbs, and the greatest danger is that one can mistake a sleeping snake for a branch and whack at it with a machete. A wounded anaconda can deliver a nasty bite, and although these snakes have no venom, the danger of infection is high.) Jaguars and pumas stay clear of humans, though I found the latter were braver about exploring camps at night and were a threat to chickens and some supplies.

The great hairy tarantulas, though alarming to look at and surprisingly difficult to kill, are not really very dangerous. They aren't poisonous, though their bite can also cause infection. Mosquitoes can be bothersome in some areas, but a combination of repellent and kerosene will usually keep them at bay. Various flies and spiders can be moderately annoying, but the kerosene deters them as well. As for leeches, well-remembered from Humphrey Bogart's nightmarish experience in *The African Queen*, I can only say that I have never yet encountered one, and would prefer to keep it that way.

By far the most bothersome of all jungle creatures are the ticks. Not the larger ones, familiar in several parts of the United States and easily removed, but tiny, almost invisible ones similar to the things called chiggers in my Texas childhood. Repellents have little effect on these tiny grass ticks, and it is all too easy to pick up a hundred of them just by walking through a few yards of high grass. The itchy welts raised by their bites are bad enough, but far more serious is the allergic reaction produced by large doses of their poison in the bloodstream. This reaction can take the form of fevers, chest pains, and coughing —much like a case of flu—and can even cause hallucinations. All the Indians I met seemed totally immune to these pests, though they disliked the sensation of ticks crawling about on their skins and were adept at finding and removing attackers I could not even see.

The greatest hazards in the bush are the smaller, venomous snakes and the constant dangers of infection. For this reason, I have always paid more attention to medical supplies than to food. One can eat local fish and game or be fed by local natives, but one cannot pop into the local hospital hundreds of miles from civilization. Infections must be treated and wounds must be tended if one is to survive, and I would rather have a good supply of antibiotics than a truckload of dehydrated foods.

I always carry a generous supply of bandages, disinfectants, and broad-spectrum antibiotics, as well as the ever-useful penicillin. I also carry a supply of needles and sutures, and a good local anesthetic. In the bush, serious wounds are common, and they must be tended without benefit of physicians. I have become fairly good at stitching up machete wounds and have even consulted doctors to improve my technique.

For the ever-present threat of snakebite, I carry the Wyeth Snakebite Kit. The serum is effective for most venom, but it is so potent that its effects must be moderated by other drugs, such as the antihistamine benedryl. And for the prevention of dysentery (and worse), I carry a generous supply of chlorine for the drinking water, as well as anti-amoebic medicines in case something gets past the chlorine. (My rule of thumb for use of chlorine is simple: If the water still tastes good, you need more chlorine.)

Outfitting an expedition can be as complicated as you wish to make it, and I have always felt that "traveling light" was good practice for boy scouts but a poor idea on a lengthy trek into the bush. Still, much fancy camping equipment can be left behind, and expensive jungle clothing (the stuff sold in sporting goods stores or through catalogs) is usually less practical than simple work clothes. I favor rough cotton trousers and short-sleeved shirts, calf-length soft-leather boots with rough rubber soles, and cotton socks that extend above the boot tops, so the trouser bottoms may be stuffed inside. This seam between trousers and socks should be doused with kerosene to keep bugs out, as should the waist band and any other openings in the clothing. (Avoid rubber boots. Nothing will keep your feet dry in the jungle, and rubber is too hot. The main purpose of boots is to protect against snakebite.)

The one absolutely essential tool for travel in the bush is a good machete. The best I have ever owned were made by a firm called Collins, and they are made from the tempered steel of old railroad rails. They are heavy and will keep a good edge, as a good machete must do, but the art of wielding one without disaster requires considerable practice. Even when one has grown accustomed to the heft and balance, there is still the problem of accurately gauging the density and resistance of the thing one is trying to cut. Many experienced hands have whacked at a vine, expecting resistance, and found that it cut like butter with the heavy blade continuing down, possibly into a foot or ankle.

The machete's uses are many, from clearing away jungle growth to chopping firewood to fighting off snakes. It is the favorite "equalizer" of the Indians of Central America, and one rarely meets an Indian over thirty who doesn't bear at least one impressive scar. I have always carried guns in the bush—my favorite .30.30 Winchester lever-action rifle for hunting game, and my .38 Smith & Wesson for show—but I would far rather have a machete at hand than a gun when confronting a snake. Pistols have no real use in the bush, but they do have a certain psychological value. Often after entering an unfamiliar native village, I have made a show of taking target practice with the .38, and I've noticed that the gun was viewed with some respect after it had knocked off a row of bottles or rocks.

There are many tricks for smuggling guns into countries (handguns can be disassembled and hidden in razor kits, rifles and shotguns can be broken down and hidden in golf bags or even umbrellas), but I have found it simpler to buy used weapons once I have arrived. Rifles for hunting can usually be shipped in without difficulty, and permits can be obtained from the consulate before you go if you're in doubt. And weapons can be left behind when you leave, especially if you're trying to bring out far more valuable gold artifacts.

Finally, there is the matter of accommodations, far from the trusty Holiday Inn. I have used sleeping bags in cold climates, but over the years I've found I prefer a small, one-man tent with a kerosene lantern for added heat. When on the move in the jungle, with no time to pitch camp, I simply use a hammock slung between two trees, with another line strung above, over which I drape a plastic sheet. This keeps off crawling bugs and other creatures that move in trees at night, and (unlike mosquito netting) it also keeps one dry. The upper line is also used for hanging up clothes and boots (upside down) to protect them from invasion by snakes or other unpleasant creatures. This line, and the ones holding the hammock, should be soaked liberally in kerosene, to keep insects from crossing it.

For a more permanent camp, I have always preferred to build a sod hut much like the one my grandparents used on the Oklahoma prairie. It is a simple structure of branches covered with sod, over a shallow excavation. I've found these huts dry, warm, and reasonably bug-free, and I've always had a rather sentimental feeling about them, as if they were a family tradition.

Most of the other things I include in my expedition kit are either items familiar to all experienced campers, or equipment that is specifically relevant to recovering treasure. One should, of course, carry emergency food rations (canned goods, dried meat, powdered eggs, and milk) and whatever libations may be required for one's peace of mind. Most of the specific tools of the treasure-hunter's trade—probes, small trowels, brushes, and spades—aren't particularly exotic and have been well-covered elsewhere throughout the book. Metal detectors, on the other hand, are such complex machines that I cannot adequately begin to describe them here. I have tried most of the leading types at one time or another: Beat Frequency (B.F.O.), Induction Balance (I.B.), Transmit-Receive (T.R.), and Pulse Induction (P.I.). All have their advantages and disadvantages. For good depth penetration, I have often used the well-known Fisher M-Scope equipment, but for all-round stability, sensitivity, and versatility, I lean toward the excellent P.I. equipment made by Pulse Induction Ltd., of No. 3 Old Pye Street in London. With their interchangeable search heads, these handy machines can be used both for broad surveying and pinpoint locating.

One's means of transportation will depend on the terrain; on the availability of machines, animals, fuel, and food; on the purpose of the trip; and often on one's ingenuity. The Land Rover (or other rugged four-wheel drive vehicle) is best for long trips where trails or roads exist, and horses can usually be rented or bought even in remote areas, with mules or burros for

243

transporting food and equipment. It is usually advisable to pick the animal that is indigenous to the region, because any animal will forage more efficiently on its home ground. When traveling in the high Andes, for instance, one should arrange to switch to the rugged little mountain ponies that can forage on the barren land between 10,000 feet and the snow line far better than animals from the lower areas. These tough little animals can survive on forage alone, though I've found that they perform better if their natural diet is supplemented with occasional portions of grain. The grain I used was the same food the Indians used as their staple, cooked up in batches once a day into a kind of stew. The Indians seemed perfectly able and content to survive on this grain alone, though they were delighted to add any game I could provide to the daily stew pot.

Living with Indians, whether in their villages or on the trail, has always been a happy time for me. They have always proven cooperative and friendly, after the initial wariness shown any stranger. Often, in fact, their very trust and warmth sometimes became a problem. I had to be careful not to become too important to the life of a village while I lived there, because the Indians had a tendency to become dependent on my medical treatment, advice, impartiality in settling personal disputes, and, to be sure, money. I was often the only source of money the Indians had ever had, and this alone gave me a position of importance I had to resist, for my own good as well as theirs.

No matter how much I enjoyed village life and Indian hospitality, I learned that it was necessary to impose rather strict discipline in the work camps. The Indians often approached a task with the notion that a whole lifetime was available in which to do it, and I found I had to establish precise working hours and pay scales, and to maintain them religiously. Often, to drive the lesson home, I would deliberately over-hire at the outset so I could make a show of discharging the least productive workers.

If this seems harsh, I can only answer that the jungle is not an easy place in which to survive, much less to accomplish a hazardous and arduous task. The jungle is anarchy. The only way to cope with it is by confronting it with order and discipline. If you can impose your order on the jungle, you will survive. If it succeeds in imposing its anarchy on you, it will kill you.

These few things I have said about living and working in the wilderness represent purely personal approaches to the problem. Possibly other explorers, more experienced than I, do things differently. But perhaps I have said enough to indicate that my technique is adequate to my purpose. And my purpose is . . . well, let's talk about that.

Where exactly can treasure still be found? The answer, really, is *everywhere*. The world is literally filled with treasures of one sort or another, from buried antiquities such as I've hunted to the legendary hoards of the buccaneers about which so much has been written.

I'm convinced, from years of research, that many of the familiar legends contain a large measure of truth. Take the treasure of Vigo Bay, for example. Certainly there was a huge naval battle at Vigo Bay, off the Spanish Coast, in 1702. And history records that at least fourteen Spanish galleons went down there with an enormous treasure aboard, estimated at close to $140,000,000 in gold and silver. Many salvage attempts have been made and some small portions of treasure have been recovered. The rest still lies at the bottom of Vigo Bay. But there it will probably remain. Even though magnetometers might be able to pinpoint metal—even beneath the forty feet of mud that probably covers the galleons by now—the detectors could not distinguish between relatively worthless cannons and gold bullion. And even if a device were sophisticated enough to make the distinction, the dredging operation would be so massive as to require huge investments in equipment, manpower, and cash.

Similarly, the legends of the missing ransom that was sent to buy Atahualpa's freedom are quite likely true. The most famous of these concerns the one supposedly collected by Ruminavi, an Inca sub-chief who ruled the northern city of Quito. Legend has it that this huge golden treasure was collected for transport

245

south to Cajamarca, but that news of Atahualpa's execution arrived before the caravan departed. When Ruminavi heard of the man-god's murder and of the approach of the Spaniard Benalcázar with armed soldiers, he supposedly sent the treasure into the forbidding Llanganati mountain region, where it disappeared. Years later, a Spanish soldier named Valverde was supposed to have found—or been led to—part of the treasure, and versions of his "derrotero" describing the location are still in the Archivo General de Indies in Seville. Unfortunately, the directions lack precision. Even so, I have known people in Quito who believe the treasure can be found and who have devoted vast amounts of time and effort to the task.

One of the most famous of all Inca treasure troves is the bottom of Lake Titicaca, south of Cuzco in central Peru. The huge gold sun-mirror from the temple was supposed to have been submerged there to keep it from Spanish hands, and there are some legends that even suggest that the great gold chain from the square at Cuzco might also have been sunk in the waters of this volcanic lake. (The mirror and the huge chain did undoubtedly exist, and neither has ever been found, so who is to say the legends lie?) In addition, many gold sacrifices were hurled into the lake to appease the angry gods, and I have no doubt they remain there to this day, buried deep in the laval mud. Many dives have been made, and a few objects have been brought up. But most attempts have ended in failure, and it is generally conceded now that the only way to get at the gold would involve draining the lake and chopping away at the cement-like mud, which becomes nearly impenetrable as it dries. Possible, yes; but far too expensive for a hunter of limited means, and probably unprofitable for anyone.

One could list the legendary treasures forever, from the sacred wells of Chichen-Itza to that most curious treasure site of all, the amazing "money pit" of Oak Island, Nova Scotia. There are treasure galleons by the hundred on the floor of the Caribbean, and there really are rivers littered with gold and emeralds. I have written of the areas I have explored and the things I have found, and I shall not attempt to speculate on the many sites of which I have little or no first-hand knowledge. There are, however, some areas that I think are so promising and/or interesting that they bear serious consideration. I won't tell you about all of them—I have to keep some professional secrets—but I will mention a few.

COCOS ISLAND lies in the Pacific about 300 miles southwest of Costa Rica, which claims sovereignty over it. It is only a few miles long, but it rises to a height of almost 3,000 feet in its center, and most of its area is covered by nearly impenetrable jungle growth. It has never been inhabited, though one attempt was made to establish a colony there before the turn of the century by a German treasure hunter named August Gissler. His colony, which originally consisted of seven families, disbanded within a few years, mainly due to constant invasion of their settlement by other treasure hunters who refused to honor Gissler's claim to be Governor and part owner of the island. Gissler stayed on for more than twenty years, a tall, bearded hermit who greeted newly arriving bands of treasure seekers with claims of precise information on the location of gold hoards. No one lives on Cocos today, except for a number of goats and pigs that have reverted to the wild, along with sizable colonies of man's most ubiquitous companion, the rat.

Most of the island's coast is rocky, with sheer cliffs and few spots at which boats can be safely beached. There are two small bays, Wafer Bay and Chatham Bay, and both have figured prominently in the island's long history of treasure seeking. Many pirates are believed to have visited Cocos, which was a natural refuge for buccaneers fleeing from attacks on Spanish shipping in the Pacific or the rich coastal towns of Central and South America. Three are well-known, the earliest being Edward Davis, who supposedly landed John Cook's ship, the *Bachelor's Delight,* at Chatham Bay in the late seventeenth century, leaving behind several chests of plundered loot. A later pirate who called himself Bonito Benito, or Benito of the Bloody Sword, supposedly buried a sizable collection of booty in a cave on the island. Though he later committed suicide to avoid capture, two of his men escaped. One named Chapelle, turned up later in San Francisco, leaving behind papers purporting to describe hidden treasure. The other survivor's name was Thompson, and there were many who claimed that he was the same Thompson who figured in the most important and tantalizing treasure cache of all.

This treasure, consisting of gold and silver bars and other articles (including, according to some accounts, a life-size gold statue of the Virgin Mary), was collected at the Peruvian port city of Callao around 1820. The treasure, from the storehouses of Lima, was threatened by the advancing Simon Bolivar, and ships were desperately sought to haul it to safety. The one ship available was the brig *Mary Dear* (or *Mary Dier* in some accounts), commanded by a Captain Thompson (or Thomson—all names vary according to the account one chooses). Eleven longboats were required to load the treasure aboard the *Mary Dear,* and she slipped out of Callao Harbor in the night, pursued by a Peruvian sloop. She made for Cocos Island, where the sloop caught up with her hours after the treasure had been hidden somewhere ashore. The crew was summarily executed, but Captain Thompson and his mate were spared in order that they might lead to the treasure. They escaped onto the island and were rescued months later by a ship that put in for fresh water.

The mate died soon after, but Captain Thompson supposedly turned up later at St. John's, Newfoundland, where he told his story to a man named Keating, who in turn led several expeditions (two are definite, and some claim there was a third) to Cocos in search of the gold. Though no proof exists that he actually found the treasure, his partner mysteriously died, and Keating himself turned up with unexplained profits which he claimed resulted from selling the gold he was able to carry away from Cocos on his person.

The island has been assaulted by one expedition after another in the last hundred years, including parties led by Keating's widow and one major onslaught by the entire crew of the H.M.S. *Imperieuse,* the flagship of the North-West British Squadron, just before the turn of the century. The island (or

248

those portions of it that are passable) has been searched repeatedly, caves have been blasted into rubble by lunatic dynamiters, and many have perished in the literally dozens of attempts to locate the millions in treasure believed to be hidden somewhere in the maze of streams and caves around the two small bays. Only one man is known to have found tangible evidence of the treasure: A single gold doubloon, dated 1788 (in the reign of Charles III of Spain), was found near Wafer Bay by August Gissler, who was haunted by that find for the more than twenty years that he stubbornly stayed on the island, searching and greeting each arriving party like a specter from the pirate past.

Cocos Island has claimed much time and money and many lives (the last two as recently as 1963), and it is possible that the treasures will never be found. But these things are certain: The *Mary Dear* sailed with eleven longboats full of treasure and she didn't have it when overtaken at Cocos Island; there are only two spots where longboats could have been brought ashore (Wafer and Chatham); and it is unlikely that such a massive load would have been carried far inland. It should, therefore, be possible to narrow the area of search to manageable proportions, and to deduce the most likely spots within that area. Using the recently improved metal detectors, which were not available to the many expeditions in the past, it may now be possible to locate this legendary treasure.

Before one tackles Cocos Island, though, it is necessary to obtain permission from the government of the Southern Province of Costa Rica, and this permission is granted only on acceptance of a cash bid, plus an agreement to turn over half of any treasure found to the government. Even so, estimates of the current value of the *Mary Dear*'s cargo run well over a billion dollars! With that much at stake, further efforts will be made—and I predict that modern equipment will make success far more likely. I hope to be the lucky man.

Cocos Island is one of the two best-known "treasure islands" in the world. The other, completely shrouded in mystery, is one of the most incredible spots on the face of this planet. It is tiny Oak Island, off Nova Scotia, and more has been written about its mysterious "money pit," first discovered in 1795 and explored almost constantly since, than about any other single treasure site in the world.

OAK ISLAND's pit was first discovered by three boys, who noted a circular depression under an oak tree and signs of chains having been attached to the branches above. The story of all the various excavations over the intervening years would fill too many pages, but what they found may be summed up fairly simply: The hole consisted of a vertical shaft, roughly 15 feet in diameter, with layers of heavy oak planking placed at 10-foot intervals, some with charcoal, coconut fibre, or ship's putty under them. At the 90-foot platform a stone was found, inscribed with strange hieroglyphics which were never deciphered (the stone later disappeared); at 104 feet down, chests or barrels were found filled with loose metal; and slightly farther down a heart-shaped stone was found. Unfortunately, at around the 100-foot mark the shaft flooded, which stopped digging and which led to the second, even more remarkable discovery: Two subterranean drains had been constructed by whoever built the underground pit, and these conduits were designed to flood the tunnel when anyone dug below 100 feet.

Later expeditions attacked the pit with various plans involving lateral shafts and blockages of the sea conduits, but all failed. Attempts to drill under the water with steam drills produced further mysteries, including three links of gold chain, bits of parchment, and an old whistle at about 150 feet, and just below that a small room made of cement! This room, estimated to be about seven feet deep and roughly five feet square, was definitely poured by human hands, in a pit 150 feet deep. And more recent drilling attempts have reached still greater depths, and have found further incredible evidence, including a heavy wooden platform at a depth of 212 feet. A small television camera, lowered into the pit and down through a hole in this platform, detected several wooden chests, a pickaxe, and what appeared to be a perfectly preserved human hand!

Millions have been spent in so-far fruitless attempts to bring up the treasure everyone assumes must be somewhere in that amazing pit, and many theories have been advanced to explain how the engineering feat, which would be difficult to match with modern equipment, could have been accomplished four hundred years ago—and without one single mention in any contemporary records! The most popular theory involves the crews of one or more pirate ships, possibly even those commanded by Captain Kidd, and evidence does indeed exist to point to ships from tropical waters. For one thing, huge quantities of coconut fiber were used in constructing the sea conduits, and the nearest coconuts are hundreds of miles to the south. For another, it is assumed that only a pirate crew—possibly with Indian slave labor—could have achieved such a feat in total secrecy, which might have been insured by simply killing the laborers when the digging was done.

Another theory involves the missing Crown Jewels of France, which disappeared at a time consistent with carbon dating of wood in the lowest drilling of the pit. This theory holds that no pirates would have gone to such unbelievable lengths to bury booty, especially since it would have been virtually impossible for them ever to have recovered it. It is argued that only a large, well-equipped, officially mounted expedition, including experienced engineers, could have accomplished such a feat, and that only the preservation of a national treasure would have justified it. Further, since any explanation runs into the problem of how secrecy was maintained, it would seem that an officially secret mission, sent out on one large ship, might well have dug the pit, filled it in, and then been lost at sea, with no survivors. All possible explanations are incredible, but I am personally inclined to think that this one comes closest to probability. Certainly *someone* dug that hole and constructed those conduits, and certainly he—or they—must have had an important reason for such an enormous undertaking. We may never know the answer, though modern oil-drilling equipment may someday be used to accomplish what past expeditions have failed to do. In any case, though I watch and wait with interest, this

251

treasure is certainly beyond the reach of any individual without a fortune to invest.

The need for great investment in equipment and manpower, plus the governmental interference such high visibility is sure to produce, has kept me from involvement in underwater salvage, though certainly the thousands of treasure-laden ships whose sinking is part of the historical record form a gigantic store of undiscovered treasure. These salvage operations are expensive, long-term undertakings, made even more difficult by the problem of distinguishing those wrecks with cargo of value from the hundreds that carried nothing more than rum or molasses. I'll leave them to the salvage outfits equipped to tackle them—with one possible exception.

GLOVER REEF and FOUR KEYS REEF, lying 8 to 26 miles offshore of British Honduras, form the longest barrier reef in the western hemisphere, second in size only to Australia's Great Barrier Reef. Many pirates and Spaniards alike came to grief here, attempting the hard passage northward, along the reef, with the strong prevailing wind blowing from the east.

The Spanish galleon was one of the most ungainly, unmanageable, top-heavy vessels that could have been designed for the open sea. Since it was almost impossible to tack the ships into the wind, the captains had little choice but to follow the trade winds. They sailed from Portobelo, Panama, with the riches of Peru and the Philippines, which had been delivered first to Panama City on the Pacific side of the isthmus, then carried overland to Portobelo on the Caribbean side. Carrying treasure from Cartagena, Portobelo, and Nombre de Dios, the galleons hugged the coast northward, heading for eventual rendezvous at Havana with the other treasure fleet from Veracruz, and then homeward to Spain.

From Portobelo, navigational logic would have dictated a northward course to Havana. However, this route brought the galleons just south and west of Jamaica, where they were easy prey to the smaller but more maneuverable ships of the pirates based in Port Royal. So the Spanish ships tended to hug the coast westward, choosing the dangers of shallow reefs and of being blown ashore in storms over the lurking pirates to the north. When they reached the Gulf of Honduras, they were compelled to sail in a relatively tight passage between the Bay Islands and the reefs. A sudden storm there could negate the best seamanship, and in spite of all efforts, a captain could find his ship driven aground on the sharp coral. Wrecks along the reef were usually a total loss, with nothing salvaged.

Untold millions in gold and silver lie in shallow water along the eastern edge of the two major reef systems. (See wrecks indicated on Thomas Jeffery's map of 1775.) Yet Glover Reef and Four Keys Reef, littered with wrecks, are seemingly unknown to modern-day treasure hunters. Salvage operations and searches have been conducted for three hundred years in the Windward and Leeward Islands, yet this reef system, ranging in depth from a few inches to no more than ten fathoms, may be the depository for more sunken treasure than the rest of the entire Caribbean.

Despite my personal reservations about underwater salvage, I did make one exploratory trip to the reefs. It was in August, 1966, a time of the year when the winds drop and the sea is usually flat. I was still recovering my health following the Paulaya River venture, and I decided a week-end outing would improve my mood. I hired Jeff Tree's new boat, which had been partially financed by our discoveries in Port Royal two years before. I took along Wilkie Cooper, a Bay Islander whose skill at free-diving for lobsters would be a great asset in a search for wrecks.

We left Oakridge in the evening, with a full moon on the smooth sea. Heading northwest from the western end of Roatán, we made for the north end of Glover Reef, arriving at noon the next day. The flat sea, bright sunshine, and clear water gave us a clear view of the bottom as we cruised north along the edge of the reef. Although I carried two maps roughly indicating the locations of wrecks, I was only mildly optimistic. In any case, our entire equipment consisted of nothing more than snorkling gear and spear guns, so salvage was out of the question.

At the north end of the reef are two points of coral rock, projecting above the high tide mark, which charts for three hundred years have designated as "The Two Spots." One of my maps indicated two wrecks near there, so when the rocks came into view ahead of us, Wilkie and I donned our snorkling gear, entered the water, and swam along the edge of the reef behind the slow-moving boat.

The water was crystal clear, and my first impression was that here were more reef fish than I had seen on any reef in the Caribbean. Every tropical fish I had ever seen was represented in profusion. This must have been what all reefs in the Caribbean looked like before the invasion of tourists with spear guns. Here, not even the local people were fishing the reefs.

Less than ten minutes after entering the water, Wilkie grabbed my arm and pointed down with his spear gun. There, clearly outlined against the sand and coral about eight fathoms below, was a huge anchor. Its wooden crosspiece was rotted away, but its hook was still embedded in the same position as when it had been dropped there, probably in a desperate effort by the crew to hold some ship off the reef. Noting the tilt of the anchor toward the reef, we swam toward the more shallow water. The ship had come to its end about one hundred yards from the anchor in three fathoms of water. Nothing of the ship's timbers remained, but a line of ballast rocks sixty feet long marked its last resting place. (Nature does not place rocks in symmetrical, straight-line piles, so ballast rocks can usually be spotted at the site of a wrecked sailing ship.)

This one had been a large vessel. Cannon, heavily encrusted with coral growth, could be seen scattered around the wreck. We spent several minutes looking for a small cannon, hopefully a bronze one, that we might be able to break loose from the coral and pull aboard our boat, but only large iron cannon were to be seen. Whatever the ship had carried as cargo was buried beneath the sand and coral.

Jeff had been told to rev the engine if he saw sharks that

254

looked aggressive, since the sound carries a great distance underwater. When Wilkie and I heard the alternating revs of the screw, we decided to postpone any further search and return to the boat. We had seen some harmless nurse sharks while making our exploration, but now we saw the reason for Jeff's concern. A very large hammerhead was slowly circling the boat.

Wilkie and I stopped and lay motionless on the surface of the water as we watched Jeff's effort to frighten the shark away. A life jacket hit the surface near the shark's head without effect, then a five-gallon gasoline can splashed near him. He continued to circle, undisturbed. Several moments passed with no apparent action from Jeff; then, suddenly, the great body of the shark darted under the boat away from us. As Jeff helped us up the stern ladder he explained the shark's odd behavior. Seeing that he couldn't frighten the shark, Jeff had thrown a large amber-jack fish, which I had caught that morning, off the other side of the boat.

After lunch, Wilkie and I saw no sign of the hammerhead, so we continued our exploration of the reef. Twice more in the afternoon we saw large sharks, but we were so fascinated with the reef that we ignored them, as they did us. In less than three hours we found evidence of three more very old wrecks. Lying on the ballast rocks of one was a small cannon, and we decided to try to get it aboard the boat. Jeff lowered a line, which Wilkie tied around the cannon. It broke loose easily from the coral in which it was partially embedded, and we went on board to help haul it up. Though the cannon was only about four feet long, it must have weighed five or six hundred pounds. In spite of all our efforts, we could not lift it clear of the water. Jeff was not too pleased with the idea of having the cannon bouncing against his newly painted hull, so regretfully we released it. We anchored there for the night, and next morning we headed back to Roatán.

In a distance of less than one mile we had seen the remains of four wrecks. The barrier reef is 150 miles long, and early maps show wrecks from one end to the other. For those who prefer underwater salvage, there can be no better hunting grounds than Glover Reef and Four Keys Reef in the northwest Caribbean. I may return there one day, though in truth, the odds are against it. My own first love is the buried treasure of the Incas and their predecessors, and there is one site I *know* is rich with as yet unexcavated treasure. It is also in the Republic of Honduras, and I may well be the only person who knows of its location.

ST. JORGE DE OLANCHO was founded by the Spanish in 1530, as a collection point for the gold being mined in several rivers of northern Honduras through the use of slave labor. The town was located on the west bank of the Olancho River, upstream from where it entered the Guayape River. Two miles north was the forbidding mountain called El Boqueron. Twice each year the gold was loaded onto pack animals for the difficult trip through the dense jungle to the coastal city of Trujillo, where it was picked up by Spanish galleons en route from Panama to Havana.

By the year 1611 there were 4,000 Spanish living in St. Jorge de Olancho, plus several thousand Indian laborers. Life was hard in this area, where summer temperatures reach 100° and winter rains turn the rivers and streams into roaring torrents. Supplies sent from Panama seldom reached the settlers, since the Paya Indian tribes in the jungles made a regular practice of raiding supply trains. Therefore, with little equipment and no other metal available, the Spanish began to manufacture all sorts of household articles for their own use out of the plentiful gold on hand. Stirrups, kitchenware, buttons, buckles, hinges, even cutlery, all were made from the readily available gold, whose abundance was confirmed in many reports sent to Spain by priests in Olancho.

In January of 1611, at the height of the rainy season, a tremendous earthquake shook a wide area of Honduras. The side of El Boqueron adjacent to the river, weakened by the rains and loosened by the quake, thundered down into the narrow canyon of the Olancho River. Thousands of tons of rock and

256

volcanic soil blocked the river, damming its waters completely.

Downstream in the town the earthquake had wreaked havoc. Most of the adobe buildings were destroyed or badly damaged, and many Spaniards lay buried in the debris of their sturdy houses while the palm-thatched Indian huts suffered little harm. By nightfall, only six hours after the earthquake, the survivors heard a tremendous roar upstream. The rain-swollen Olancho River had formed a lake behind the landslide of El Boqueron, and the pressure of rising water had breached the dam. Within minutes, a wall of water thundered downstream, completing the destruction of St. Jorge de Olancho.

Fewer than two hundred Spaniards survived the catastrophe. The rubble of the once flourishing town was abandoned, and the survivors made their way northwest, where they founded the present town of Olanchito (Little Olancho).

Armed with an 1857 report by an English mining engineer named William V. Wells and my collection of seventeenth- and eighteenth-century maps of the area, I decided to look for the old city site. Wells, who had been exploring gold mining possibilities for a California mining group when Indians led him to the ruins, reported that a few adobe walls were still standing and that the location of the main plaza could be traced. I had no way of knowing whether those walls would still be standing more than a century after Wells' report, but since the area where the town might have stood was narrowed considerably by its relation to the river and its distance from El Boqueron, it seemed worth a try. It seemed certain that a fortune in gold must lie buried in those ruins. In addition to the hundreds of gold utensils and other gold being stored there for shipment to Trujillo, it was reported that still another life-size gold statue of the Virgin Mary had never been recovered from the ruins of the church.

In 1965, while awaiting completion of the dredge I was to take up the Paulaya River, I decided to spend a few days in search of the site. Taking along Wilkie Cooper as an interpreter, I drove the 120 miles of dirt, dust, chuckholes, and hairpin

257

turns to Juticalpa, Honduras. We left the Land Rover there as security against the horses we hired, and the next morning we set out for El Boqueron, rising visibly from the jungle fifteen miles to the east. Following a good trail, we reached the base of the mountain at noon and made camp on the Olancho River.

Wells' report had indicated that he had no difficulty finding Indians who could lead him to the site, and I felt it should be equally easy for us. But after four days of traveling upstream and downstream, questioning Indians on both banks of the river, we found no one who had ever seen the ruins described by Wells. The only explanation likely was that the heavy annual rains had simply crumbled and washed away the few walls still standing in 1857.

From the early descriptions of the town I knew that it should be downstream from El Boqueron, on the west bank of the river before it entered into the Guayape River. This would entail a search of approximately three miles, through thick bush heavily infested with snakes. I hired eight Indians to clear trails through the bush, and after four days of work we came to a flat area extending well back from the river two miles downstream from El Boqueron.

As the flat area was cleared, fragments of old walls began to appear. I soon saw the foundations of many buildings. Here, I was certain, was Olancho. I would have liked to stay there and work the site, but I had no electronic equipment along and there was little I could do without it. Reluctantly I filed the site for future reference and returned to San Pedro Sula, to complete preparations of the dredge. Finding the treasure site, and knowing that no treasure hunters had been there before me, was almost satisfaction enough. By now the bush will have grown up again, hiding the city and the wealth of gold which has to be there scattered beneath the ruins. Perhaps I'll return there one day, or perhaps someone who reads this book will find the treasure of St. Jorge de Olancho.

Throughout this chapter, and in the chapters preceding, I have indicated the areas and even the specific locations I am convinced—from extensive research and personal exploration—

258

are rich with treasure. I am still certain there is pirate treasure on the Morant Keys, and modern metal detection devices have grown sophisticated enough to locate it even in the presence of salt water. There is still gold in the Paulaya River, and I'm sure there are rivers in Ecuador where emeralds wash down from the mountains each year. And there is that third chest left by the Mitchell-Hedges expedition on Roatán Island. During the years when I lived on Roatán, I often looked out across Port Royal Harbor to the spot where I knew that chest to be, and I knew that each new improvement in metal detectors made the search for it that much more feasible. But I was a resident then, and I didn't want to court trouble with the local authorities. I have thought of the chest often, though, and maybe someday . . .

Finally, of course, there is the vast storehouse of treasure buried in ancient mounds and tombs throughout Peru, Colombia, Ecuador, and much of Central America up to the Yucatán Peninsula. I have not scratched the surface of this huge residue left by many centuries of men in many varied civilizations, and I could not do so in a dozen lifetimes. But I have tried, and I shall go on trying, and perhaps I shall again have the satisfaction of locating a treasure of antiquity, of bringing it out to the world, and of seeing it on view in one of the major museums of the United States or Europe. The financial rewards, though often substantial and of very real interest to any treasure hunter, are only part of the motivation, for me at least. The adventure into remote regions, the testing of long weeks of research against the actual sites, and the thrill of discovery are the things that send me back, time and again, into places where few outsiders have ventured. And it is those things that I will remember years later when I see the artifacts I unearthed on display for the enjoyment and enrichment of millions who would not otherwise have this direct contact with the glories of mankind's past.

Treasure hunters have often been accused of defiling tombs and of despoiling archaeological sites, thereby interfering with scholarly pursuits. The truth is that treasure hunters have often

259

*discovered* these sites, as in the case of Coaque. And, as with Coaque, most treasure hunters have dug carefully, disturbed a relatively minor amount of the site, and removed only small amounts of the total materials available for archaeological study. I opened fewer than fifty graves at Coaque, out of the hundreds of thousands that must be there. There is ample room for archaeological study of the artifacts and culture of this ancient city, now that it has been rediscovered and partially explored— by a treasure hunter.

The truth, of course, is that many noted archaeologists have been treasure hunters at heart, and many of the greatest discoveries of recent times have been made by men who were more adventurers than scholars. Ancient Troy was discovered by Heinrich Schliemann, who made off with its fortune in gold; the Venus de Milo was smuggled out of Greece by a man named Brest and delivered to the Louvre (which promptly misplaced several vital parts); Sir Tomkyns Hilgrove Turner acquired the Rosetta Stone as a military prize in the Napoleonic Wars; Giovanni Belzoni, who excavated Abu Simbel and opened the Second Pyramid, was frankly a treasure hunter and a showman; and Lord Elgin's two hundred cases of material "discovered" at the Acropolis brought him £35,000 from the British Parliament. It has been estimated that as much as eighty-five percent of the ancient art in the British Museum was smuggled out of its country of origin and then purchased by the museum, and the curator of the Cleveland Museum has estimated that ninety percent of the antiquities in *all* museums may well have been acquired in this manner.

To the charge that I have committed sacrilege by disturbing the dead, I can only answer that thousands of years have passed and entire cultures have come and gone, of whom we can know little without studying the artifacts that were part of their daily lives. The only way these artifacts can be found is by careful excavation, and I cannot see that the digging of an archaeologist is any less a spiritual violation than that of a treasure hunter. In fact, the treasure hunter, with limited resources and full knowledge of the value ancient objects have, is less likely to disturb large areas than the eager armies of graduate students with an entire summer to spend at pick and shovel.

And finally, to the charge that I am a footloose and irresponsible adventurer, I can only say that I may have contributed more to the knowledge and enjoyment of mankind than I ever would have at an office desk, and made a good deal less money doing so.

I do not regret one minute of the years I have spent chasing after treasure. I only hope I have many more years to give to my chosen occupation.

There is so much left to find.